Practising Journalism
Values, Constraints, Implications

Editor

Nalini Rajan

SAGE Publications
New Delhi   Thousand Oaks   London

First published in 2005 by

Sage Publications India Pvt Ltd
B-42, Panchsheel Enclave
New Delhi 110 017
www.indiasage.com

Sage Publications Inc  **Sage Publications Ltd**
2455 Teller Road 1 Oliver's Yard, 55 City Road
Thousand Oaks, California 91320 London EC1Y 1SP

Published by Tejeshwar Singh for Sage Publications India Pvt Ltd, phototypeset in 10/12 Century Schoolbook by Prism Graphix, and printed at Chaman Enterprises, New Delhi.

Library of Congress Cataloging-in-Publication Data

Practising journalism: values, constraints, implications/editor, Nalini Rajan.
    p. cm.
  Includes index.
  1. Journalism—India. 2. Journalistic ethics—India. I. Rajan, Nalini, 1954-
PN5374.P73   079'.54—dc22   2005   2005015653

ISBN: 0–7619–3378–6 (Hb)   81–7829–521–0 (India-Hb)
      0–7619–3379–4 (Pb)   81–7829–522–9 (India-Pb)

Sage Production Team: Sarita Vellani, Shinjini Chatterjee, Jeevan Nair and Santosh Rawat

Contents

List of Figures

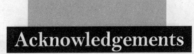

Acknowledgements

I owe a special debt of gratitude to Omita Goyal. The truth is that her constant encouragement and enthusiasm for this project gave me the energy to relentlessly pursue my contributors for their articles. My special thanks to N. Ram and Robin Jeffrey for readily giving me permission to use their published work for this volume. N. Ram's article appeared as an editorial in *The Hindu* (27 August 2003), while Robin Jeffrey's article appeared under a different title, 'Breaking News', in *The Little Magazine* (Volume IV, Issue 2, 2003).

I would also like to thank the following persons: Shinjini Chatterjee at Sage for her patient, good-natured responses to my incessant nagging; the anonymous reader of this manuscript who highlighted the flaws in the first draft of my Introduction; my colleagues and friends, Mahalakshmi Jayaram, Sreekumar Menon and R. Vijayaraghavan for editorial assistance; Sashi Kumar, Chairman, Media Development Foundation, for institutional support; Sadanand Menon for generous assistance in providing me with contacts; Ayesha Begum for help in translating Harivansh's Hindi draft; B. Bhanu for keying in the manuscripts; the students of the Asian College of Journalism for helping me sustain my faith in the values of the profession; and, last but not least, all the contributors to this volume who have greatly enhanced my understanding of journalism.

Nalini Rajan
June 2005

introduction

nalini rajan

*t*he history of journalism is not linear but a series of criss-crossing loops. The way in which these loops are constructed is witnessed in the struggles of a liberal vision of journalism as a crusading vocation against the different currents of scepticism and pragmatism in the media. Admittedly, the idea of ethics in journalism is being challenged today by market-driven objectives. Nevertheless, as most of the articles here inform us, it may be an ideal still worth pursuing. This edited volume, comprising 26 contributions from working journalists, freelance writers, journalism teachers, media practitioners and others involved with the media in one way or another, attempts to examine some of these struggles, mainly in the Indian context.

This volume is not envisaged strictly as a textbook for a journalism school, but more as a general collection of essays reflecting the fascinating spectrum of practices, trends and visions within the journalistic profession. When I got all the papers, I was quite excited by the variety of ways in which the craft is practised and viewed. It is this excitement that I wish to impart to the reader, both inside and outside the profession. This indeed is the modest aim of the book.

Conventional books on journalism have been dominated by biographies of well-known practitioners of the craft or by institutional histories. The first essay in this collection by B.R.P. Bhaskar is also a history of sorts of the press. If, in the 1950s, Hindi, English and Urdu papers dominated the Indian media scene in terms of numbers and circulation, Hindi and English newspapers continue to do so in the early twenty-first century, while the Urdu press has slipped way down the ladder in terms of circulation.[1] This essay is really more than a history, since it is also concerned with issues like proprietorship and freedom of the press. Article 19 in the Indian Constitution guarantees freedom of speech and expression with reasonable restrictions. It does not guarantee freedom of the press or other media. In a curious way, the interpretation of the two freedoms—freedom of expression and of the press—has given rise to paradoxical situations when they have been at cross-purposes with each other. For example, in 1960, the Indian government's attempt to fix a price–page schedule in order to curb the monopolistic tendencies of big newspapers and promote the cause of a free press was effectively challenged in the apex court as being unconstitutional and violating the freedom of expression guaranteed in Article 19(1)(a). This ruling, in a sense, paved the way for the flourishing of monopolistic practices in the media.

Periodically, in its history, journalism has undergone shifts in conception, and that has something to do with the way this craft is practised. The more news gathering and news presentation are linked to ethical concerns, the more the humanistic nature of the profession is stressed. Clearly, this shift in perception all over the democratic world has something to do with the liberal faith, following the European Enlightenment tradition, in the connection between the word, its audience and human action. Harivansh's moving account of the phenomenal rise of a paper like *Prabhat Khabar* as the number one Hindi paper in the Jharkhand area is the sort of 'feel-good' account that the media is aching for today. Against all the media-related shibboleths of the inevitability of tabloidisation, dumbing down and marketing pragmatism, the story of *Prabhat Khabar* is a tribute to the journalist's faith in the values of the profession. The paper's success teaches us an important lesson—*commitment to an ideal, rather than to profit making, is all-important.* By linking information to credibility and political activism, *Prabhat Khabar*'s success shines like a beacon in the last decade, which has been characterised by media sensationalism and economic liberalisation.

We also have N. Ram recalling the journalistic values or functions articulated by Noam Chomsky and Edward S. Herman.[2]

---

[1] M.H. Lakdawala discusses this point in his article in this volume.
[2] Edward S. Herman and Noam Chomsky, *Manufacturing Consent: The Political Economy of the Mass Media* (New York: Pantheon Books, 1988).

These are the credible-information function, the critical-adversarial or watchdog function, the educational function and the agenda-building function. In addition, given the peculiarities of the Indian context, Ram mentions values like truth telling, freedom and independence, justice, humaneness and contributing to the social good. All these values apply equally to the print, broadcast and online media. Despite the fact that one is the editor of a leading English-language paper in a metropolitan centre and the other heads a small—albeit successful—Hindi-language paper in a predominantly tribal belt, both N. Ram and Harivansh stand for the same cardinal values in the journalistic profession.

Indeed, as practitioners begin to define the media's guiding values and principles, the route between journalism and the humanities or social sciences is becoming well traversed. After all, everything that the journalist says or writes today is likely to constitute the historical 'archive' for the social scientist working two or three decades later. If this is the case, every journalist has a great responsibility not only to tell the truth but also to understand the context of the subject on which she is writing or broadcasting. The question is, if values and principles inform the profession, and since social scientists as a group are preoccupied with the connection between facts and values, is a journalist also a social scientist? There are two opposing views on the subject, both of which are articulated in this volume.

According to one view, even if there are similarities between the roles of the journalist and the social scientist, there is a distinction between news (acquaintance *with* something) and truth (knowledge *about* something). Dilip D'Souza's description of investigative journalism is clearly confined to news. It consists of checking and crosschecking facts, maintaining a steady flow of news reports on the investigations, several follow-ups, and a hard-hitting conclusion based on all the damning evidence collected. This is the stuff of the news reports on the Bofors gun scandal, the St Kitts forgery case, the Babri masjid demolition, the 2002 Gujarat carnage, the stock market scam, the coffins scandal, the petrol-pump misallocation episode and, last but not least, all the tehelka.com exposés in recent years. The tragedy no doubt is that seldom any punishment commensurate with the crimes is meted out, following the scams. Indeed, given the rate at which the crimes are committed by those in power, a certain level of ennui or fatigue creeps in among the readers, and the vocation of investigative journalism—perhaps the essence of the profession—is itself in trouble.

But there is a more important distinction between the two roles. A journalist has greater responsibility to present news credibly—this is the credible-informational role referred to by the Chomsky–Herman model—than does the social scientist when she presents her conclusions in an academic publication. The reason is that the mass media get much wider coverage than academic publications, and mistakes get amplified in the former. With specific reference to the investigations conducted by the now defunct website, tehelka.com, Mukund Padmanabhan provides a sharp critique of its credible-informational role. The critique here does not relate to the veracity or credibility of the information, but to the means that the website employed to get it. While discussing two recent undercover investigations conducted by the website—one on match-fixing in Indian cricket and the other on corruption in defence deals—Padmanabhan convincingly reveals the online journalists' insensitivity to issues relating to the privacy rights of the individuals involved directly or indirectly in the cases. While 'contributing to the social good'—one of the journalistic values enumerated by Ram in his paper—can often trump privacy rights in investigative reporting, those (like the tehelka.com investigators) who rely largely on impersonation, deception and spy cameras are likely to cross the thin line that separates ethical and responsible journalists from the paparazzi.

The truth is that in the name of investigative reporting, journalists can violate the privacy rights of their informants and often expose them to unprecedented danger, especially in the context of tyrannical, non-democratic regimes. Valerie Kaye provides an impassioned account of the way in which even journalists working with the most respected broadcast network in the world, the BBC, can be sometimes insensitive to the consequences of their reporting—in this case, on the alleged tortures and kidnappings by the military junta in Argentina in the 1970s, which involved interviews with some of the victims. The ethical issue that arises here relates to the extent to which a journalist should protect her/his source and honour the privacy rights of her/his informants, even if the final report contributes to the social good. The answer will depend on how the media differentiate between the 'social good' and the 'selling good'; or between editorial and marketing functions. To quote Ram on this subject: 'Great newspapers with a soul know where to draw the *lakshman rekha* and how to give primacy to the editorial functions.'[3] Many believe that these are the core values of journalism, and these are the principles that empower the media—whether it is print, broadcast or online.

The second view envisages a much closer link between the journalist and the social scientist and is articulated by some contributors to this volume. In order to be aware of subtleties of meaning and signification in different fields of interest, the media practitioner is expected more and more to become an 'expert'. The emerging genre of journalism as an applied social science stands in sharp contrast to the traditional stance of journalism as a humanistic enterprise. But it represents more than a new social science approach (truth or knowledge about something) as against an older journalistic tradition (news or acquaintance with something). Many reporters, who become conscious of the high degree of responsibility attached to what they write or say, see themselves as 'scientists' engaged in the vocation of 'fact finding'. These same reporters also challenge the divide between news and truth. According to them, journalists should go beyond merely acquainting people *with* things and provide them with knowledge *about* things. This calls for a study and understanding of the research methods employed by social scientists today. As Philip Meyer puts it: 'To cope with the acceleration of social change in today's world, journalism must become social science in a hurry.'[4]

Not only is there an imperative for specialised knowledge, there is also a corresponding need to master new technologies. Journalists the world over have benefited from computer technology to find, analyse and explain data; that is, to turn raw data into information for stories. However, outside the United States and Western Europe, claims Steven Ross, journalists often fail to use the computer for this purpose. They believe that little or

---

[3] See N. Ram's paper in this volume.
[4] Philip Meyer, *Precision Journalism: A Reporter's Introduction to Social Science Methods* (Bloomington: Indiana University Press, 1973), p. 14.

no relevant data is available, and that much of the data that might be available is unreliable. Americans, on the other hand, often believe that teaching computer techniques in less developed countries is a waste of time due to perceived lack of skills and technology in such countries. In reality, data software and hardware are readily available, and journalists in developing countries often have an educational base equal to or greater than is typical in American newsrooms. Educational materials and teaching methods must be adjusted to local conditions, however. Slow Internet connection speeds can sometimes be a problem, but that issue is minor and fast disappearing. Ross's well-illustrated article lucidly describes the issues involved in the context of teaching computer-assisted reporting in South India in recent years.

While positively reviewing the different technical treats on hand in contemporary journalism's menu card, Mahalakshmi Jayaram draws our attention to the dangers of identifying the role of the journalist with that of the technician. Indeed, if the media are to be imagined as facilitating a democratic public sphere, then the journalist's role, too, must be conceived as much more dynamic. Journalists are not technicians who mechanically impart an information package to readers and viewer–listeners; instead, assuming the role of transformative intellectuals, they treat their audience as reflective agents, question how information is produced and distributed, utilise debate and discussion, and render ideas and opinions critical and meaningful. In fact, one of the key differences between the older print media and the various kinds of new media is the interactive nature of the latter—like the phone-in mode in the broadcast media and the discussion boards in the online media. While some have welcomed the democratisation of journalism with devices like blogging that blur the boundaries of writer/publisher and reader/buyer, others are worried about the limited access to technology in Third World countries. While conceding the latter, Jayaram also cautions us against going overboard about the former, lest we forget the crucial journalistic values of providing credible information, adopting the role of watchdog of society and educating the readers.

Both these perspectives discuss the different ways in which the roles of the journalist and the social scientist intermesh;

equally, both are concerned about the use and abuse of the media's power in society. Although the power of the media has been emphasised by many theorists, there are others who demur. The media, some pragmatic critics maintain, constitute but one of the many processes in society and are indeed surpassed in importance by economic interests and even family values. Ironically, the realms of economics and the family have historically constituted the 'private' bulwark in Europe against the power of the monarch, especially in the sixteenth and early seventeenth centuries. The rise of journalism was possible, in the following century, when the bourgeois public space emerged as individuals started making public and political use of their reason. Indian journalistic writing, for its part, gathered momentum only towards the end of the eighteenth and early nineteenth centuries. As is well known, many newspapers and periodicals were started during that period as part of the nationalist movement in an attempt to create a free public space for debate, protest and agenda building. However, these democratic values were confined to the public sphere; the private realm of the household continued to be the preserve of traditional and conservative values.[5]

Nearly two centuries on, feminist scholars and women journalists have questioned the division between a public political sphere and a private non-political sphere of the household—although such sensitivity to nuances may not always be reflected in the media. By claiming that the private—that is, the household—is also the political, women journalists and activists have forced the media to direct some of their attention to gender issues. As Pamela Philipose explains in the second section of this volume, coverage of gender issues in the Indian English language media—both print and broadcast—since Independence has varied from almost-total absence in the 1950s and 1960s, to moderate coverage during the height of feminist activism in the 1970s and 1980s, to dilution of gender concerns during the 'backlash years' of the last decade of globalisation and liberalisation. 'Gender coverage' today implies focusing on female celebrity lifestyle or on women's involvement in scandal and crime.

[5] See Meera Kosambi, 'Gender Reform and Competing State Controls Over Women: The Rakhmabai Case (1884–1888)', in Patricia Uberoi (ed.), *Social Reform, Sexuality and the State* (New Delhi: Sage Publications, 1996).

This, too, is the case with much of the regional-language media. In an engaging essay on recent trends in the Tamil language press, V. Geetha points out that it is not as if gender-related stories are not saleable in the media. They certainly are—especially if the dénouement of the narrative promises to be physically, or at least emotionally, titillating. So, apart from the pin-up girls, Tamil popular magazines revel in 'female victim' tales. Thus, despite their 'soft Hindutva' ideology, some popular Tamil magazines also project fairly comprehensive 'victim' reports on Muslim women. Compared to these, small literary journals in Tamil at least confront caste and community politics head-on, even if they are more cautious about seriously addressing gender issues. In sum, if there is coverage of gender in the Tamil media, it is usually of the sensational variety.

If serious gender issues have dropped off the media's radar screen during the last decade, the fate of a subject like agriculture— which concerns the lives of more than 60 per cent of India's population—may well be imagined. Devinder Sharma reminds us that agriculture makes news only when corporate interests are involved—for instance, when multinational corporations are involved in developing genetically altered crops. As far as the media are concerned, agriculture is an 'up-market' subject when promoting the interests of agribusiness and international trade; it is dubbed a 'down-market' subject when issues like farmers' suicides, the public distribution system or land-ownership patterns are concerned. Ironically, the British media have stood up rather well to the corporate onslaught against the interests of farmers and the environment; the Indian media are content to adopt what Noam Chomsky calls 'the role of the missionaries of the corporate world'.

In a parallel development to these trends in rural reporting, there is a similar dichotomy in urban reporting today. As Kalpana Sharma points out, celebrity or 'Page 3' journalism dominates the content in newspapers. Some newspapers now sell editorial space on the society pages. The old city 'beats', of regularly covering the municipality, health, labour and civic issues, are now almost completely erased. The city is thus divided into 'citizens' who pay taxes and deserve their privileges, and 'others' who are assumed to drain the state's resources and contribute to the ugliness in the urban landscape by inhabiting the slums.

Do the media intrude actively into our collective psyche and reconfigure the very categories of thought and action? If that is the case, in some instances the media help the public think differently and more innovatively; in other instances, they facilitate thought that is rigid, action that is irresponsible and beliefs that are stereotypical. After it had reached its peak as a public profession in Europe, journalism registered a decline in the late nineteenth century by making private life, in the form of economic issues, a matter of public concern. In the early twenty-first century, the Indian media are singularly preoccupied with the imperatives of the market. When the media indulge in piece-meal and fragmented reporting on the urban and rural poor, the processes that lead to rural and urban deprivation are obfuscated and it becomes extremely difficult to mobilise public opinion against the state on these matters.

Even if mainstream media publications have been preoccupied with the leisure class and business interests—areas that were confined to the 'private' sphere during the early days of journalism in Europe and India—the 'alternative' media have dared to be different. Darryl D'Monte refers to one such publication, the *State of India's Environment* (SOE) report, brought out by the Centre for Science and Environment (CSE) in New Delhi. In this case, says D'Monte, the media have not only performed their credible-information role by accurately reporting the news, they have also undertaken the educational role by providing alternative perspectives on environmental issues. By combining the functions of research and reporting, the media are sometimes capable of blurring the boundary line between social science and journalism.

The truth, however, is that journalistic goals, especially in the mainstream media, are generally not made with a view to influencing decision-making in political life; they are merely expected to maximise personal economic security. As a result, in this neo-liberal phase, political decision-making is left to the elite politicians. In all this, what is in jeopardy is not merely the ability of the media to be creative, but the very capacity for conceptual thought. Moreover, since vibrant social and political processes depend on the existence of an autonomous and thinking public, the present media culture is likely to endanger the survival of democracy itself. In such a climate, journalists, by and large, have taken a backseat in terms of playing their intellectual roles as watchdog and educator.

It seems that at its worst, journalism confuses the public by inundating them with trivial information along with contradictory opinions that cancel each other out. In the third section of this volume which deals with the constraints faced by the media, Bindu Bhaskar explains why public opinion, media content and the actions of government interact in complex and uncertain ways. Unfortunately, the media's current preoccupation with trivia and 'infotainment' has crowded out informed opinion on livelihood issues that affect the majority of Indians. Even more unfortunately, those like Amartya Sen, Prabhat Patnaik, Aruna Roy and Arundhati Roy, who delve deeper into livelihood issues today also happen to be outside the media.

Against the grain of all those arguments trashing entertainment and favouring information, Robert Brown claims that the problem with the Indian media is not that there is too much entertainment, but too little. And what little there is tends to be crude and debasing. If the British media have always viewed information and entertainment as two sides of the same coin, the Indian media are uncomfortable with providing entertainment to its audience, given the sobering backdrop of large-scale deprivation. Entertainment, if subtle and sophisticated, does not dumb down, but brightens up the news. Interestingly, Brown claims that the importance of being entertaining as well as earnest has been grasped by the weekly newspaper, *Tehelka*, the new avatar of the website, tehelka.com. It is likely that the reader, being a rounded human being with a multidimensional appetite for news, is happy to accept the protean *Tehelka*—viewed varyingly even in this volume as part idealist, part trickster, part entertainer.

The traditional-minded Indian print media may look down on entertainment, but certainly not on writing style. The overriding impression of journalism in the minds of laypersons and practitioners alike is that it is somehow connected to literature. The reason for such an idea is that journalistic writing is always associated with 'good' writing, which in turn is associated with literature. That style continues to be an important component of journalistic writing is emphasised by Nirmal Shekar in the second section of this collection. According to Shekar, this is especially true of the sports journalist in the print media. From being a poor country cousin to the political or business journalist, the sports journalist has now emerged as a glamorous and powerful figure. There is, however, a difference between the broadcast and print journalist. Given satellite television's penchant for chasing the sensational and for image building, it is left to the print journalist to write the story in a style that is both appealing and innovative in order to wean away the television audience that is fed on a diet of seductive visual images. The sportswriter can compete with former players who attend matches and contribute columns for papers only on the basis of her/his writing style. Sadly, in comparison to their British or American counterparts, Indian sportswriters have a long way to go in terms of developing the art of creative storytelling. This, says Shekar, is the challenge currently faced by Indian print journalists.

At its best, then, journalism is practised not only from the point of view of style, but also its interaction with a historical context, where it contributes to the creation of networks of communication and the reinforcement of democracy. Ashish Sen, in the last section, discusses the role of community radio in a population that has a sizeable section of illiterates, and laments the fact that initiatives in this regard are so few. What exactly is the relevance of community radio? Sen claims that its relevance lies in its inclusiveness and its public advocacy role, hence, its positive implications for the future.

As many practitioners will insist, these different journalistic ideals hold good even in the age of globalisation. Instead of being a passive mirror to society, a journalist today has an enlarged responsibility to understand an event within its context, interpret it accordingly, and then decide on the narrative and style s/he employs. In other words, a news item in any of the media should not simply be viewed as an isolated event; it has a context and should be linked to processes and opened to interpretation. This last idea of 'being open to interpretation' is likely to put a question mark on the cardinal principle of objectivity.

Indeed, the principle of objectivity has come under attack for the most part of the twentieth century from linguists and philosophers of science, among others. Journalists, especially reporters, have also joined the bandwagon by problematising the principle of pure objectivity. Lawrence Liang explains why the urban reporter must take into consideration the fantasies, ambiguities and innovations of society that interrogate the neat categories of public and private, legal and illegal, subjectivity and objectivity. Describing the 'schizoid' relationship between legality and illegality in post-colonial cities in the Third World, Liang describes the proliferation of illegality, from housing to pirated compact discs. Therefore, no journalist can function effectively in post-colonial cities today armed only with the modernist categories of legality and rationality.

Because objectivity is hard to pin down in definition as well as in practice, journalists prefer to discuss the notion of 'fairness', that is, covering different sides of a story to achieve some kind of 'balance'. The truth, as S. Anand claims, is that there is hardly any balance in the media with respect to some issues, say, like caste. Anand maintains that there are gross imbalances in both the coverage of dalit (former untouchable castes) issues by Indian journalists and their representation in Indian media institutions. The Indian media may not adopt an anti-dalit stand, but they certainly practise casteism by omission. Statistical studies of media organisations reveal that hardly any dalit is employed as a journalist. When self-professed secular and progressive liberals in media houses in the country practise such exclusion, says Anand, it is far more appalling than the openly anti-dalit stance of groups like the Rashtriya Swayamsevak Sangh (RSS) or the Ranvir Sena. Moreover, there seems to be a silent conspiracy in the media, whereby in all news reports, dalits are always marked or identified, whereas the upper castes remain unmarked or invisible. At the end of this hard-hitting critique of the media, Anand turns the spotlight on himself and renders visible his own brahminical, and thus 'marked'—origins.

There is another kind of serious imbalance in the media, and that is the location of the Urdu-language media within their framework. M.H. Lakdawala informs us that the falling circulation figures of the Urdu press, which began in the 1980s especially in Delhi, Uttar Pradesh and Bihar, could be related to its poor editorial quality, the fact that contributors are rarely remunerated, and the low literacy levels within the community. At least 103 Urdu papers have ceased publication in the last five years, and another 100 are likely to follow suit. According to Lakdawala, even the credible-information function of the Urdu press is at stake, since most papers are only interested in pushing stereotypes about the different communities in the country. Lakdawala claims that Urdu media houses do not use modern technology, and Urdu journalists are encouraged to write like religious preachers. The result is that, with the exception of a few innovative Urdu papers like *Inquilab* which, claims Lakdawala, must be encouraged, even Urdu-language students prefer to buy cheaper and better quality English-language papers.

Apart from the issues of class, caste and community that have affected the profession, a practising journalist should be aware of other structural constraints. Praveen Swami points out that journalists involved in reporting conflicts are rarely conscious of the multiple pressures that operate in conflict zones like Kashmir. This is the reason that excessive dependence on uninformed informants can lead to half-baked knowledge, rumours or lies masquerading as 'truth' in a report in the print or broadcast media. Many journalists reduce conflict zones to spectacles and simply ignore the hard reality of the lives of ordinary human beings. Thus, as the old adage goes, truth is the first casualty of war and of conflict reporting. Furthermore, in conflict zones, there is the serious problem of media houses surrendering to terrorist fiat and the Kalashnikov.

The journalist's own bias is not the only element that contributes to imbalance or unfairness in conflict reporting. Shyam Tekwani discusses the concept of 'embedded journalism' in the context of the recent war in Iraq. In earlier times, the war correspondent travelled informally with a particular unit or battalion, usually for an unspecified duration, and managed to remain independent of government control and censorship. With the Iraq War, the US government formalised the policy of 'embedment' by handpicking assignments for journalists and assigning them to units. The positive side, says Tekwani, is that embedding offers unprecedented opportunity to journalists to report facts from the front. The negative side, of course, is that embedded reporters have to sign a contract with the military that charts out what can and what cannot be reported. More importantly, journalists who opt out of the embedding plan are 'freezed out' by the government and, on occasion, even harassed. The distinction between patriotism and fair or objective reporting becomes fuzzy in such instances.

To use a journalistic cliché, then, media products, whether the printed word, the broadcasted sound or visual, or the virtual space, reflect not only their editors' concerns, but also those of the public in both the state and civil society. In the last section of this volume, Robin Jeffrey brilliantly illustrates this point in his analysis of the Hindi-language press, whose circulation has more than trebled since the early 1990s. What this implies in real terms is that 30 years ago a newspaper would have reached the village schoolteacher's house in the Hindi-speaking belt once a week; today, the newspaper reaches every literate villager's house in time for some newsreading along with breakfast. More importantly, the spread of newspaper literacy facilitates the creation of a robust public sphere in civil society, and this could take the form of news reports or even letters to the editor that are actually appeals to the government to take corrective action. Indeed, this is the general transition the world over from face-to-face village communities, to imagining the nation-state with the help of the printed word.[6] In other words, a journalistic tradition that was started towards the end of the eighteenth century in India as part of an anti-colonial struggle to create a public sphere, is kept alive in different ways even today, despite monetary pressures, as part of the nation-building process.

In a country like India, with a substantive illiterate population, much of this imagination relating to nation building will depend on the visual media. S. Gautham discusses the struggle of television news producers and documentary filmmakers to create free and public spaces in the broadcast medium, given the fact that much of it is controlled by the Indian state. Indeed the state has been secretive with respect to the functioning of its own media, repressive with respect to the privately-owned or independent media, and arbitrary with respect to exercising its power of control of censorship. It is this last aspect—censorship—that is picked up and parodied by K.P. Jayasankar and Anjali Monteiro. According to them, the censor's simplistic assumptions of fixed meanings, the instrumentality of language, conscious intentionality of the language user and its predictable impact on the receiver are necessarily flawed, and this in turn leads to the impossibility of complete censorship, as it were. After all, there

---

[6] See Benedict Anderson's *Imagined Communities: Reflections on the Origin and Spread of Nationalism,* revised edition (London and New York: Verso, 1991).

will always be subtle and insidious subversions that are likely to escape the censor's scissors.

Citizenship, like democracy itself, is part of a historical tradition of struggle to appropriate forms of knowledge and values in the public space. However, these values do not have any transcendental significance outside the lived experiences and social practices of individuals who constitute public life in any polity. When the media, owing to market imperatives or euphoria with technology, ignore the cultural and ideological dimensions of individual experience, they deny the ground on which individuals learn, speak and imagine. When the media confine their attention to a small section of society, they deny democratic citizenship to the vast majority in the polity.

If statistics are to be believed, a large part of the Indian public (54 per cent) is under 25 years of age. The last essay in this collection by Anjali Kamat reminds us that the market-driven corporate image of the youth as constituting a homogeneous group of shallow and apolitical elements could not be further from the truth, if the participation of a staggering 10,000 young people at the World Social Forum in Mumbai in January 2004 is anything to go by. The paradox is that members of the media criticise the youth (as a general category) on the assumption that they are the largest consumers of the 'Page 3' trivia that the media themselves dole out! Instead of succumbing to vicious cycles of marketing or flatulent self-fulfilling prophecies, says the writer, the media could resort to more creative strategies and fresher narratives that could prove to be an inspiration to young people.

In short, it would seem that even though the history of journalism proceeds in criss-crossing loops, the values of the profession, though in need of modification to fit particular historical contexts, essentially remain the same from one generation to the next.

PART I
The Core Values

1

flourishing papers, floundering craft: the press and the law

b.r.p. bhaskar

$f$rom about 330 daily newspapers with a total circulation of 2.5 million copies in the early 1950s[1] to 5,638 newspapers with an estimated circulation of 59.1 million copies in 2001,[2] the Indian press has registered phenomenal growth in the past half-century. A Press Commission, which attempted a comprehensive survey of the newspaper scene in the early years of Independence, found that Hindi, the most widely spoken language, accounted for the largest number of dailies (76), closely followed by Urdu (70), and together they commanded sales of about 592,000 copies. The English-language press dominated the field: 41 newspapers in that language had a combined circulation of about 697,000 copies, which was 28 per cent of all newspaper sales. By 2001, Hindi was at the top of the table in terms of both the number of newspapers (2,507) and the number of copies sold (23.4 million, or 40.47 per cent of the total). The combined circulation of all English newspapers was only 8.7 million copies.[3] A detailed analysis of the way newspapers in the different languages grew during this period will reveal a skewed pattern.

In the colonial period, there were two categories of newspapers: those under British ownership and those under Indian ownership. The British-owned newspapers had white editors and supported the colonial regime. They habitually referred to the Indian-owned newspapers as the 'native press'.

---

[1] Report of the Press Commission headed by Justice G.S. Rajadhyaksha.
[2] Report of the Registrar for Newspapers in India, 2002.
[3] Ibid.

The Indian newspapers dubbed their British-owned rivals 'Anglo-Indian contemporaries'. While Indian publishers were active in both English and the local languages, the British companies brought out only English-language publications. In Kolkata (Calcutta), the birthplace of the Indian press, *The Statesman*, a British-owned newspaper, led the field, with *The Amrita Bazar Patrika* and *The Hindustan Standard*, both under Indian ownership, as its major challengers. In Mumbai (Bombay), too, the market leader was a British-owned newspaper, *The Times of India*. Its main nationalist competitors were *The Bombay Chronicle* and *The Free Press Journal*. The scene was different in Chennai (Madras), where *The Hindu*, one of the oldest nationalist newspapers, was ahead of *The Mail*, a British-owned newspaper.

When the British rulers decided to divide and quit, the British newspaper owners sold their businesses and left. Seth Ramakrishna Dalmia, a leading industrialist, took over *The Times of India* Group and a Chennai businessman acquired *The Mail* along with several non-newspaper firms. *The Pioneer* of Allahabad, which too was under British ownership, went to another industrial house. The owners of *The Statesman*, who had stakes in non-newspaper ventures as well, appeared to be in no hurry to quit. This annoyed the nationalists, whose sentiments were expressed by *The National Herald* in an editorial: ' ... with the attainment of freedom, it was not in the country's interest to allow foreign interests to run a newspaper like *The Statesman*'. It added: '*The Statesman*'s past policy is well known and a newspaper circulating in two neighbouring countries, which have been at war in Kashmir, and trying to be neutral is extremely irritating.'[4] Eventually, *The Statesman*'s foreign owners also pulled out. They turned over their shares to a consortium of Indian industrialists, including the Tatas and the Mafatlals.

Towards the end of the colonial period, G. D. Birla, a leading industrialist, had obtained controlling shares in *The Hindustan Times* of New Delhi. It marked the beginning of industrialists' incursion into the nationalist press as well. Ram Nath Goenka, an ambitious entrepreneur, picked up shares of the Madras edition of *The Free Press Journal*, and using it as a launching pad began building a newspaper empire under the banner of *The*

---

[4] Editorial, *The National Herald*, Lucknow, 11 September 1949.

Indian Express. The new owners of *The Times of India* bought a struggling New Delhi newspaper and converted it into a leading national daily. *The Times, Hindustan Times* and *Express* groups also went into the Indian languages. The predatory instincts of the big business press, which V.K. Krishna Menon dubbed 'the jute press', led to fears of the Fourth Estate ending up as an appendage of big business, cutting out diversity of opinion and endangering press freedom. The Indian Federation of Working Journalists (IFWJ), founded in 1950 as a trade union, demanded governmental intervention to check monopolistic trends and ensure press freedom.

The Constitution of India, while enumerating various freedoms, made no mention of freedom of the press. To begin with, the Constitution of the United States, too, had been silent on the subject. However, the omission was quickly rectified in circumstances that are worth recalling. Many federating states were unhappy that the Constitution did not include a Bill of Rights, and refused to ratify it unless this lacuna was removed. Their resolute stand forced the federal leadership to sponsor a set of 10 amendments. The first of these provided, among other things, that 'Congress shall make no law ... abridging the freedom of speech, or of the press'.

The press, as an institution, was still in its infancy when the US Constitution was framed. The Indian Constitution came more than 175 years later, by which time the press had won recognition in the democratic world as a powerful institution that deserves to be counted among the 'estates of the realm'. Yet the Indian Constitution-makers did not deem it necessary to incorporate in it a provision to forbid laws that impinge on press freedom. Their lack of sensitivity to the issue can be attributed to the circumstances prevailing at the time. World War II was only a year behind when the Constituent Assembly began its work. At the time the press was still reeling under the impact of wartime censorship. Large parts of the subcontinent were witnessing communal strife. Assuming that conditions were ripe for revolution, the communists launched an armed insurrection. The new rulers thought they needed the repressive laws enacted by the colonial regime to face the situation.

Soon after the Constitution came into force the Madras government barred the entry of *Crossroads*, a pro-communist weekly published from Bombay, into the state. The journal's editor, Romesh Thapar, filed a writ petition challenging the validity of the ban. The Supreme Court struck down the Madras order as a violation of the constitutional guarantee of freedom of speech and expression. Its judgment sanctified freedom of the press as an integral part of the freedom of speech and of expression enshrined in the Constitution. However, since the Constitution allowed the state to impose reasonable restrictions on fundamental rights, it was open to the government to place curbs on it. To get over the problems arising from the *Crossroads* verdict, Parliament enacted the Press (Objectionable Matters) Act 1951, which empowered the government to confiscate or demand security from publications.

There was no organisation of newspapermen that was strong enough to resist such legislation. The All India Newspaper Editors' Conference (AINEC), of which editors of prominent newspapers were members, was formed during the colonial period primarily to ensure cooperation between the regime and the press. Its record was one of collaboration. At the 1950 session of the AINEC, Prime Minister Jawaharlal Nehru said that the government did not believe in a controlled press. It was ready to accept a free press with all its faults. The AINEC thanked him for that commitment. Its response drew derisive comments from IFWJ President M. Chalapathi Rau, who was the Editor of *The National Herald*. He wrote:

Nothing less could have been expected of the Prime Minister. But was it a cause for expression of gratitude that the government were showing great consideration in not getting the Constitution amended? Such an unintelligent attitude on the part of the press would be unthinkable in any other free country.[5]

Chalapathi Rau voiced concern about the repressive laws.

The existence of the Supreme Court is no excuse for the continuance of obnoxious laws. They mean harassment, licence for the executive, work for the courts. While freedom of the

[5] Editorial, *The National Herald*, Lucknow, 5 December 1950.

press is inherent in freedom of expression, which the Constitution guarantees, the AINEC legal experts still harp on the theme of a separate enumeration of press freedom, forgetting that it is the provisions in Article 19 which have to be amended. The Prime Minister believes that the press is free; so does the Home Minister. They mean that, whatever may be the laws, the press is free in practice. Why not then amend the laws and allow the victims of bad laws to avoid litigation and harassment?[6]

It was in response to IFWJ's demand that the Government of India appointed a press commission, headed by Justice G. S. Rajadhyaksha, to inquire into the state of the press and make recommendations for its healthy growth. The Commission's terms of reference covered a wide gamut of subjects including control, management and ownership of newspapers, relationship between the owner and the editor, and service conditions of journalists. Its 11 members included the presidents of AINEC, IFWJ and the Indian Language Newspapers Association.

One problem that the Commission faced when it began the inquiry was the absence of information about newspapers. No one knew how many newspapers were published in the country and what circulation they commanded. Readers had no means of knowing who owned the newspapers they read. Gathering information was not easy. Letters that the Commission sent out to some newspapers were returned undelivered. It asked the Centre to create an agency to gather data on newspapers and publish a report each year. Finding that many journalists worked under miserable conditions, it recommended legislation to ensure satisfactory working conditions and prescribe wage scales for them periodically. It also called for the creation of a Press Council to look into complaints of breach of journalistic ethics. In the course of time the Centre enacted legislation to give effect to these recommendations.

The inquiry revealed an uneven media landscape. The large newspapers dominated the scene by virtue of their reach and revenues. The English-language newspapers, based in metropolitan cities, garnered the bulk of the advertisement revenue.

---

[6] Ibid.

The small and medium newspapers had a precarious existence. Monopolistic tendencies were in evidence. 'The ultimate goal of Indian society has been very clearly defined in the directive principles embodied in the Constitution,' the Commission said in its report. 'This is to secure and protect a social order in which justice—social, economic and political—shall inform all the institutions of national life.' It was, therefore, of the view that the 'power of the holder of a monopoly to influence the public in any way he chooses should be regulated and restrained.'

With *The Statesman* still under British owners, the Commission considered the question of 'ownership of newspapers and periodicals by nationals of other countries and even by foreign governments'. It said:

> We consider it highly desirable that proprietorial interests in daily and weekly newspapers should vest predominantly in Indian hands. We consider *The Statesman* a notable exception, which has for long been associated with Indian journalism and has become more or less an Indian institution. Even so, on general principles, we consider it desirable that there should be Indianization both of capital and of the staff, especially at the higher levels. This would apply also to commercial and economic weeklies such as *Capital, Commerce,* etc. Similarly, we would view with disfavour any attempt to bring out Indian editions of foreign periodicals which deal mainly with news and current affairs. On the other hand, we see no objection to the publication of local editions of technical and specialist periodicals, with the participation of Indian capital and labour.

When Leo Jay Margolin, the representative of a US syndicate, said in New Delhi that his group wished to buy newspapers in India, Chalapathi Rau likened his mission to Commodore Perry's Pacific adventure.[7] The government granted permission to the US magazine, *The Reader's Digest,* to publish an Indian edition. Later, at the instance of the Information and Broadcasting Ministry, the Cabinet decided that 'no foreign-owned newspaper or periodical should, in future, be permitted to be published in

---

[7] Editorial, *The National Herald,* 11 September 1949.

India.'[8] It accepted in principle the Press Commission's recommendation that foreign newspapers and periodicals, which dealt mainly with news and current affairs, should not be allowed to bring out Indian editions. While not overruling the decision to permit *The Reader's Digest* to publish an Indian edition, it resolved not to permit the periodical to bring out editions in any Indian language.

The Commission estimated that the 330 dailies had an aggregate circulation revenue of about Rs 60 million and advertisement revenue of about Rs 50 million in 1952. The large English newspapers published from metropolitan cities accounted for the bulk of newspaper sales and cornered a lion's share of the advertisement revenue. It suggested a ceiling of 40 per cent on space devoted to advertisements in a newspaper. It also wanted the selling price of a newspaper to be linked to the number of pages that it provided. These measures, it hoped, would enable small and medium newspapers to face the stiff competition from large ones and protect diversity of opinion in the press. The big business press opposed the proposals, viewing them as an attempt to fetter it. The IFWJ asked that the proposals be implemented to check monopolistic tendencies. All journalists did not share the working journalist movement's concern over industrialists' domination of the press. S. Mulgaokar, Editor of *The Hindustan Times*, argued that the financial viability of the big business press was 'a safeguard against the play of at least extra-proprietorial pressures'.

According to him, the big business press had three distinct advantages.

First, without exception, it eschews sensationalism. Secondly, it is in a position to hire the most professionally competent journalists and to attract to its pages the best outside talent for a discussion of public issues. Thirdly, it is the only section of the press that shows some concern, though unfortunately in a diminishing measure, for coverage of foreign news of significance.[9]

---

[8] Cabinet resolution dated 13 September 1955.

[9] S. Mulgaokar, 'The Press in Free India', in A.G. Noorani (ed.), *Freedom of the Press in India* (Bombay: Nachiketa Publications Ltd., 1971), pp. 17–18.

Although the government, in pursuance of the Press Commission's recommendation, enacted in 1956 the Daily Newspaper (Price and Page) Act, it did not take any immediate steps to give effect to its provisions. In 1960, as political polarisation in the country was intensifying, it ended years of hesitation and issued the Daily Newspaper (Price and Page) Order to enforce a price–page schedule. It was immediately challenged in court, not by any of the large metropolitan newspapers, who were its primary targets, but by a Marathi daily, *Sakal* of Pune. Some small newspapers joined the litigation on the government's side.

It was contended on behalf of *Sakal* that the Act and Order curtailed the freedom of the press inasmuch as it was compelled to raise the selling price by one paisa or reduce the total number of pages. If it raised the selling price, its circulation would be adversely affected and if it reduced the number of pages its right to disseminate news and views would be violated. In either event, there was interference with the right under Article 19 (1) (a). It was also contended that the Order allowed the Central government to reserve the power to permit issue of supplements, except those on 26 January and 15 August. This would place the newspaper at the mercy of the government, which would amount to interference in its freedom of expression.

The Supreme Court declared the Act and the Order unconstitutional. It ruled that 'the right of freedom of speech cannot be taken away with the object of placing restrictions on the business activities of a citizen.'[10] It said:

Freedom of speech can be restricted only in the interests of the security of the state, friendly relations with foreign states, public order, decency or morality, or in relation to contempt of court, defamation or incitement to an offence. It cannot, like the freedom to carry on business, be curtailed in the interest of the general public.[11]

While advocates of the price–page schedule had viewed it as a means of promoting the cause of democracy by ensuring plurality of opinion, the court came to the opposite conclusion. It held

---

[10] AIR, 1962, SC 305.
[11] Ibid.

that 'since its objective is to affect directly the right of circulation of newspapers which would necessarily undermine their power to influence public opinion, it cannot but be viewed as a dangerous weapon which is capable of being used against democracy itself'.[12]

The *Sakal* judgment put an end to legislative attempts to help small newspapers by creating a level playing field. More than a decade later, the government attempted to achieve through an executive order what it could not do through legislation. The order sought to restrict newsprint allocation through what came to be known as the Ten-Page Order. The Supreme Court struck down that as well.

The Registrar of Newspapers in India, in his annual reports, continued to draw attention to the growth of monopolistic trends. When the report for 1971–72 appeared, Chalapathi Rau commented that 'despite all the talk about curbing monopoly, including press monopoly, the hold of monopoly in the newspaper industry continues to grow steadily'.[13] He pointed out that the big business press was getting a lion's share of newsprint and government advertisements:

There is little point in the proud announcement that the total number of dailies in the country has gone up to 821, a 50 per cent increase in the quinquennium ending at the end of 1971, when it was seen that of the total newsprint available, more than half goes to nine of the 98 common ownership units. These nine groups get 1.04 lakh (104,000) metric tonnes out of the total 1.94 lakh (194,000) metric tonnes available for all dailies, and a total of 1.13 lakh (113,000) metric tonnes of the 2.24 lakh (224,000) metric tonnes available for dailies and periodicals together. Seventy-two of the common ownership units cornered about 1.74 lakh (174,000) metric tonnes or 77.7 per cent, while nine of them got 65.6 per cent out of this.

But this is not the whole story. Two common ownership units of big business houses—including *The Express* Group of the Goenkas with 14 dailies and eight periodicals—cornered almost a quarter of all available newsprint. Without burdening

---

[12] Ibid.
[13] Editorial, *The National Herald,* Lucknow, 7 May 1973.

the reader with the whole range of figures provided by the
Registrar, it may be said that the 'freedom of the press' over
which the Goenkas, the Jains, the Birlas and the Tatas raise
a howl all the time is in fact the freedom to corner newsprint
increasingly and prevent the growth of medium and small
newspapers which alone can sustain genuine democracy.[14]

He added:

The monopoly press is never tired of pretending that it is not
dependent upon the government, that the government are in
fact creating problems for it. The Press Registrar has avoided
giving details, but has at any rate said that nine 'big' dailies
secured between one-quarter and one-half of their advertisement revenue from government sources, and 21 'big' dailies
between 10 and 25 per cent.[15]

He took the opportunity to demand reintroduction of the price–
page schedule and imposition of a ceiling of 40 per cent on the
space a newspaper can allot to advertisements. The IFWJ, too,
campaigned sporadically for steps to check the growth of monopoly.
However, the government did not pursue the matter seriously. At
one stage Indira Gandhi considered legislation aimed at restructuring the ownership of newspapers but the proposal was not pur-
sued. However, during the Emergency, her government promul-
gated an ordinance to prevent publication of objectionable matters.

In 1977, the Janata government set up a second Press Commission, with Justice K. K. Mathew as Chairman, to report on
the state of the newspaper industry. For some reason, small
and medium newspapers took less interest in its work than the
big ones. Seventy-six newspaper undertakings publishing128
dailies responded to its summons. However, only 50 of them—
31 big, 10 medium and nine small—provided the data it sought.
The Commission found that 90 dailies published by these undertakings accounted for 57.67 per cent of the total circulation of
daily newspapers.[16]

[14] Ibid.
[15] Ibid.
[16] Report of the Second Press Commission (New Delhi: Government of India,
1982).

The Commission noted that a major problem of small and medium newspapers was shortage of capital. To illustrate the point, it narrated the story of two Gujarati newspapers, *Jansatta* of Ahmedabad and *Loksatta* of Vadodara, which had ended up in *The Indian Express* stable in 1968. As the newspapers ran into financial trouble, their owners approached the Government of India for help. The Information and Broadcasting Ministry wanted to help but the Press Council, which was consulted, said a direct government loan would in principle be improper as it might impair the freedom of the press. The Council suggested the setting up of a Press Finance Corporation with an independent board as a long-term solution to the problem of failing newspapers.[17]

The Commission stated in its report that since the 1960s several European countries such as France, Italy and Belgium were providing subsidies or soft loans to newspapers to overcome financial difficulties. Norway and Sweden gave automatic subsidies to all newspapers whose circulation was between 2,000 and 10,000. The Commission, however, did not favour subsidies for two reasons:

> First, we do not have in India the problem of mergers and a diminishing range of choice of newspapers as is the case in the USA and several western countries. Secondly, in the prevailing atmosphere of animosity between political parties and the tendency to exercise executive discretion for the advantage of the party for the time being in power, a system of direct financial subsidy to individual newspapers would be liable to be misused.[18]

The Information and Broadcasting Ministry did pursue the idea of a Newspaper Finance Corporation. But the Finance Ministry shot it down. It was of the view that a special wing could be set up in the National Small Industries Corporation to give soft loans to newspapers.

Table 1.1, constructed using data gathered by the Mathew Commission, confirms that big newspapers increased their share of the circulation during the early decades of Independence.

---

[17] Ibid., Vol. I, p. 93.
[18] Ibid., p. 94.

Table 1.1: Circulation Share of Different Categories of Newspapers

Year	Big Newspapers		Medium Newspapers		Small Newspapers	
	Number	Circulation Share	Number	Circulation Share	Number	Circulation Share
1952	6	17.1%	35	35.8%	289	47.1%
1960	19	28.0%	50	20.8%	331	51.2%
1965	35	47.0%	111	34.4%	338	18.6%
1970	41	50.0%	91	29.4%	388	20.6%
1975	42	48.7%	96	27.8%	429	23.5%
1979	61	56.6%	115	23.5%	514	19.9%

Source: Compiled from data gathered by the Mathew Commission.

The table shows that the growth of newspapers was uneven. Initially, there was continuous rise in the number of big papers as well as their circulation share. In 1970 there were 41 big newspapers and together they accounted for half of all circulation. One more newspaper joined the group by 1975 but the circulation share of the big papers was down to 48.7 per cent.

Between 1952 and 1960, the number of medium newspapers rose from 35 to 50 but their circulation share fell from 35.8 per cent to 20.8 per cent. In the next five years, their number increased dramatically to 111 but their circulation share went up to only 34.4 per cent, which was below the 1952 level. By 1970 their number dropped to 91 and circulation share to 29.4 per cent. In the next five years the number of medium newspapers rose to 96 but their circulation share fell to 27.8 per cent. By 1979 the number of papers went up to 115 but circulation share declined further to 23.5 per cent.

Small newspapers registered improvement initially, with their number going up from 289 in 1952 to 331 in 1960 and their circulation share from 47.1 to 51.2 per cent. That was apparently the best period in the saga of small newspapers. In the next five years, their number improved marginally to 338 but their circulation share fell precipitously to 18.6 per cent. That took them to what was apparently the worst period in their history. While the number of small papers continued to rise, their circulation share, after going up to 20.6 per cent in 1970 and 23.5 per cent in 1975, slid to 19 per cent in 1979.

Both big and medium newspapers suffered a setback in 1975. This may be attributed to the reading public's disenchantment with the censored press of the Emergency period. Since the press

scene differs widely from region to region, detailed sector-wise
studies are necessary to fully explain all the erratic movements
reflected in the chart.

Table 1.2 relating to big newspapers, which is also based on
data contained in the Mathew Commission's report, shows the
uneven growth in the different language segments.

Table 1.2: Big Newspapers in Different Languages

Language	1960	1965	1970	1975	1979
Hindi	—	1	2	2	5
English	2	5	6	7	10
Bengali	—	2	2	2	2
Gujarati	—	—	—	3	3
Kannada	—	—	—	1	1
Malayalam	—	2	4	4	5
Marathi	—	1	3	2	3
Tamil	—	1	2	1	1
Total	2	12	19	22	30

Source: Compiled from data gathered by the Mathew Commission.

As we can see from the table, in 1960 there were only two newspapers with a circulation of more than 100,000, and they were
both in the English language. Five years later, there were 12
such newspapers, and they included seven in five Indian languages. Bengali and Malayalam had two each, and Hindi, Marathi
and Tamil one each. In the next five years, the number of big
newspapers went up to 19, with the Malayalam and Marathi
press adding two each and English, Hindi and Tamil one each.
By 1975, the number went up further to 22. While one Marathi
newspaper and one Tamil newspaper went out of the list, three
newspapers in Gujarati and one in Kannada joined the big league
for the first time. This shows that even during the Emergency,
which affected big and medium papers in the country adversely,
the press in some regions registered significant growth.

The post-Emergency period witnessed a newspaper boom as
the press came out with stories of excesses which could not be
reported as they happened because of censorship regulations,
and the public lapped them up. This explains why the number of
newspapers with a circulation of 100,000 or more shot up to 30
by 1979. Newspapers in English (10) and Hindi (five) accounted
for half of them. Newspapers in Malayalam (five), Marathi and

Gujarati (three each) and Bengali, Tamil and Kannada (one each) made up the rest.

We need to remember that big newspapers did not pop up from nowhere. They had started as small or medium newspapers and grown in terms of circulation and stature. Evidently, as the small newspapers' share of circulation was shrinking, some of them were making the transition to the medium category and some in that category were graduating to the category of big newspapers. While many newspapers that made it big during this period belonged to the big business press, there were also many who grew by overcoming challenges from that section.

Again, detailed sector-wise studies are needed to get a full picture of the pattern of growth of newspapers in the country. Data relating to circulation of newspapers in English and a few other languages in the early 1970s are analysed here to give an idea of the complexity of the pattern.[19]

The English-language press led the field with seven newspapers selling more than 100,000 copies each. They were *The Times of India* (253,251), *The Indian Express* (198,602), *The Statesman* (195,321), *The Hindu* (192,176), *The Hindustan Times* (146,401), *The Tribune* (110,629) and *Amrita Bazar Patrika* (101,871). All except *The Tribune* had their headquarters in metropolitan cities. Four of the seven belonged to the big business press. Two Hindi dailies had circulations in excess of 100,000: *Navbharat Times* (176,849) and *Hindustan* (153,086). They belonged to *The Times* and *Hindustan Times* groups, which had links with prominent industrial houses. The largest Marathi dailies, *Loksatta* (129,420) and *Maharashtra Times* (122,128), were part of *The Express* and *Times* groups.

If all this seemed to justify apprehensions about a few industrial houses dominating the media, the Bengali, Gujarati, Malayalam and Tamil press had a different story to tell. To begin with, the market leaders in these languages did not have links with industries. However, the owners of some of these newspapers did develop interest in non-newspaper ventures later.

As *The Hindu* and *The Indian Express* forged ahead in Chennai, *The Mail* (25,533 copies) was in the doldrums despite

---

[19] The circulation data has been drawn from INFA's *Press and Advertisers, Year Book* (Delhi: INFA Publications, 1974). The audited circulation figures relate to the first half of 1973.

its industrial connections. It had made a fatal mistake in not turning into a morning newspaper during the war years as *The Hindu* did. In Mumbai, *The Free Press Journal* (36,622) slipped to third place after *The Times* and *The Indian Express* (66,856). The pro-left *Patriot* showed briefly that the big business press was not unbeatable. It edged past *The Statesman* (22,923) and *The Times* (32,087) to claim the third largest sales in New Delhi with about 37,000 copies after *Hindustan Times* (71,086) and *The Indian Express* (49,554).

In several state capitals and small cities, English language newspapers likewise demonstrated the ability to hold their ground in opposition to the metropolitan newspapers and their local editions. *The Deccan Chronicle* sold about 21,200 copies in Hyderabad against *The Hindu*'s 14,529 and *The Indian Express*'s 6,131. In Bangalore, *Deccan Herald* with 37,637 copies was far ahead of *The Hindu* with 10,355. In Patna, *The Indian Nation* (9,860) was in the lead and *The Searchlight* (8,625), which belonged to the *Hindustan Times* group, a close second, while Kolkata's *Statesman* (1,498) and *Amrita Bazar Patrika* (1,156) were way behind.

The first quarter-century of freedom saw a blossoming of the provincial press. Advertisers, particularly consumer goods manufacturers, eager to reach out to the middle class in the newly emerging urban centres, began patronising the provincial newspapers. In the wake of increasing urbanisation, local advertising also grew. These trends benefited the state-level newspapers in English as well as the regional languages immensely.

Navbharat Times and *Hindustan*, belonging to *The Times* and *Hindustan Times* groups respectively and published simultaneously from both New Delhi and Mumbai, were able to establish themselves quickly as the leading Hindi dailies. However, regional newspapers continued to dominate cities like Patna, Lucknow, Jaipur, Bhopal and Indore. *The Times* group went into Marathi and Gujarati too. *The Express* group, which made the most inroads into the Indian languages market, published newspapers in Tamil, Telugu, Kannada, Marathi and Gujarati, besides Hindi. All the chains steered clear of Bengali and Malayalam.

The second quarter-century of freedom saw a blossoming of the district press. In this period, advertisers, wanting to extend their reach further, began patronising the district newspapers. According to the latest report of the Registrar of Newspapers for India, there were 171 common ownership units in 2001, and they brought out 817 publications.[20] It said:

> In the 'big' category were 169 dailies and tri- or bi-weeklies. In the 'medium' category, the number stood at 573 and in the 'small' category 587. The big dailies had a share of 46.11 per cent in the total circulation of the daily press, the medium accounted for 42.05 per cent and the small only 11.84 per cent.

These figures point to a reversal of the monopolistic trend of 1979 when big newspapers had 56.6 per cent of all circulation. The medium newspapers were better placed than earlier with 42.05 per cent of the circulation. However, the small newspapers' share had declined from 19.9 per cent to 11.84 per cent.

An interesting fact brought out by the report is that corporate newspapers were lagging behind those under individual ownership. Newspapers owned by joint stock companies accounted for only 43.51 per cent of the circulation. As much as 45.68 per cent of the circulation was held by newspapers owned by individuals.

Hindi newspapers, which registered a comparatively small growth in the first quarter-century, took a big leap in the second. As against five newspapers with circulations in excess of 100,000 in 1979, there were a few with circulations of one million or more at the turn of the century. None of them belonged to the big business press. While in the former period metropolitan newspapers spread to the states, in the latter period state and district newspapers were pushing into the metropolises. Leading the brigade were *Amar Ujala, Dainik Jagran* and *Dainik Bhaskar.*

Amar Ujala, which began publication at Agra in 1948, established editions in Delhi, Chandigarh and Punjab, besides a dozen centres in Uttar Pradesh. *Jagran,* which made its appearance in another district town of UP in the early1940s, had a score of

---

[20] Ministry of Information and Broadcasting, *Press in India 2002, Report of Registrar of Newspapers for India* (New Delhi: Government of India, 2002).

editions in eight states. *Bhaskar,* launched at Bhopal in 1958, also had almost as many editions in as many states. These newspapers boasted of circulations between 1.3 million and 2.1 million[21] and were still growing. The big business newspapers with immense resources appeared to be powerless to stop their advance. One reason for their remarkable success was the use of new technologies that made remote editions less expensive than before. The big business newspapers were slow in taking to new technologies.

The quick advances made by these newspapers revealed a linguistic divide. While the metropolitan newspaper establishments with strong moorings in English failed in the Indian languages, the Hindi newspapers could not replicate their success in English. Forays into English by *Bhaskar* and *Jagran* were disasters.

In the second quarter-century, Marathi, Gujarati and Telugu joined Malayalam, Tamil and Bengali in the list of languages with fast growing newspapers. What role social, economic and political developments played in the differential growth of newspapers in the various languages is another matter that calls for detailed study.

In retrospect, it would appear that the apprehensions of critics of big business press like Chalapathi Rau were not entirely well founded. In this context, it is worth noting that the Ambanis, who built a big industrial empire in a short while, came a cropper in the newspaper field. The virtues that admirers like Mulgaokar found in the big business press were also misplaced. Far from resisting sensationalism, newspapers like *The Times of India* became its ardent devotees as profit replaced popular concerns as the prime factor in the newspapers' scheme of things.

A discerning observer can see signs of a sea change in the character of the press. To begin with, the role model of the Indian newspapers was Britain's quality press. In the 1940s, a Tamil newspaper, *Dina Thanthi*, adopted the style of Britain's popular press and built up a large circulation. In the 1960s, the International Press Institute started bringing in foreign experts, directly or through its Asian and Indian associates, to help the Indian

---

[21] ABC figures given in Indian Newspaper Society, *Press Handbook 2003– 2004* (New Delhi: INS, 2004).

newspapers with new ideas. They were all from the popular stream and promoted the techniques of popular journalism. Yet, until recently, popular journalism had few takers in the country. Now, however, the situation has changed. Tabloidisation has played a large part in the growth of newspapers in all the language segments that registered significant expansion of circulation in the last few years.

The Times of India has set a new trend by switching from quality to popular journalism to beat long-established rivals. In Bangalore, it raised its circulation from less than 25,000 copies in January–June 1996 to 230,000 in January–June 2001, while the share of the market leader *Deccan Herald* declined marginally from 131,898 to 121,724. *The Times* achieved its phenomenal growth through a multiple strategy, which included, on the marketing side, a hefty price cut, and on the editorial side, trivialisation of news. It did not make all its gains at the expense of other newspapers. This is evident from the fact that the others lost fewer than 25,000 copies during this period. Obviously, popular journalism helped *The Times* to find a large body of new readers. Similar developments are taking place in other parts of the country as well. They point to the dawn of a new era characterised by flourishing newspapers and floundering journalism.

2

defining the principles of
ethical journalism*

n. ram

*t*he Hindu, founded on 20 September 1878, is the oldest surviving major newspaper of Indian nationalism, by which we
mean the great socio–political movement that won freedom for
India from colonial bondage and helped consolidate the gains of
Independence in every sphere of national life. The world has
undergone a sea change since a President of India inaugurated
the newspaper's centenary celebrations in Chennai on 5 September 1978. It is but fitting that in its 125th year, *The Hindu*
re-committed itself to its larger societal and public service mission. Within that framework, it has set itself the goals of up-
holding and strengthening quality and objective journalism in
respect of both news and opinion, and continually achieving
higher standards of journalistic performance in an increasingly
competitive milieu. The long-term strengths of this newspaper
have been independence, seriousness, newsiness, credibility,
fairness, balance and critical spirit. It has become clear to large
numbers of readers as, well as to those within the organisation
who bear responsibility for the newspaper's future, that these
traits needed replenishment and reinforcement. In consequence,
The Hindu recently undertook a restructuring and reorienta-
tion of its editorial operations, and indeed a correction of course.

The background and context of this editorial re-direction are
important. By and large, the claim can be made that the Indian
press retains its historical strengths and its soul. It also retains

---

* This paper was first published as an editorial in *The Hindu,* 27 August
2003.

a relatively high degree of diversity and pluralism, reflecting the vast regional, linguistic, socio-economic and cultural heterogeneity of a subcontinent. There are indications, however, that this diversity has come under pressure and could even be under long-term threat; and that concentration of circulation is growing in several market sectors. As a recent scholarly analysis of the economics of media diversity in India puts it, 'in each market segment within each kind of media business there is a real threat of domination of a kind that dilutes the basic tendency towards diversity and pluralism characteristic of the Indian media market place', a trend that has 'adverse implications for serious and good journalism'. Revolutionary technological advances have made it possible for newspapers to be more attractively and speedily produced. They have transformed production values, including the use of colour and graphics, almost beyond recognition. They have given accessibility a new meaning by creating new news and information delivery vehicles and enhancing existing channels of distribution.

quality journalism

However, objective processes of socio-economic and media development, intensifying competition within the press and from the other news media, above all television, and other kinds of economic and political pressures have introduced serious problems. Higher levels of manipulation of news, analysis and public affairs information to suit the owners' financial and political interests; prejudice and propaganda masquerading as professional journalism; the downgrading and devaluing of editorial functions in some cases; the growing willingness of newspapers in 'the drive for dominance' to 'tailor editorial styles to target the space created by ... homogenizing influences ... in segmented markets'; Murdoch-style price wars and aggressive practices in the home bases of other newspapers to overwhelm and kill competition; and creeping corruption are deeply worrying tendencies.

   The only answer to all this can be journalism of high quality, rooted in well-defined principles, clear-sighted, ethically and professionally sound, determined to put editorial values first, responsive to the needs of readers and the market within clearly worked out journalistic parameters, and willing to transform its methods and practices to take full advantage of changing technology and times. *The Guardian* in England has proved that journalism of this kind can more than hold its own against Murdochism. It needs to be added that such journalism cannot flourish by itself. It must go hand in hand with good, state-of-the-art business practice, which bases its long-term strategy on a balanced appreciation of the fundamentals and core values of journalism and the evolving needs of a dynamic society. *The Hindu,* which was launched 125 years ago as a weekly newspaper by six young nationalists who borrowed a rupee and three quarters to print 80 copies, is today a daily with a circulation of over 925,000 copies printed in 11 centres and published by a Rs 4 billion company. Advertising revenue now accounts for 80 per cent of its total revenues. In the contemporary age, there can be no walls separating editorial functions within a newspaper. There can also be no walls between the editorial and marketing functions of a newspaper in the sense of ruling out exchange of information, insight and experience, consultation and cooperation. Great newspapers with a soul know where to draw the *lakshman rekha* and how to give primacy to the editorial functions.

framework

Convergence and the arrival of online journalism and generally the 'new media' (defined as digital, interactive and multimedia) are expected to revolutionise the field of journalism, although the direct impact thus far has been less than predicted. Newspaper journalism as well as the business side of news operations must grasp the opportunities with both hands and ensure that the online product is at least as good as the hard copy. What is already clear is that given the big problem of information overload on the Net, the virtues and core values of journalism will prove invaluable. This means that the capability to select, to distinguish between the important and the unimportant, the significant and the trivial, to interpret and place in context news and public affairs information, and to do all this to a rigorous deadline, will win out in the new media.

What is the conceptual or theoretical framework in which such journalism can flourish? The idea that information, and especially the press, can play a substantive and even a crucial role in the formation of public opinion in society and in shaping public policy on major social, political and economic issues is an appealing one in intellectual and socio–political terms. The discovery that, on vital matters such as mass hunger, deprivation and a sudden collapse of entitlements, timely and relevant information makes a qualitative difference to the way public opinion is shaped and official policy is made to respond is a great boost to the self-image of professional journalism. The long-term Indian press experience, set in a larger context, suggests a set of functions that serious newspapers have performed with benefit to society. These are (a) the credible-informational, (b) the critical-investigative 'watchdog', (c) the educational and (d) the agenda-building functions. In addition, there is the well-known propaganda or 'manufacture of consent' role played by the dominant news media, a negative function that harms society and the people's interests.

The credible-informational function, which has something to do with a rule of law tradition, can be seen as a prerequisite for the critical function. On the other hand, it is this second function that gives the credible-informational function a new, substantive content in relation to society. Experience teaches us that if the critical function weakens or gets eroded, the credible-informational function might fade away through sheer disuse. The critical function can also be conceptualised as a 'watchdog' role, which is to say it can involve either constructive cooperation or adversariality in the public interest depending on the circumstances. Under ideal circumstances, the purpose and tendency of press reporting, criticism, investigation and even 'watchdogism' may be to improve the government or reform the system. But under other circumstances, the more substantive and progressive function may legitimately turn into a 'destabilising' role in the sense that the press tilts effectively against what begins, as a result of the communication impact, to be popularly and politically perceived as unjust or corrupt or otherwise unacceptable government policy. The Hindu's 125-year history illustrates, time and again, the role of an independent newspaper in the two contrasting sets of circumstances. It was founded with the proclaimed objective of helping to 'reform' a British Raj that had, eventually, to be done away with for the simple reason that it was inherently unjust, oppressive and imperialist. *The Hindu* also took on a role of 'constructive cooperation' in the first flush of Independence and during some other phases in recent decades. However, it played an adversarial as well as watchdog role in its detailed coverage of the Arbuthnot Bank crash scandal in the first decade of the twentieth century. Eight decades later, it played the same role more aggressively in its sustained investigation of the Bofors corruption scandal.

A newspaper cannot claim to be great merely by performing the first two positive functions. It must also play a strong educational role in society. Over the long term Indian newspapers have been performing this function, to an extent, in areas such as politics and public affairs, the economy, foreign policy, business, science and technology, school and higher education, literature, the arts, especially Indian classical music, and sports. However, this educational role has been performed far below potential. When the educational function is taken up systematically and imaginatively by Indian newspapers, exciting results are likely to follow. The fourth function involves socially conscious newspapers working hard to trigger agenda-building processes to help produce democratic and progressive outcomes. This function is derived from the first three functions. But when the agenda-building function attains critical mass, it becomes an autonomous, proactive role vis-à-vis society—a process in which *The Hindu*, as India's national newspaper looking to the future, would like to play its due part.

principles

Conventional wisdom in the West, and especially in the United States, has posited a *laissez faire* conception of a libertarian press with unbridled rights that no government and no external agency could be allowed to touch. The social responsibility theory arose in reaction to this posture. For all the criticisms and objections levelled against it, the conception of socially responsible journalism has come to stay. Several theorists have formulated principles that should guide such journalism. In keeping with the values of India's historical civilisation, which has respected, cherished and conserved diversity and pluralism, and the universal modern values of enlightenment, democracy, secularism and justice, *The Hindu* has worked out for itself a set of five principles as a template for socially responsible and ethical journalism.

The first is the principle of *truth telling*. This essentially means that a newspaper must aim for factuality, accuracy, verification, 'anticipating the likelihood of error', providing context, background, reasonable interpretation and careful analysis. It means also probing deep and investigating in a tough-minded and resourceful way to uncover facts of significance that are either concealed or are inaccessible for some other reason. There are different categories of writing in a newspaper, especially in an all-round newspaper like *The Hindu*. The three broad categories are *news reports, news analyses and interpretative pieces* and *opinion pieces,* including editorials and articles expressing various kinds of opinion. The C.P. Scott dictum, 'Comment is free but facts are sacred' sounds old-fashioned in the contemporary journalistic context; we do know that all news writing involves an element of judgment and selection, which might be called subjective. However, the lines separating the three categories of writing have virtually disappeared in most newspapers, and editorialising in news reports has become rampant. This newspaper, which was also affected by the 'editorialising as news reporting' virus, is determined to buck the trend, restore the professionally sound lines of demarcation, and strengthen objectivity and factuality in its coverage.

freedom and pressures

The second principle is that of *freedom and independence.* Freedom of the press was not easily won in modern India, even if it tends to be taken for granted today. Denied before Independence by a battery of anti-press colonial laws and authoritarian practices, this freedom, which is enviable by the standards of the less developed world, flows from Article 19 of the Indian Constitution and has been put on a pedestal by judicial interpretation. The Supreme Court of India has held that freedom of the press is a combination of two fundamental rights, Article 19(1)(a), 'the freedom of speech and expression', and Article 19(1)(g), 'the freedom to practise any profession, or to carry on any occupation, trade or business'. The first is clearly the principal component. It is subject to 'reasonable restrictions' that can be imposed by law for the purposes specified under eight heads in Article 19(2)—and for no other purpose. Article 19(1)(g) is, however, subject to 'reasonable restrictions' that can be imposed by law 'in the interests of the general public'. The restrictions must also meet judicial standards of reasonableness. In practice, some of these 'reasonable restrictions', notably those provided for in the criminal defamation and criminal contempt of court laws, have become unreasonable and illiberal, constituting pressure points and even encroachments on the freedom of the press. This newspaper is determined to oppose and resist all unreasonable restrictions on a free press. It is of the considered view that statute changes have become necessary to eliminate the mischief. To safeguard Article 19 freedoms, defamation must be de-criminalised, and the sky-high powers assumed by the higher courts to act as 'judges in their own cause' (not allowing even truth as a defence against criminal contempt of court) must be taken away by Parliament and the people.

The third component of the template is the principle of *justice*. Conceptions of justice vary widely, from the classical liberal to the Rawlsian to the radical and revolutionary. No professional prescription can be laid down for which conception a journalist or a newspaper must follow. One level of justice is fairness, judged by widely accepted standards of reasonableness. A fairness doctrine can be laid down in a quite precise and enforceable way; it can indeed be codified in terms of professional ethics. But justice is much more than 'fairness' in this sense. A progressive approach to justice that can be of real value to a serious newspaper is the theoretical concept of entitlements, human capabilities and functionings developed by Amartya Sen. Given Indian realities, this concept can be a powerful tool for triggering journalistic interest in socio-economic and other forms of deprivation and in the development of specialised capabilities for covering deprivation in an informed, interesting and accessible way. Thus, constructive pressure can be put on the system and momentum generated for public action in a critical area where independent India has performed extraordinarily poorly in any international comparison.

The fourth principle is that of *humaneness*. To ask for this consistently from the news media is not to aim too high. National media coverage of the 2002 Gujarat carnage has been justly praised for its 'honesty, integrity ... and humaneness'. However, the coverage of the same experience by some leading newspapers in that state lacked both truth and humanity. Covering a severe drought, starvation deaths and mass distress tends to be, at the same time, an exercise in truth telling, independence and humanity. *The Hindu* believes that socially responsible journalism must make its commitment to the principle of humaneness more explicit, immediate, wide-ranging and nuanced.

for the social good

The fifth principle is that of *contributing to the social good*. Professional journalism must not become agitation and propaganda, but there is strong ethical and social justification for a journalism that contributes, within its constraints and to the best of its ability, to peace and to the resolution of conflicts in society. Thus journalism that stands for the social good must take a clear stand against raining down death, anarchy and chaos, with high-tech weapons, on masses of innocent people and devastating a country under the pretext of bringing about a 'regime change'. Opposing communalism as a political mobilisation strategy and also every form of fundamentalism and extremism; advocating the principles of secularism—the equality and non-discrimination principle as well as the principle that religion, however significant it may be in the life of the people, should not be used to incite hatred or exploited for political gain—and the path of uniting people for development and social transformation tasks; resisting chauvinism and divisiveness in the name of caste, language, ethnicity, river waters and so on; improving relations with neighbouring countries; arguing for democracy, rationality, science and education; demanding that all children of schoolgoing age should be in school and that the unconscionable practice of child labour should be eliminated; demanding that female foeticide through sex-selective abortion not be tolerated and comprehensive measures be adopted to improve the sex ratio in the population—in the eyes of most reasonable people, these are ways of contributing to the social good. However, there are bound to be disputes over what is socially good, as divided reactions to such horrors as the demolition of the Babri masjid, the Gujarat pogrom and terrorist atrocities in Jammu and Kashmir show. It is the social responsibility of a serious newspaper constantly to remind political leaders that the politics of hate, bigotry, communalism and chauvinism is guaranteed to produce a vicious cycle featuring violence, tension and instability in society.

Is it too much to demand from the socially intelligent media that they must discern or discover in a free and independent way what is true, what is democratic and just, what is humane, what is socially good, and to avoid the traps that abound in the professional arena and the marketplace? *The Hindu* is clear it is not.

3

prabhat khabar: an experiment in journalism

harivansh

*p*rabhat Khabar is an experiment in Hindi journalism. When readers, hawkers and newsagents were given gifts amounting to millions of rupees by other newspapers as part of their 'aggressive marketing' tactics, none of this influenced the editorial policy of *Prabhat Khabar*. When in the 1990s, newspapers were sold at lower rates to attract new readers, capital-starved *Prabhat Khabar* did not join the price war. When it was generally accepted in journalism circles that 'entertainment' and 'information' were the principal virtues of newspapers, *Prabhat Khabar* raised high the flag for development issues. When it was quietly agreed in this age of free market and globalisation that ideals and values have no place in journalism, *Prabhat Khabar* considered ideals and values to be its very basis (see the figures in the Appendix for examples of front page news in the paper).

When we started working in *Prabhat Khabar* in the 1990s, I remember reading some research on the content of Hindi journalism that had an abundance of rumour, gossip and sensationalism. This finding coincided with a period when it was announced that newspapers had become a product and were no longer a mission. However, things began to change slowly. *Prabhat Khabar* started giving information on science, information technology, economics and the comparative financial progress of different states. Simultaneously, the paper became the torchbearer for various ethical agitations in civil society. It did not imbibe the liberal and market-oriented view of the 'consumer as king', but accepted the Gandhian principle that 'readers are the

masters'. The nearly bankrupt *Prabhat Khabar* was given a new
lease of life 15 years ago by a committed young team.

When we started the work to set the newspaper back on its
track, no one could have imagined that one day it would become
such a success in Hindi journalism. Much of this success came
from the paper's efforts to reach out to its readers. In 1990–91,
Prabhat Khabar conducted 'readers' courts', where readers could
interact with journalists and discuss ways of improving the paper. In villages and at the block level, interactive programmes
like '*Prabhat Khabar* at your door' were conducted. The newspaper linked itself to information about the people's movements,
and during elections, conducted voters' awareness campaigns.
It thus not only became a part of the cities but also of the villages. By conducting such awareness programmes, *Prabhat
Khabar*, despite the absence of huge funds, became a very popular newspaper in Jharkhand. From the most backward region of
Bihar, Ranchi—which is now the capital of Jharkhand state—
the almost defunct *Prabhat Khabar* forged ahead and is today
published from five centres in three states.

Before Jharkhand became a separate state, *Prabhat Khabar*
spearheaded the task of providing the intellectual stimulus and
energy to the agitation for a separate statehood. The newspaper
also published a special series on Jharkand at that time in its
editions in Ranchi, Jamshedpur and Dhanbad. People used to
say that the agitation had come to a standstill everywhere, except on the pages of *Prabhat Khabar*. Thus the paper had, from
the beginning, an emotional relationship with the structure of
the new state.

In 2000, with all the political discussion of making Jharkhand
a separate state, a big newspaper house arrived in Ranchi with
much pomp and show. It even managed to entice 33 staff members from *Prabhat Khabar* with promises of huge salaries. The
larger paper no doubt hoped that a severely crippled *Prabhat
Khabar* would cease publication. However, the statistics of the
National Readership Survey (NRS)[1] reveal that, despite the conspiracy, *Prabhat Khabar*'s circulation actually doubled over the
last four years. In February 2003, another big Hindi daily (claiming to be the highest selling paper), *Dainik Jagran*, launched

---

[1] National Readership Studies Council, *National Readership Survey* (Mumbai:
NRSC, Audit Bureau of Circulation, 2004).

three editions in Jharkhand: in Ranchi, Jamshedpur and Dhanbad. Despite its aggressive marketing and publicity, it has had hardly any impact in this region. Why have the efforts of such big newspapers been fruitless? To my mind, this is because *Prabhat Khabar* has always associated itself with public issues and conducted a direct conversation with the people.

How did it all begin? Two weeks before we actually started working in *Prabhat Khabar*, Sanjeev Kshitij and I went to Ranchi. The then Director, D.S. Sharma (from whom I learnt how to be patient and disciplined), came to our hotel to meet us. Mr Sharma and Sanjeev then went to the *Prabhat Khabar* office. I requested Sanjeev to give me his impressions of the place. As for me, the day I started working would be the day I would go for the first time to the office of *Prabhat Khabar*.

After being associated with the well-known Hindi weekly of *The Times of India* group, *Dharmyug*, (which had the highest circulation in the Hindi-language press), followed by the weekly *Ravivar* from the *Ananda Bazar* group in Kolkata, I now had to contend with *Prabhat Khabar*! Its circulation then was approximately 500. Being a journalist in metros like Mumbai or Kolkata is very different from being one in Ranchi, particularly with an almost defunct organisation. It is the difference between the glamorous journalism of Central government politics and metropolitan cultures, on the one hand, and journalism of the jungles and mountains, on the other. In those days, questions relating to one's career graph were of great importance. Many of my friends and journalist-colleagues had already warned me of the impending end of my journalist life. Well-wishers did not want me to go to a small and unknown place and get lost there. Senior journalists from Delhi–Mumbai (from whom I learnt much about journalism) were extending offers to join them.

The truth was that I was drawn to the simple life of the tribal community in Jharkhand. My meetings with missionaries and activists in this community (while working with *Ravivar* and *Dharmyug*) had made a huge impression on me. The ladder of success in journalism in metropolitan cities—indeed many of my journalist friends had chosen this path—can easily lead to power, wealth, fame, glamour and parliamentary politics. But my calculations were different. I had left my previous jobs as lecturer and Reserve Bank officer and opted for 'journalism' in order to be part of a changing society. Indeed, my father, who was a farmer, regretted throughout his life that I had quietly left my officer's job in the Reserve Bank.

During my younger days, I felt that journalism was a powerful tool to break the social complacency around me. My background did not allow me to think about personal security, of things like a house, vehicle, property or a bank balance. Our generation was habitually very careless about these things. The people from whom I learnt about culture or social etiquette, and in the company of whom I spent most of my time, were purposeful and honest. Perhaps they were poor, but they had pride. My companions were innovative, restless, always enthusiastic about doing something new, and willing to face dangerous challenges. If I had succumbed to the present trend of thinking only about my future, owing to the pressures of market arrangements in a globalised world, I would not have come to Ranchi. I would not have got the experience of working in *Prabhat Khabar*.

So, in my hotel room in late 1989, I was restless to hear about Sanjeev's first impression of *Prabhat Khabar*. As soon as Sanjeev entered the room, I sensed the situation from his facial expression. There is a big risk involved here, he seemed to be saying. I started getting apprehensive. With a heavy heart and fears about the future, we returned to Kolkata that evening. During late-night train journeys, when the world sleeps, when there is a rule of silence, it is my favourite pastime to look intently out of the window. That night I could not think about anything other than *Prabhat Khabar* and questions about my future. That night is still fresh in my memory.

In the life of every human being there is a turning point when decisions have to be taken. Given my stubborn determination not to turn back, I knew what I would do. It was necessary to choose between singing glorious songs praising a group of power brokers or taking up dangerous challenges and do something new. I had already chosen. I believed that a magnificent defeat was far more prestigious than a victory gained at the cost of self-respect. By the time I reached Kolkata, I had resolved to try my luck in this seemingly impossible task in *Prabhat Khabar*.

After a week, we returned to Ranchi. For the first time, on 22 October 1989, I entered the premises of *Prabhat Khabar*. For about 10 days, my team members and I observed everything.

There were nearly 240 people working there. Composing, production, seating arrangements, everything was in disarray. Two old composing machines comprised the life of this newspaper. The machine used for printing the eight pages of the newspaper was decrepit. The circulation and advertisement departments—not to mention the editorial department—were overflowing with people. The total work was to print 500 copies of a six-page newspaper. Most of the copies were given away free. After a long time, we found out that many of these free copies had been given away to some readers throughout their lifetime!

Since the news agencies were closed, we were forced to cut and paste news from other newspapers, which were our main source of news. It was the first time I heard about this 'cutting–pasting' style of journalism. Old decrepit machines (which were repaired often) were used to print the headings. If the headings did not print properly, then they were written by hand. There was no system at all. There was no value for time. No planning was done. There was no supplement or Sunday edition. Who would provide the stationery? There was no provision for this. There was no allotment of responsibility anywhere. Who was doing what work? Who was in control of what? In the personnel department there was no record of employees. There was a big difference between the information given by the old organisation about the people engaged in work and the information we got on 22 October 1989, at the time of the 'takeover'. We had to face 'functional anarchy' directly. It was the first time we had to face such a disorganised situation. It was a time for losing courage, patience and self-control at every step.

Initially, I had told the new management that I would take up the responsibility of the editorial department. But right from the first day I knew that it was necessary to make every department professional. It is easy to start a new job, but to set right things that have gone off-track is close to impossible. Therefore, a list was prepared of well-known people in the newspaper industry. We decided to get suggestions from these people regarding production, circulation and marketing. These experts were also invited to attend the discussions of the top team of our organisation.

Given the rising power of the visual media in the early 1990s, the only way a newspaper could survive was by providing substantial and fresh information to readers. The *Ranchi Express* was already a very successful newspaper. From Ranchi, Jamshedpur and Dhanbad, *Aaj* was published and sold for just one rupee. The idea of a third newspaper standing up to these two powerful, well-established newspapers was daunting, to say the least. When there was little chance of success, it was hard to see a future beyond one-and-a-half months. In those early days, I tried my level best not to allow my pessimism about the future of *Prabhat Khabar* to percolate down to my enthusiastic team members.

There was no end in sight to the work of setting right this disorganised place. Since there was a chronic shortage of time, the *Prabhat Khabar* team started work at 9 in the morning and continued till 3 or 4 the next morning. This routine continued for five or six years every day; in every department, people stayed back in the office to complete their work. In those early years, perhaps no one in our office ever had any leisure time during weekdays.

In November 1989, on the twin occasion of Jawaharlal Nehru's centenary and the festival of Diwali, we planned a special supplement. We requested various well-known, national-level writers to write for us. The problem, however, was that we did not have the infrastructure to print anything, leave alone a supplement, beyond six pages. Strangely enough, if a team has courage, interest and zeal, then nothing is impossible. Even though we were less than a month old, we managed somehow to bring out the special supplement!

Our first collective attempt was to streamline every department. Our priority was to organise the editorial department, starting from the duty chart and meetings with reporters, to maintaining rules of editing and a code of conduct for the workers. This system was imposed on everyone, from the editor downwards. It was a violation of the code if profiles of the editor were published in our newspaper. Developing an impartial work-style favourable to journalism was the editorial priority. It was decided that only one correspondent would attend a press conference and that that person would not accept any gifts. These values I had learnt from people like Dharamveer Bharati, Editor of *Dharmyug*, who had taught me the ABC of journalism.

For our team, there was another challenge: how to frame an editorial policy? We had to decide on the content of the paper. Our idea was not to foster unhealthy competition among the bigger newspapers in the Ranchi area—then south Bihar. The aim of *Prabhat Khabar* was simply to become a better Hindi newspaper. The tradition of publishing information according to the wishes of the editor was stopped. Instead, we framed an open policy for every topic and asked co-workers to function according to it. The moral conduct to be followed was always discussed during our meetings. With this transparent policy, we struggled from the beginning to create an identity of a good, clean and modern newspaper.

Today, in this age of globalisation, newspapers are raising slogans for 'localisation'. From *The Times*, London, to the big newspapers of the country such as *The Telegraph* or *The Times of India*, the incidents in the life of a common man or woman may now constitute the lead in a newspaper. But in those days, there were severe constraints imposed on the exposure of the 'local' in big newspapers. Only incidents related to the lives of important personalities could constitute the main lead in the newspaper. In Hindi journalism, the situation was even worse. We broke with this sorry tradition in the initial stages of *Prabhat Khabar* by publishing local events that are important in the lives of ordinary people as the lead on the first page of the newspaper. This was perceived by some to be a very bold experiment. Others considered it to be a foolish step. The fact of the matter was that we started acquiring an identity in the eyes of our readers. This step also brightened our own prospects in *Prabhat Khabar*.

Within two or three months, our team had acquired its own editorial voice. Instead of focusing on topics related to politics, crime and sensational content, we gave importance to local talents, toppers in schools and colleges, successful farmers, women and shopkeepers. We published stories about the lives of ordinary people who struggled for success and excellence. *Prabhat Khabar* decided that instead of reports about specialists, prosperous people and the ruling class, it would focus on the joys and sorrows of ordinary people.

During this early period, the electricity tower fell down because of a cyclone in Ranchi. The government had announced that there would be no electricity in the city for the next 15 days.

The situation of the city telephones and hospitals can well be imagined. Officials used the generators provided by the government and led a relaxed life, while the public had to suffer. *Prabhat Khabar*, in the role of an activist newspaper, invited people to join in an agitation against this announcement. This agitation was headed by women and other ordinary people.

By this time, the madness of innovation had crept into our minds. Big functions, publicity-expansion in millions of rupees— these are important steps. But we did not have the luxury of unlimited funds at our disposal. Instead, we made pamphlets and arranged for their distribution. Our agenda was publicity, daily meetings with the editorial and circulation departments, and sustained work on new ideas. Towards this end, we had to rise above narrow considerations of religion, caste and society.

In the days when religion and caste were the main topics of discussion in Hindi newspapers, *Prabhat Khabar* was the first newspaper in Bihar to publish the inside story and pictures of the Bhagalpur riots. On the one hand, a few powerful groups wanted to suppress the actual news and photos of the riots; on the other, a few groups wanted to take political advantage of the atrocities. Our belief has been—and continues to be—that every citizen of our nation should be respected in any situation.

One important incident in the early 1990s forged the identity of *Prabhat Khabar*. The Ayodhya issue was in the news at that time. Hindi newspapers had published rumours as headlines and thereby fostered communal tension in society. There was curfew in Ranchi, and rumours about the number of dead people were rife. There was a competition between different papers to exaggerate the number. Some newspapers were putting up banner headlines that 200 to 400—even 800—people had been killed. Not only this, the number of people who were 'dead' varied in the eight editions of a single newspaper. Exaggerating facts and producing wrong facts—perhaps this had never happened on such a scale in independent India! There was no accountability or fear of the law. The Press Council wrote a sternly-worded report about this phenomenon, exposing six big Hindi newspapers. For our part, in *Prabhat Khabar*, we were publishing the correct information, that only six people had died in the Ayodhya dispute, with the help of our old friend, who was the Editor of the Lucknow *Navbharat Times*, and of the BBC team which had been present there.

Around the same time, our circulation department informed the then Director D.S. Sharma that there was no demand for *Prabhat Khabar* in the market. People were dubbing it a 'Muslim' newspaper and distributing pamphlets against it. (I, too, had received several threatening letters.) We told Mr Sharma that we had to decide whether to stand for the truth or resort to rumour-mongering. Need I mention the fact that our entire team opted for the former? Some of the newspapers which had earlier sold lakhs of copies on the basis of lies and rumours are today almost on the verge of closing down. *Prabhat Khabar*, which sold 500 copies to begin with, now has around 10 lakh readers, according to the NRS.[2]

This was the period when the term 'advertorial' had already taken root. Advertisements were published in editorial form. There were market pressures on the media. Our top team decided that when it was a question of the good of millions of people, we would rather choose the side of the public than that of commerce and advertisements.

Our priority was to become the voice of the people in a locality. We provided a forum for the oppressed tribals and urged official recognition of various tribal languages, like Nagpuri, Mundari, Kudukh and Khadiya. For the first time, we identified intellectual voices among the tribals. As part of a novel experiment in Hindi journalism, we started new columns to publicise the local affairs of the region. Questions about the forest and the land and water problems of Jharkhand have always been considered important by us. Thus displacement and progress also became important issues to be dealt with. *Prabhat Khabar* started campaigns against those who had made the forests a pastureland.

In 1992–93, our newspaper published several investigative reports on the cattle-fodder scam, which the rest of the country came to know about in 1996. *Prabhat Khabar* had a leading role in exposing this scam, and, later on, various big and famous newspapers of the country gave *Prabhat Khabar* the credit for being the first to expose it. In 1997 a BBC team arrived from London and made a film on the issue, and also acknowledged the role of *Prabhat Khabar* in this regard. But what was the cost

[2] National Readership Studies Council, *National Readership Survey* (Mumbai: NRSC, Audit Bureau of Circulation, 2004).

of exposing the scam? Criminals (who were protected by the then state government of Bihar) entered our office and threatened us. At every step, we were harassed by the police and other administrative officers.

After the formation of the new state of Jharkhand, the same work culture and corruption continued. We raised our voice against this phenomenon and paid the price for it. The electricity department in Jharkhand threatened *Prabhat Khabar* with dire consequences for publishing news about corruption there. Those who feel that corruption is not a serious issue are mistaken. *Prabhat Khabar* has tried to bring to light issues like the misuse of government facilities, wastage of money on half-completed jobs, lack of accountability and the lies of politicians. Our correspondents visited every village with the programme '*Prabhat Khabar* at your door'. We heard about the sufferings of villagers from our readers. A list of basic problems was framed and was published on an ongoing basis. During the voters' awareness campaigns, readers were told about the importance of their votes. We also brought to light the activities of honest leaders. We discovered, in interior villages, various tribal leaders (who had been ministers or members of parliament) ploughing fields in villages and living a life of deprivation.

In the early part of the 1990s, news about starvation deaths started coming out from the Palamau area. We used the power of journalism to fight on the side of the people suffering from hunger. A people's committee was formed in Ranchi, and people like Dr Siddharth Mukherjee, Tridev Ghosh and Colonel Bakshi came forward to offer help. The committee asked the people to contribute towards providing some immediate relief to those who were suffering, by donating items like food and clothes. Processions were taken out. Meetings were held. The names of those who had donated to this cause were published in the newspaper. The experience of getting involved in social issues empowered *Prabhat Khabar*. And such power or strength cannot be obtained from market publicity or by giving gifts.

In 2002, *Prabhat Khabar* again published news about deaths due to starvation in a village in the Palamau area. It is notable that six months prior to the printing of this news, the state government had declared this area as drought-stricken. According to the law, when an area is declared to be drought-stricken, relief work should be immediately commenced in that division. But the work had not been started and an affidavit based on the news published in *Prabhat Khabar* was submitted in the Daltongunj court.

As soon as the news about the starvation deaths was published in our newspaper, government ministers flew in by helicopters to visit the area. A big battalion of officers occupied the streets of this area. There were no roads, no electricity and no water. Although the government admitted that relief work had not been carried out here, it refused to acknowledge the fact that people had died of starvation. According to the official version, people had died of various illnesses.

Prabhat Khabar published whatever was said by the government very prominently but it also sent its correspondent to these villages for a period of 10 days. These villages were not the ones visited by the government representatives, and the paper continued to publish reports of starvation deaths. At last the Jharkhand government wrote a threatening letter to *Prabhat Khabar* on the grounds that it was publishing inaccurate information. Till that time, the other newspapers had been either silent on the issue or simply published the government version of events.

News about the starvation deaths reached the ears of the economist, Jean Drèze, who visited Kusumatand village and stayed there for four days. This incident was covered by the national newspapers. Drèze himself wrote articles in the English-language newspapers. In *Frontline* magazine,[3] Bela Bhatia and he mentioned the fact that the Jharkhand government had threatened *Prabhat Khabar* for printing the news on starvation deaths. Later on, the High Court started monitoring this issue. The other newspapers then started publishing news of the starvation situation and the Jharkhand government started its relief work.

With these experiences, it became clear that new techniques had to be adopted and strong attempts made for networking in rural areas. At a time when even the country's big Hindi news-

[3] Bela Bhatia and Jean Drèze, 'Starving Still in Jharkhand', *Frontline*, vol. 19 (16), 2002, www.frontlineonthenet.com/fl1916/19160850.htm.

papers were not engaged in this sort of thing, *Prabhat Khabar* started linking the faxing system to the villages in 1991. This attempt to link ourselves to modern technology helped us in the progress of our paper.

After this our 'top team' began wondering how to start editions of the newspaper in Jamshedpur and Dhanbad. Shortage of funds was a big issue. Our team members, K.K. Goenka and R.K. Dutta went to Jalandhar and purchased a 'third-hand' black-and-white machine at a nominal rate. The machine being used for printing in Ranchi was declared as scrap and replaced by the third-hand machine. The '(almost) scrapped machine' was installed in Jamshedpur. After that it was taken to Dhanbad. Then the third-hand 'Orient' machine installed in Ranchi also started giving problems. For two to three months, Goenka, Dutta and I used to stay back in the office till 5 or 6 in the morning because the newspaper's distribution was being delayed.

The Patna edition of *Prabhat Khabar* was launched in 1996, the Jamshedpur edition in 1997 and the Dhanbad edition in 1999. We launched our Kolkata edition in 2000.

So in Jamshedpur we started *Prabhat Khabar* with the nearly scrapped, black and white eight-page printing machine with minimal infrastructure. Before we started new editions at any place, we rented a guest house there. In Jamshedpur, all of us, starting from the chief editor to the clerk, stayed together. Goenka and Dutta had a list of useful household tips for every guesthouse. The wooden boxes which were used to transport the machines were used as benches to sleep on. With hardly any expenditure, arrangements for acquiring bedspreads and other necessities were made. All of us did odd jobs like cutting vegetables and cooking meals. For several years our top team members travelled in second class compartments in trains and even on buses. How did we deal with the publicity and expansion of the newspaper? For this, too, new ways were devised. Today, people who spend crores of rupees for every edition would surely laugh at our tactics in such matters. Our team decided that just as a person would open a recurring deposit account in the bank as a safeguard against financial crisis, we would open recurring accounts of Rs 5,000–10,000 each for the different editions of *Prabhat Khabar*. Thus, we were able to purchase land for the offices of *Prabhat Khabar* at Dhanbad, Jamshedpur and Ranchi.

But not all our experiments succeeded, especially in the early years between 1990 and 1995. For the first time in Hindi, a weekly newspaper about financial news (called *Karobar Khabar*) was published by *Prabhat Khabar* from Kolkata. But we could only bring this newspaper out for about two years. For women, a magazine called *Ghar* was started and this was published for about four years. Today this magazine is being published by the *Jagran* group as *Sakhi* and is doing very well. We also started a fortnightly magazine that focused on social problems. After some time we had to stop this as well. All these experiments were initiated without much investment. The only serious mistake we made was to burden our already overworked editorial staff in *Prabhat Khabar* with the extra responsibility of looking after these magazines!

In the meantime, we were also hassled by administrative problems. According to government rules, after six months of publishing, a newspaper is expected to submit an application to the Ministry of Information and Broadcasting, Government of India, in order to obtain recognition as a publication. Next, an application has to be submitted to the state government for registration. The state government grants its own 'recognition' certificate after it has investigated the affairs of the paper and ascertained that everything is in order. For several years in succession, we at *Prabhat Khabar* fulfilled all the formalities and were chasing the Bihar government authorities to grant recognition certificates for the Patna, Dhanbad and Jamshedpur editions. The Patna edition was finally recognised in the year 2002, after six years of waiting. But we did not succeed in getting recognition for the Jamshedpur and Dhanbad editions, nor did we get any explanation for the delay.

Despite all these problems and against all odds, we have carried on our work at *Prabhat Khabar*. Over the years, there were many hopes that the Hindi newspapers—given their rootedness in the culture of the people—would raise their voices against the different kinds of exploitation taking place throughout the country. But most big Hindi newspapers tend to imitate the style of English newspapers and become spokespersons for the 'haves' of society. Why is this so?

With globalisation, the mainstream media in Hindi journalism are losing their cultural roots and are only concerned about promoting the interests of the middle class. In the big newspapers, a new stream of journalism favouring the Page 3 lifestyle is gaining momentum. This involves leading names and faces in the fields of cinema, fashion, politics and the bureaucracy, and focuses on topics like beauty, sex, love affairs, titillating behind-the-scenes political events, expensive clothes, costly ornaments, the latest fashion trendsetters, the world's best hotels and so on.

A second important problem is the contribution of Hindi literature to the Hindi-speaking world. Earlier, till the 1970s, Hindi writers tried to represent the changes that were taking place in society. Now consider the writings in Hindi over the past 10 years. How many Hindi readers and writers know what innovations are being brought in by the various states in the country on the financial front? Until issues related to 'non-fictional' topics are given importance, it will not be possible to break free from the shackles of a backward society. Especially in the past 15 years, the content of big Hindi newspapers has become fictional and sensational. Poverty, suffering, unemployment, social atrocities, backwardness—these are no longer topics of interest in Hindi journalism in the twenty-first century.

In the Hindi media, it has become a habit to shamelessly publish false information. Even if this happens on a single day, it could mislead a lot of readers. But such 'serious mistakes' take place every week, while smaller ones are committed every day. Yet, there is no accountability—not to the readers, to society, or even to one's own organisation. Frequent transfers, postings, new contracts—all of these have become a pastime for senior journalists. Indeed, if this trend continues, Hindi-language journalism is likely to have the same unstable and undesirable trajectory that politics enjoys in the Hindi-speaking belt today.

Translated from Hindi by Ayesha Begum and Nalini Rajan.

appendix

prabhat khabar: *changing the lives of people*

Fig. 3.1A: *Prabhat Khabar*, Front Page, 24 November 2004

Fig. 3.2A: *Prabhat Khabar,* Front Page, 23 April 2005

Fig. 3.3A: *Prabhat Khabar,* Front Page, 4 May 2005

उग्रवाद खत्म होने तक विकास कार्य रोकदें

संक्षेप
सीबीआई ने की थापर से पूछताछ

खास बातचीत में नामधारी ने कहा

राज्य के कुछ छोटे-बड़े अधिकारी उग्रवादियों को लेवी देते ही नहीं, बल्कि छहे पहुंचाते हैं

धौनी को डीएसपी पद का ऑफर

कोयला कर्मचारियों को सौ फीसदी डीए देने पर सहमति

सरकारी कर्मियों का अर्जलीव 300 दिन

20 सूत्री कार्यक्रम में झारखंड फिसड्डी

॥ शुभ आमंत्रण ॥

लोकप्रिय आयुर्वेदिक उत्पादों के निर्माता मेघदूत ग्रामोद्योग सेवा संस्थान आपको आमंत्रित करते हैं.

250 घरोंवाले गांव में 55 तालाब

4

investigative journalism: those who expose us[*]

dilip d'souza

Some years ago, I visited some slum-dwellers in Baroda. That was at a time when I held a media fellowship from the National Foundation for India in Delhi, to meet and then write about India's denotified or ex-'criminal' tribes. These are communities that the British listed (or 'notified'), via the 1871 Criminal Tribes Act, as criminal. While independent India repealed the Act in 1952, a half-century later these people are still seen as criminal. This grossly mistaken perception naturally colours the way they live.

In Baroda, the slum I visited is home to about a hundred families from one such tribe, the Bajanias. In fact, the slum is called Mani Nagar Bajaniavas. When I visited Mani Nagar that day, these Bajanias spoke to me most of all, and animatedly, about their problems with the Municipality. In particular, they had things to say about two ongoing struggles: first, to get water; and second, to stop the Municipality's efforts to demolish their huts to make space for flats for Baroda's middle and upper classes. Such municipal efforts are commonplace in our cities, but even so, they take on an added poignancy when applied to the residents of Mani Nagar.

I began to feel this when the Bajanias, explaining their situation, produced several pieces of paper that they had saved for years, urging me to examine them. No doubt this squirrelling away of paper is itself an intriguing facet of the lives of denotified tribes.

---

*Shorter and modified versions of this paper appeared in *Seminar* and www.indiatogether.org in September 2003.

There were a lot of water bills, going back nearly 25 years.
The oldest one belonged to Nathabhai Veljibhai Vaghela. Dated
30 August, 1975, it was for the year between 1 April, 1975 and 31
March, 1976. On it was the water charge for those 12 months:
Rs 2.14. Nathabhai also showed me a bill 13 years younger. Dated
6 August, 1988, it applied to the year 1988–89. This bill demanded
Rs 18 for water. In 13 years, there had been a nearly ninefold
increase in the charge for water.

Seventy-year old Khudabhai Jivabhai had the most recent
bill to show me. It was dated 2 November, 1998, and asked
Khudabhai to pay Rs 252 for water for the year 1998–99. In 10
years since 1988, the Municipality had multiplied its water fee
another 14-fold.

In other words, when I visited Mani Nagar, the charge for the
Baroda Municipal Corporation water to this one colony of
hutments was nearly 120 times greater than it was just under
25 years ago. That outstrips inflation by a mile: Tata's reliable
Statistical Outline of India[1] provides the information that the
wholesale price rose approximately fivefold over the same period. It struck me that day that there probably is not a single
investment that has, over a quarter-century, increased in value
as much as the cost of Baroda water to several hundred of its
poorest residents.

This, for a single municipal tap that serves the entire slum of
about 600 people. Now hold that thought while I put this in
some context. It was 80 years ago, the Bajanias told me, that
the Maharaja of Baroda gave their ancestors this land to live on.
They were then part of a wandering minstrel tribe, making a
living by playing music at weddings and such like. (The name
Bajania comes from the word 'bajana', to play an instrument).
The land—then part of Majepur village, well outside the limits
of Baroda—was a royal reward to one Bajania troop for a performance at some long-forgotten royal wedding.

The Maharaja's word was then law. If it was to prove inadequate decades later, at the time it was enough for those two
dozen musicians and their families. They did not bother asking
the Maharaja for written titles and other such legal niceties.

---

[1] Tata Services Ltd, *Statistical Outline of India* (Mumbai: Tata Services Ltd,
Department of Economics and Statistics, 1998–99).

Giving up their wandering, the band of Bajanias built themselves homes and have lived here ever since.

Also among the papers the Bajanias showed me was a judgment from the Ahmedabad High Court dated 28 April, 1993. This was the outcome of a case they had filed to halt the destruction of their homes by the Municipality. In their arguments, they explained to the Court how the Maharaja had granted them the land. Clearly, it was not a persuasive explanation. Dismissing their petition, the Court observed:

> [The appellants] submitted that they are in possession [of the land] pursuant to some grant in their favour by some ruler of Baroda State. In support [of this] submission no evidence was produced before [the Court] .... The appellants therefore do not have any claim on the land and therefore they cannot be permitted to [occupy it].

So much for royal decrees.

When I returned from Baroda, I wrote an article about these people based on the various papers they had shown me. I wanted to explain the uncertain state of their lives and the reasons for it: in short, the story their papers told me.

That is a somewhat long introduction, but there is a point to it. My article brought me a few letters in response. One completely floored me. 'A good piece of investigative journalism,' wrote this appreciative reader. I was grateful for the praise, but also startled. Not because it was a poor effort—I thought I had written a good piece. But in my mind, the phrase 'investigative journalism' has always referred to sustained campaigns by intrepid reporters, doggedly pursuing secret leads and Deep Throats over months, then revealing to an astonished world findings that can bring down entire governments. Of course, even a generation later Watergate remains the classic example, but there have been others as well. That this person saw my article in the same way was flattering. But could this one report, based on a few hours spent with some slum residents, together with ordinary inferences drawn from their papers, really qualify as 'investigative'?

Perhaps I am making too much of this incident. But I wonder if there is not a lesson somewhere in here about journalism: that standards and public expectations have sunk so low that even the most trivially analytical article is held up as 'investigative'. Yet I'm hardly making the case that investigative journalism—the real thing, Deep Throats included—is dead. Not at all.

Consider the investigation of Enron's doings, practically from the moment the US firm came to India in the early 1990s to build a power plant in coastal Maharashtra. Various groups, activists and journalists diligently analysed every aspect of the project: from the way clearances were sought and given to financial agreements to human rights aspects. Cases were filed based on these issues, and fought all the way to the Supreme Court. It is a different matter that apart from issuing judicial rebukes, no court saw it fit to call a halt to the project.

One petitioner, Abhay Mehta, wrote a book about this pursuit,[2] that is an indictment not so much of Enron but of the Indian bureaucrats and politicians who betrayed the Indian interests they were supposed to serve. Enron, wrote Mehta, 'did what most business houses would have done to secure [the best possible] deal': the most lucrative contract in its history. On the other hand,

> [T]he problem lies mostly with us—the Indian nation state of India and all that term represents or should represent. At the core ... lies our inability to deal with or look after our own interests and to take responsibility for our actions or the lack thereof.[3]

For years, through changes in the state and Central governments, people like Abhay Mehta were laughed at, or simply ignored. Yet when Enron's house of cards came crashing down in India, and very soon after that in the USA too, their analyses proved to have been spot on. Take just one feature of the Enron project: the price of power. When the plant began supplying it, there were wails of outrage at the price it was charging Maharashtrian consumers. From between Rs 3 and Rs 4.25 a unit in mid-1999[4]—an already high figure—it rose to Rs 7.80 a

---

[2] Abhay Mehta, *Power Play: A Study of the Enron Project* (New Delhi: Orient Longman, 2000).

[3] Ibid., p. 177.

[4] *The Hindustan Times,* 8 July 1999.

unit by the end of 2000.[5] At the very same time, Tata Electric had power available for sale at Rs 2.20 a unit. Enron, though, had an absurd contract which forced the state to buy its more expensive product instead. (Absurd, that is, from the point of view of power consumers. From where Enron stood, it was a brilliant agreement.)

But this contract had been examined by the likes of Abhay Mehta, and Enron's high prices had been foreseen, if futilely. In September 1996, for example, a Pune-based non-government organisation called Prayas did a detailed analysis of the project. In its report, it came to the conclusion that the most 'likely' scenario was that 'the tariff [for Enron power would be] Rs 3.45 at the [plant]. According to the Chief Minister [then Manohar Joshi of the Shiv Sena party], the end user has to pay about double the [plant] tariff.'[6] By my calculations, the double of Rs 3.45 is Rs 6.90. Enron power was actually selling at nearly a whole rupee more by the end of 2000. But who paid any attention to Prayas's 1996 warnings?

Another example of meticulous investigation was the 1992 exposé of the infamous stock scam in Bombay by Sucheta Dalal in *The Times of India*. Checking and crosschecking of figures, a steady stream of follow-up reports, and a damning conclusion: the men involved had no escape from the noose that Dalal and others drew. That they escaped nevertheless, in the sense that nobody, to my knowledge, has ever been punished for that swindle, is a commentary on our society and its law and order mechanisms, but not on the investigation itself.

Enron, the stock scam, and let us not forget the work of that feisty website, tehelka.com: investigative journalism is certainly alive. So with stories like these that inspire journalists like me, why the note of pessimism with which I began this article? One, stories like these remain few, exceptions rather than the rule. Naturally I do not mean that investigative stories should be all that fills our newspapers. But if I can think of just three prominent examples through a decade (we can, I think, safely ignore my article on Baroda's Bajanias), that's a trickle. Not just that; in a country as filled with corruption as India is, there are plenty of scams that could stand to see the light of day. So it is also that

[5] Sucheta Dalal, *The Indian Express*, 3 December 2000.
[6] Prayas, *Occasional Report* (Pune: Prayas, Energy Group, September 1996).

corruption and crime flourish because the media pay too little attention, dig too infrequently and rarely deep enough.

Two, stories are hardly followed beyond initial reports. In fact, I suspect too few of us journalists understand the power and necessity of following a story up, down and everywhere. We find glamour in an initial exposé and feel that our job ends there. (To their credit, the journalists who went after Enron and the stock scam kept following up, and that really explains their triumph.) So we have daily tales of crimes in various quarters, but rarely news about what happens to the perpetrators. This is probably why so many of us complain about widespread corruption, but have a poor idea of the true extent of it, or of the specifics of individual scandals. This is probably also why the corrupt flourish and steadily increase the scale of their corruption.

Three, crimes and scandals come at us at a fearful rate. Off the top of my head, in no particular order, here are 15 Indian outrages—in the sense that each outraged us at one time or another—over the last two decades: the Bofors gun scandal; the urea scam; the fodder scam; the St Kitt's forgery case; the Delhi Sikh massacre, in 1984; the Jain diary case; the stock scam; the Gujarat violence in 2002; the J.J. Hospital glycerine adulteration deaths in 1986; the Mumbai (Bombay) riots in 1992–93; the Mumbai bomb blasts in 1993; Sukh Ram's telecom scam; the LPG allotment scam; the Babri Masjid demolition case; and the coffin scam.

Quite a list? But think of this: even as I type out these words, I remember others that I have not listed. The inevitable fallout of this cascade of crime is that public memory for what seem like momentous scandals is short. Worse, a certain ennui sets in, a fatigue with the treadmill of scams, an inability or unwillingness to recognise and feel outrage at crimes. Every journalist must battle this feeling among readers. What suffers, then, is their capability and keenness to work on investigative stories. What's the use, I've heard journalists say, when our readers don't give a damn? Stick to the fluff story about Miss Beautiful Smile at the Miss India contest!

Four, nobody of any consequence—in our 58 years after Independence, nobody—has ever been punished for their crimes. Maybe this lament is heard in other parts of the world too, I do not know. But it is certainly heard, and often, in India. Look again at that list of 15 crimes. In not one of those cases—in two decades, not one—have we managed to punish a single powerful or semi-powerful figure. In most of them, there is not even any kind of trial underway. And if there is, it waffles along quarter-heartedly.

Take Sukh Ram. Tens of millions of rupees in illegal cash were actually found in his bedding. For weeks in 1995, he frantically resisted efforts to arrest him. Yet today, while his case meanders through some dusty court, he remains a powerful leader in Himachal Pradesh. Today, Sukh Ram joins hands to form governments with the very people who once demanded his arrest. And in too many circles, he is a great hero. 'I don't care what money he took,' a principal of a school in Himachal Pradesh told me once. 'Without him we would not have had phone service!' Which is as telling a comment on our tolerance for corruption as any. And those stashes of cash? Who cares?

Many journalists are discouraged by this phenomenon too: not only are the guilty never punished, not only do the politically connected wink at punishment and collude to evade justice, but ordinary people show a remarkable willingness to forgive and forget. What use investigative journalism?

Five, the criminals themselves prosper despite being exposed, or perhaps because they are exposed. I have already spoken of Sukh Ram, and the adulation he commands in his home state. Take Bal Thackeray of the Shiv Sena party, named in innumerable press reports for his role in instigating riots in Mumbai in 1992–93. In its 1998 report, the Srikrishna Commission that inquired into those riots said this about him: '[L]ike a veteran general, [Thackeray] commanded his loyal Shiv Sainiks to retaliate by organised attacks on Muslims .... The attacks on Muslims by Shiv Sainiks were mounted with military precision with lists of establishments and voters' lists in hand.'[7]

What could be clearer? But naturally Thackeray remains unpunished. He rode those riots into power in Maharashtra in 1995. Today, he is a revered 'Hindu Hriday Samrat' (Emperor of the Hindu Heart—an actual title that was 'conferred' on him by adoring supporters), a man before whom everyone from industrialists to cricketers to Bollywood stars scrape and bow.

---

[7] *Report of the Srikrishna Commission* (Mumbai: Government of India, 1998). The Commission was constituted by the Government of India to probe the Mumbai riots of 1992–93.

Take Harshad Mehta, the prime figure in the stock scam. That this man was never punished was just a footnote in his career after the news of the scam broke. He became a sought after speaker, a columnist in several publications, admired and envied for his 'success' at 'beating the system', whatever the 'system' was, and no matter that his 'success' wiped out the savings of any number of far less 'successful' people. He had his own heavily trafficked website (www.harshad.com) and a Harshad Mehta Fan Club (members were promised that 'good markets or bad, you will make money').

Writing in *The Telegraph*, a paper that carried a Mehta column, Parthasarathi Swami summed up the 'popular refrain' of these fawning fans: 'Please send us some tips; email us before you post it'.[8] That is, fans did not want him punished, they admired him and wanted only that he share his secrets so that they could benefit too. So not only do ordinary people show a willingness to forgive and forget crimes, but there are enough of us to actually glorify them and their perpetrators.

Six, investigators themselves face vicious reprisals. Consider what happened, three years on, as a result of Tehelka exposing the rot in the way we buy arms. The government set up an inquiry into the scandal. Defence Minister George Fernandes resigned. Not long afterwards, while the inquiry that was going to establish his guilt or otherwise was still underway, he returned to office with a ringing endorsement from his Prime Minister. The inquiry itself came to a shuddering halt when the judge conducting it resigned. Under a new judge, it meanders on aimlessly. In other words, the rot remains. Meanwhile, the government mounted an inquiry into tehelka.com itself, hounding its investors and driving the site out of business. The message? *This is what happens to those who expose our crimes.*

But worse than that backlash was that journalists with their own sympathies for those in government gloated over Tehelka's troubles. They carped about its methods and glossed over the chicanery some intrepid reporters uncovered. Example: on hidden camera, Tehelka actually caught the then Bharatiya Janata Party (BJP) President, Bangaru Laxman, accepting a bribe. The clip of him taking the cash was shown widely, over and over again, on

---

[8] Parthasarathi Swami, *The Telegraph*, Calcutta, 28 July 1997.

television. Yet the rediff.com columnist Arvind Lavakare explained away Laxman's grubby grabbing thus:

> Now look at the treacherous 'testimony' against Bangaru Laxman, BJP president. Although it did not, once again, prove any wrongdoing, it cast an incalculable damage on the man's reputation. Consider that (sic) one sequence in the publicised Tehelka transcript that ran as follows:

> Tehelka: Rupees or dollars?

> Laxman: Dollars. You can give in dollars.

> The above 'quote' of Laxman was given a eight-column headline in *The Asian Age,* but with the exclamation mark (!) after 'Dollars'. The observant would have wondered why, if Laxman had reportedly wanted dollars as offered by Tehelka, did he accept payment in rupees? ...

> The mystery lies in that exclamation (!). What Laxman in all probability said was 'Dollars??' with an exclamation of shock in his tone, and 'You can give dollars??' with another exclamatory tone. But *Tehelka* must have just clipped away the exclamation marks in its transcripts while the audio in its tapes was just too damned garbled to reveal the exclamatory tone.[9]

Notice that Lavakare is not trying to say that Laxman did not take the money; he even acknowledges that he did (in asking 'why ... did he accept payment in rupees?'). But he diverts attention from that with a feeble, though wordy, hypothesis ('in all probability') about exclamation marks after 'dollars.'

This is the climate in which investigative journalism is both mired and must operate. So in a climate like this, with all these obstacles to battle, why would any journalist want to dig? And in a climate like this, what qualifies as investigative journalism for some readers? Answer: one column based on a few hours spent with slum-dwellers in Baroda. Even so, the remarkable thing is that there are still substantial investigations that happen, still diligent journalists who do them. In a climate like this, those things inspire me.

---

[9] www.rediff.com/news/2001/mar/24arvind.htm.

5

publicising the private: the right to privacy against media intrusion

mukund padmanabhan

*t*he issue of privacy has not received much play in discussions in the Indian media. An important reason for this is the manner in which the media have conducted themselves. Journalistic practices in the United States and Britain—for that matter in most of the West—have thrown up an array of ethical dilemmas surrounding the issue of privacy. Such dilemmas stem from a broad and perplexing question: how do privacy rights enjoyed by individuals square up with the media's role in publicising information?

Indian journalists are fond of pointing out that the media in this country are far more responsible than their counterparts in other countries. After Princess Diana and her companion were killed in a car crash in France, there were self-congratulatory articles that drew attention to the welcome absence in India of that aggressive, privacy-invading, journalistic half-breed: the paparazzi. The Indian media, one journalist remarked, would go only so far to sell more newspapers or get higher viewership ratings, no more.

There is a considerable measure of truth in this. By and large, the Indian media recognise that even public figures have the right to private lives. Film stars are an exception, being often the subject of titillating gossip and sexual innuendo. However, the argument in favour of making this exception is that film stars themselves court a certain kind of publicity to stay in the public eye. As a result, the unwritten privacy rules that prevail for others do not apply to them.

I do not wish to examine the merits of this argument here. The point is that unlike in many other countries, the private lives of most public figures (politicians, industrialists and other celebrities) generally fall outside the purview of prying media eyes. Complaints of the usual kinds of privacy invasion by journalists—intrusion on seclusion, publication of private facts and portraying in a false (but not necessarily defamatory) light—are rare in India. Although many journalists would attribute this to ethical practice, a possible explanation is that the country does not have, unlike the United States for instance, a set of privacy torts in place.

Two recent undercover investigations conducted by the (now defunct) website, tehelka.com have shown that the privacy issue cannot be ignored by the Indian media. Both took recourse to a form of journalism that depends on false pretences and misrepresentation to gain entry. Both relied heavily on a controversial investigative tool: the hidden camera. And both justified the means used in terms of public interest, which Tehelka describes as 'the final touchstone of all journalism'.

The first undercover investigation, Fallen Heroes, was a story on match-fixing in Indian cricket. Conducted in mid-2000, soon after the website was launched, the investigation made extensive use of a former Test cricketer, Manoj Prabhakar, who secretly filmed conversations with officials and former players on behalf of the website. At one level, the videotapes were a part of Prabhakar's attempt to substantiate his allegation that he was offered a bribe by former captain, Kapil Dev, to play poorly against Pakistan. At another level, the tapes purported to show that cricket match-fixing was prevalent and that top players, officials and possibly even politicians were involved in the racket. The tapes did not provide direct evidence of misconduct, but they provided the basis for an extensive criminal investigation into the match-fixing phenomenon.

The following year, Tehelka followed this up with Operation Westend. Two reporters posed as arms dealers of a non-existent company trying to sell non-existent fourth generation thermal imagers and, by doing so, gained shockingly easy access to the military establishment. The purpose of the investigation was to show how ingrained bribery and inducement are to the process of striking defence deals. To hammer home this point, Tehelka did not stop with merely secretly taping defence officers, arms agents and politicians it had conversations with. It actually paid bribes to some, most notoriously to Bangaru Laxman, the President of the Bharatiya Janata Party (BJP), who was caught greedily accepting a wad of cash on film.

The methods used by the website went well beyond secretly filmed conversations, but Tehelka, possibly aware of the repercussions, did not disclose this when it went public with the exposé. The website arranged call girls for some army officials it was stringing along and then proceeded to secretly film them having sex. When this information eventually became public, the website defended itself by claiming that the army officials had demanded that call girls be arranged, and that it had acceded to these forceful demands only to keep the story alive. But this explanation has a disingenuous ring. It fails to explain why the call girls and the army officials were secretly filmed in the act. Did Tehelka initially plan to use these tapes as a part of the exposé and then hold them back because better sense prevailed?

The impact of the two undercover investigations was immediate. The cricket exposé resulted in an extensive and open-ended Central Bureau of Investigation (CBI) inquiry into the phenomenon of match-fixing. At the end of the inquiry, the CBI concluded that a criminal case could not be made out. The reason was simple and was apparent from the very beginning. Fixing a match is not a crime under Indian law. At first appearance, the obvious recourse might have been to the Indian Penal Code section on cheating. But there is a problem here. Who cheated whom? Can those who placed illegal bets be deemed to have been cheated by those who allegedly fixed a match? The CBI report was referred to a committee set up by the Board for Control of Cricket in India (BCCI). Some cricketers against whom the CBI found *prima facie* evidence of match-fixing were slapped with life bans or served with suspension notices. As for Operation Westend, the defence transactions and procurements caught on videotape were referred to a Commission of Inquiry.

By and large, media reaction to the cricket and the defence exposés either ignored the ethical issues involved in conducting undercover investigations of this kind or referred to them in a passing or cursory way. To some extent, the attitude of the

Central government was responsible for deflecting attention from privacy issues. Some incidents, including the arrest of Tehelka journalists and the onslaught against one of its investors, lent the impression that the Centre was engaged in a systematic attempt to crush Tehelka. If the truth was otherwise, there was no effective attempt to correct it.

Tehelka defended its use of surveillance gadgets like the hidden cameras and false identities on the ground of public interest. The website argued that its recourse to such methods for Operation Westend was justified because it was 'of vital public importance and national security'. The implication here is simple: the public or social importance of the story outweighed issues such as intrusion and privacy. In other words, the ends were important enough to justify the means.

If such a defence has a familiar ring, it is because public interest is commonly invoked to defend journalistic invasion of privacy. This is hardly surprising. Our understanding of privacy is intimately linked to our notion of what constitutes the public interest. In this classic definition of what constitutes privacy and its invasion, Section 652D of the Restatement (Second) of Torts in the United States of America provides:

> One who gives publicity to a matter concerning the private life of another is subject to liability to the other for invasion of privacy, if the matter publicized is the kind that (a) would be highly offensive to a reasonable person, and (b) is not of legitimate concern to the public.

The right to privacy is not absolute; it has never embodied the principle that 'privacy must never be invaded'. In their seminal 1890 article 'The Right to Privacy' in the *Harvard Law Review,* Louis D. Brandeis and Samuel D. Warren explicitly excluded material that was in the public and general interest while laying out the case for the right to privacy. The notion that public interest can trump the right to privacy goes back a very long way. So does the Tehelka style undercover journalism that relies on deception or misrepresentation as a technique to gather information. In 1887, a woman reporter feigned mental illness to be admitted into a New York lunatic asylum. Her story on the abuse of patients won her acclaim and led to a grand jury investigation and legal reform. In 1904, another American journalist did an undercover investigation of the slaughterhouses in Chicago, his articles providing the impetus for federal food legislation. In 1972, the Pulitzer Prize was awarded to a journalist for a series of articles on voting irregularities, the information for which he gathered by concealing his true identity to secure a position with the Chicago elections board.

There may have been some questions raised about the deception involved in gathering such information. But on the whole, the articles referred to above generated more praise than criticism. Examples such as these abound. What they suggest is the existence of a general consensus that undercover journalism, which relies on deception, is justified under certain conditions. This raises the obvious question: what are the conditions that need to be satisfied to legitimise deceptive, privacy-invading journalism?

It is difficult, in fact probably impossible, to lay down a tight set of sufficient conditions that morally sanction the use of deception. However, most people would agree that a few necessary conditions must prevail in order to legitimise irregular information gathering techniques. The first such condition is the obvious one, which has already been referred to at some length. All information gathered by irregular, privacy-invading techniques must have a larger social purpose or a public interest. As we saw, the very notion of privacy is defined or understood in juxtaposition to such a purpose or interest. 'Public interest' and 'larger social purpose' are broad expressions and do not lend themselves to precise definition.

Having held that the 'right to privacy does not prohibit any publication of matter which is of public or general interest', Brandeis and Warren were aware of the difficulties in arriving at an exact or watertight categorisation of what matters are private and what are not:

> In general, then, the matters of which the publication should be repressed may be described as those which concern the private life, habits, acts, and relations of an individual, and have no legitimate connection with his fitness for a public office which he seeks or for which he is suggested, or for any public or quasi public position which he seeks or for which he

is suggested, and have no legitimate relation to or bearing
upon any act done by him in a public or quasi public capacity.
The foregoing is not designed as a wholly accurate or exhaus-
tive definition, since that which must ultimately in a vast
number of cases become a question of individual judgment
and opinion is incapable of such definition; but it is an attempt to indicate broadly the class of matters referred to.[1]

A number of the controversies relating to privacy invasion revolve around the fundamental difficulty of clearly demarcating
the public from the private. In many cases, the line is thin and
vague and decisions on whether privacy has been violated rests
on 'individual judgment and opinion', which are based on complex
and contentious value judgments. Such conceptual ambiguity is
one reason why the media should exercise caution when exercising judgment on matters that have a bearing on privacy.

Obviously, the mere fact that an undercover investigation was
motivated by a larger social purpose is not enough to justify it. If
this were so, there could be no dispute about the legitimacy of
most such investigations. There is no reason to disbelieve, or at
the very least, no way of disproving, the notion that Tehelka's
undercover investigations were prompted by nothing more than
the public interest; that Fallen Heroes was underpinned by the
desire to establish that match-fixing was rampant in India's best-
loved game and thereby put an end to this shameful practice once
and for all; and that Operation Westend was conducted only to
expose how rotten was the entire system engaged in making defence procurements. So what, if any, are the other moral yard-
sticks against which the Tehelka investigations should be assessed?

There are some broad rules or principles that must govern
the assessments of investigations that employ irregular, privacy-
invading methods.

1. Such invasions of privacy must be directly linked to the larger
   purpose of the investigation.
2. Information may be gathered by irregular means only when
   it cannot be obtained by other and less offensive means.

---

[1] Louis D.Brandeis and Samuel D. Warren, 'The Right to Privacy', *Harvard
Law Review*, 1890.

3. The public or social importance of the information acquired must outweigh the damage of the injury caused by the privacy violation.
4. All information that is not germane or irrelevant to the larger purpose of the investigation must not be made public.

These are broad rules and their application to specific instances will involve a measure of subjectivity, and will necessitate making some value judgments. For instance, there is no objective measure to weigh the social importance of the information a journalist gathers against the damage or injury he causes by violating privacy rights. There is also no settled way of deciding whether information procured irregularly could have been gathered otherwise. However, it is broad rules such as these that shape, if often in a reflexive, unthinking way, the positions we adopt towards irregular journalistic practice.

How do the Tehelka investigations stand up when assessed in the light of these rules? The truth is: Not very well. This, I suspect, was the basis for the widespread discomfiture or uneasiness with the methodology of the investigations. The website failed to ensure adherence to any of the broad rules listed above. For instance, its use of call girls is a blatant violation of the linkage principle in Rule 1. The larger purpose of Tehelka's story was to show the corruption and greed that accompany defence deals. What does secretly filming army officials having sex with call girls have to do with this? What does it add to the story beyond demonstrating that the corrupt were also lascivious? The answer is plain: Nothing.

Tehelka has argued that it could not have carried out either Fallen Heroes or Operation Westend without resorting to unconventional methods. Here, it is important to assess the worth of the evidence gathered by the two sting operations. Consider Fallen Heroes. All that the cricket investigation established is that there was a general belief among former players, officials and others that match-fixing and bribery were rampant in Indian cricket. There was nothing it unearthed which proved, beyond reasonable doubt, that a particular cricketer was engaged in match-fixing.

Fallen Heroes of course resulted in a CBI inquiry, which concluded, as pointed out earlier, that there was no basis for pressing criminal charges against those the agency suspected may have been involved in match-fixing. The agency based such suspicions on the evidence of cell phone calls made by some cricketers to bookies or vice versa, and confessional, self-incriminatory statements made by a couple of cricketers. The CBI's report formed the basis of another inquiry commissioned by the Indian cricket board (BCCI). This one indicted four cricketers, two of whom were banned for life and two were suspended for five years. Ironically, Kapil Dev, the man who was in many ways the target of the Tehelka investigation, was cleared in both the CBI and the BCCI inquiries. In a further ironical twist, Manoj Prabhakar, the man who Tehelka used for the sting operations, was found 'guilty' of match-fixing and slapped with a five-year suspension. Not surprisingly, Tehelka has never been able to adequately explain the colossal incongruity of having employed a cricketer who was implicated in match-fixing to blow the whistle on the phenomenon—and that too by conducting an elaborate undercover operation.

Whether the public importance of what was unearthed by Tehelka outweighed the injury caused by privacy violation is something about which there are likely to be different opinions. The overwhelming media reaction to those who had been caught accepting cash on film was that they had received their just deserts. But as Sevanti Ninan pointed out in an article in *The Hindu*,[2] much of the videotaped material is unsubstantiated loose talk. In more than one place, the boasts of unsuspecting arms dealers, who seemed more than happy to flaunt their contacts in the corridors of power, have been peddled as if they constituted solid evidence. As for Tehelka's use of the call girls, the information gathered—assuming that any was gathered at all—is surely incommensurate with the injury caused by invasions of privacy. Even call girls have privacy rights and the contracts to hire them for sex did not include permission to secretly film them in the act. Violation of privacy comes under the law of torts, but by soliciting call girls, Tehelka's methods breached the existing provisions of criminal law.

Investigations that rely on impersonation and spy cameras are bound to unearth large amounts of information that are

---

[2] Sevanti Ninan, 'Who Cares for Ethics?', *The Hindu,* 1 April 2001.

totally unrelated to its larger purpose. Tehelka made no attempt at all to edit out the irrelevant information, thereby breaching Rule 4. In Fallen Heroes, one of those secretly videotaped was former film actress Anju Mahendroo, whose apparent connection with cricket does not go much beyond a friendship she enjoyed with a famous all-rounder decades ago. The transcript unearths nothing of relevance. However, it occupies 10 pages of the book that Tehelka published of its investigation and contains references to such things as cosmetics and beauty parlours. The same is true of Operation Westend. It seems that Tehelka was oblivious of the need to edit out what was superfluous and therefore insensitive to the issues relating to privacy that emerged out of its investigation.

In 2003, on the eve of the Chattisgarh State Assembly election, *The Indian Express* published pictures and transcripts of a secretly-filmed videotape that showed BJP leader Dilip Singh Judeo accepting money, apparently in connection with a commercial contract. *The Indian Express* did not film the incident. It received the tape from an unknown quarter, checked it for veracity and then ran the story.

The issues that this 'scoop' throws up are somewhat different. I do not wish to go into this here beyond saying that undercover journalism, although relatively uncommon in India, did not stop with Tehelka. India has neither a privacy law nor a set of privacy torts in place.

Experiments in other countries towards formulating a fully-fledged privacy law have thrown up a typical difficulty—that of framing regulations in a manner that does not unreasonably hamper the freedom of the media. What this means is that the media must evolve their own rules to deal with privacy issues. Undercover investigations must follow some general rules and this paper has attempted to spell out a few, albeit in a general way. It has also attempted to assess or evaluate the Tehelka investigations against the background of these principles. In so doing, one hopes they cast some light on the kind of issues that journalists need to be alive to when they employ irregular techniques, such as deception and spy cameras, to unearth information.

6

the untold story of television coverage

valerie kaye

One of my most memorable experiences as a fledgling television researcher was the day, just a short while after I had started working for BBC on its flagship television current affairs programme, *Panorama*. I was approached in the corridor by a harassed-looking producer. 'You don't know anyone who can speak Spanish do you?' he asked. 'I'm off to Argentina in two days time and I need an interpreter, and we daren't use a local person.' 'Why not?' I asked naively. He told me, 'The situation there is so tense that they would either be a spy or else we would be putting them into danger by using them to film illicit material.' 'Actually,' I said, 'I speak fluent Spanish.'

And two days later, after a brief telephone grilling by a Peruvian journalist checking up on my Spanish, I was off. I had spent time as a print journalist, mainly for a specialist health publication, and had been on a two-week contract with the BBC. It is hard to imagine nowadays that anyone can be employed for just two weeks. I had spent that time researching a film on industrial diseases, and subsequently found myself winging off to South America as a researcher for the team.

The year was 1979. The reason for the film was that the World Cup was due to be played in Argentina later that year and the Argentine government was very keen to propagate an image of a civilised country, Western in outlook, democratic in its institutions, really more part of Europe than anarchic Latin America. We were out to prove otherwise.

The military junta was in control of the country, headed by General Videla whom we planned to interview. The country had been plunged into chaos by repeated guerrilla and Montonero attacks and by a terrorising military which seized thousands of people who were suspected of any sympathy or link with anti-government forces. Often people were not arrested openly, but unlicensed police cars would pull up outside their houses and they would be bundled inside. Their relatives would go for news at police stations, but usually to no avail, and often they would never be seen again. They became known as the '*desaparecidos*' or disappeared ones, and 'to disappear someone' became part of the common language. The triple A (AAA) death squads were operating and it was a time of national terror. This was the background into which I, a youngish and naïve girl, was jetting.

I was the sole interpreter for the crew, apart from the time when we did get to interview President Videla, and I rapidly became exhausted translating every interview, spending my spare time translating magazine articles, and helping the crew sort out any practical problem they might have. I don't think that nowadays a researcher would be expected, in her spare time, to go and get the reporter's watch strap repaired, as I did, although these things depend on the personalities of the people involved. I certainly earned my crust, around £80 a week as I remember.

The process of accreditation was lengthy; we all had to present ourselves at government offices and after providing the necessary documentation, we were given press passes. The fact that we were from BBC TV gave us a lot of credibility. Certainly this respect for the BBC which in the end gave us so much freedom to manoeuvre within Argentina, was abruptly withdrawn when the film was finally broadcast—but I am getting ahead of myself.

We then went through a series of interviews with government officials, members of the military junta, trade union officials and other quasi-official people. At the same time we were secretly filming dissidents, relatives of the *desaparecidos,* and so on. The two strands to our filming had to be kept separate and secret as we knew we would be deported if discovered. All the rolls of secret filming—in those days we used film which lasted for 10 minutes per roll—were taken immediately to the airport and shipped back to the UK for fear that they might be discovered.

When filming in this tense atmosphere, the film crew becomes a cohesive group, a strong unit where personality clashes are often frequent. Ours was no exception. I grew to loathe a couple of the crew members and I am sure the feeling was mutual. It made for very difficult filming conditions in what was already an extremely testing environment. We worked together, ate together and spent all of our time together, and it was no wonder sparks flew.

At one point we flew up to the north of Argentina and then took a tiny helicopter, manned by a government pilot, to see how the northern jungle was being cleared. We were in two different helicopters as they were small and could not accommodate our bulky gear. On the way back, a violent storm blew up. We found ourselves in mid-air, stationary for two hours, in very cramped conditions, being buffeted by a fierce wind, torrential rain and extraordinary thunder and lightning. I feared for my life. We got back eventually, having lost radio contact with the other helicopter and fearing they had crashed. It was a hellish experience.

It certainly made me wonder why I was there in the first place. I had been more terrified than I have been before or since then, and nearly 30 years have now gone by. I was working my butt off, to use a very apt American phrase, for people with gigantic egos who treated me as less than slave labour, and who I knew would reap the credit for the film in the end. Two crew members saw me as part of the perks of the job in that they would make sexual innuendoes constantly, frequently ask me to go to their hotel rooms for a 'massage', and generally would treat me as a sexual object.

And the film itself? We had already put people's lives in danger by filming them talking about their disappeared children. Of course we took pains to make sure we were not followed when we filmed at their houses, but you could never be sure. The atmosphere was always twitchy, we were always aware we might be followed when doing these interviews, that we were being spied on when filming despite our precautions, and that whereas we were safe, our interviewees were not. It took a life-threatening helicopter ride to put it all into perspective.

We got back to Buenos Aires and flew off again to Cordoba to conduct some more covert interviews. We lived a life of extreme tension, doing our official interviews with President Videla and other military officials on the one hand, and on the other hearing horrendous stories from people whose children had just vanished into thin air. What was impressive was the fact that often, almost immediately after arriving at a hotel and checking in, I would receive a telephone call. It was always an anxious voice: 'Please come down to the lobby of your hotel,' he or she would intone desperately into the receiver. And downstairs would be a distraught parent who would tell the film crew, with me translating of course, about young daughters or sons who had gone missing several months ago when the triple A death squads were operating at their peak. Visits to the local police station were stonewalled, although neighbours would often report that unmarked police cars had taken them off.

Of course, we wanted to film some of these interviews, but were always refused. 'I just wanted you to hear my story, to bear witness to this horror we are living through, but I don't dare be filmed. No, I would never see my child again', was the invariable response. My director became frustrated and angry: 'Valerie, you are just not trying hard enough. We *need* this interview for the film. Try and persuade her. She can be blacked out, no one will recognise her.' I did my bit. Of course, everyone was totally dependent on my translations. None of these people spoke English and I was the only crew member who spoke Spanish. At the same time, I was tremendously aware that people's lives, for the first time in my life, did depend on me. We were in a country that was undergoing a tumultous civil war. There was, at this time, no shooting on the streets, no rationing, no fear of aerial bombardment. However, there was a sadistic military junta in power, despite the superficial charm of President Videla when we interviewed him, total press censorship, and daily disappearances. These people, we came to know later, were, probably while we were there, being tortured in police stations or military barracks and then killed. Anyone talking to the foreign press about this was likely either to be picked up and tortured themselves, or their child would be killed. My heart was not in my interpreting.

We arrived at the penultimate day of our trip. I seem to remember we had been in Argentina for around three weeks altogether, but this was 1979 and my memory of this has become faded. Not so what happened next. I find I have total recall of our shameful swansong.

The director and reporter summoned me. Things were extremely tense, more than usual. 'We are going back to the UK tomorrow, but there is an essential element of the film we haven't got yet. We have not got anyone on film who has been tortured. It all depends on you Valerie. You have got to find someone. Go to the Human Rights office, sit there all day until they come up with someone who has been tortured who will talk about it on film. We can black out their faces, but we have got to have this interview. And we'll make sure that our boss back in London knows who got it.'

What choice did I have? Like an obedient puppy, I planted myself in the Human Rights office, manned by cautious but brave volunteers. I told them what I wanted. I sat and waited for may be six hours, I don't remember. Around 7 P.M. I was told they had someone who would speak on camera about being tortured, two people in fact, young students. I telephoned the hotel and shortly after the crew arrived. We filmed these two young people, back to camera, the camera focusing only on my worried face. I wanted my contract extended and I had done the most I could do, and I prayed the students would be protected. They told a harrowing tale of being kidnapped by the police, tortured repeatedly and then unexpectedly released. The director and reporter were delighted.

The next day we said our goodbyes. The director and reporter were flying back to the UK to edit the film, and the rest of the crew and I were flying on to Chile to make another film. The director thanked each member of the crew effusively for their hard work. Strangely, he seemed to miss me out. Hadn't I done what he wanted? Hadn't I got the interview he told me was essential? And how could they have made the film without my research and interpreting skills?

We flew to Chile for another highly nerve-wracking experience making another secretive political film. Back in the UK, I was summoned to see the editor of *Panorama*. 'Well, I just wanted to tell you that we will not be renewing your contract at the end of the month.' That was it—no explanation was given, and it was not for me to say how I thought I had been invaluable to the film. The director did not like me, although he did admit he could not have made the film without me, and that was that. I ended my short time with the *Panorama* crew on a sour note.

I had had what many later told me was a typical researcher's experience.

And the film? It caused a storm in Argentina when broadcast. Official protests from the Argentine military junta were made. When I visited some years later, I was told that the local bourgeoisie had been scandalised, as they knew nothing of the torture and did not believe our evidence on the film. And what happened to the two young students who had so bravely given me their evidence? I'm afraid I have no idea. That's what happens in these current affairs documentaries. Everything and everyone is sacrificed for the sake of the film. I was told that they could be recognised even though their faces were blacked out, but I have never heard anything about them since.

PART II
Specialisation within the Craft

7

the greening of india's scribes

darryl d'monte

*i*f any proof is needed of the fact that the environment has become a major issue in Indian journalism, it is provided in the *Green File* brought out by the Centre for Science and Environment (CSE) in New Delhi. Every month, it puts together clippings from major English and Hindi dailies and comes out as a 200-odd page document.

The list of newspapers from which it culls news items and comment articles is by no means complete. Not only are many smaller papers excluded but so are smaller editions of mass-circulation dailies, not to mention those in other languages. Indeed, it is the regional media which are currently experiencing a boom, since English readership has virtually plateaued. As fellowships awarded annually by the CSE indicate, regional-language journalists have far more serious concerns, as a rule, than English-language scribes. Even so, a mere glance at the '*File*' is sufficient indication that environment is still a major subject for the print media. There are also other compendia of environmental stories, like that put out quarterly by the Council for Promotion of Rural Technology (CAPART) and the Tata Energy Research Institute (TERI).

Environmental journalists cut their teeth on such early controversies as the threat to the Taj Mahal from the Mathura oil refinery (see Fig. 7.1) and the proposal to build a hydel plant in the monsoon forests of Silent Valley in Kerala, both in the 1970s. The journalists would not have described themselves as such, and many still do not, preferring to swear by the 'generic' nature of their profession rather than the brand.

Fig. 7.1: Taj Mahal: Threatened by the Mathura Oil Refinery

Note: Picture shows base of a minaret being repaired.
Source: Photograph taken by the author.

Prior to that, there were a few journalists who had been studying the Chipko Movement in Garhwal, Uttar Pradesh, and other
people's movements in various parts of the country. Prominent
among these was Anupam Mishra of the Gandhi Peace Foundation in Delhi, who till today is unrivalled in his intense involvement with the environment movement. The late Anil Agarwal
was by any reckoning the doyen of such journalists and had also
widened the very scope of journalism to a critique of development itself. These were some of the pioneers of environmental
journalism and many of their bylines still command the attention and respect of readers throughout the nation.

Among the Hindi writers, Om Thanvi, once Resident Editor
of *Jansatta* in Chandigarh, and Mukul Sharma of *Navbharat
Times* in Delhi, stand out. The former has contributed to the
nation's knowledge of traditional water-harvesting techniques
in Rajasthan, while Sharma had written series of articles in his
daily newspaper, indicating his ongoing commitment to a cause.[1]
Today, the bulk of environmental journalists are freelancers.

[1] Mukul Sharma, *Landscapes and Lives: Environmental Dispatches on Rural
India* (Delhi: Oxford University Press, 2001).

To add to the vigour of the environmental movement, many activists also double as journalists and vice versa. The best known example is Sunderlal Bahuguna, who was not only a stringer for a national news agency but also a prolific freelancer. On occasion, he has been known to handwrite features in trains and buses on his way to address meetings in remote corners of the country. Claude Alvares, who lives in Goa and is a vehement campaigner against the degradation of the environment of this pristine coastal state, was also someone who commuted effortlessly between journalism and activism, or often played a dual role at one and the same time. Bittu Sahgal in Mumbai has extended his concern for conservation to bringing out a monthly titled *Sanctuary,* an Indian version of the *National Geographic.* In Kerala, the writer and poet Sugathakumari has been passionately devoted to causes such as the preservation of Silent Valley, in defence of which she composed a poem.

The CSE has given institutional shape to this otherwise amorphous body of green scribes. It has given a number of young journalists the opportunity to do fieldwork through the scholarships it offers every few months, with funds from the Central government, for six to eight weeks. Following the Bhopal gas tragedy in 1984, there is also the recognition of the need to collect and disseminate information, apart from the fact that it was journalists like Praful Bidwai, the late Ivan Fera and Arun Subramaniam, who not only were the first to document what was happening in Bhopal from the scientific data available, but also were at the forefront of the campaign to ensure that the victims obtained a fair deal. An offshoot of Eklavya—an activist organisation in the town—was formed only for the purpose of disseminating information on the tragedy. It exists even today, and has since spread its concerns to campaigns against big dams and other environmental issues.

In the late 1980s, a further step forward in granting recognition to environmental journalists as a breed in their own right was taken with the formation of the Forum of Environmental Journalists of India (FEJI). The initiative in forming such a national forum came from UN ESCAP in Bangkok, which coaxed member countries in the region to band together under an umbrella organisation called the Asian (now Asia–Pacific) Forum of Environmental Journalists. It has so far been holding a number of meetings in the region and has been instrumental in forming a loose network of journalists in these countries.

One realisation that is rapidly dawning is that countries in the region are very similarly affected by man-made disasters. The effect of these processes can be fruitfully studied by media persons from these countries. For instance, FEJI undertook a three-nation study of the degradation of the Himalayas in Nepal and its effect on river systems, right down to the deltas in Bangladesh. Thus, journalists from Nepal, India and Bangladesh conducted a joint study of this problem. Similarly, South-east Asian countries like Indonesia, Thailand, Malaysia and the Philippines could examine how the demand for tropical timber is depleting their scarce natural resources.

I have attended a number of conferences on environment and the media, including one on the Amazon in Brazil, and it is becoming quite obvious that the interest in this area can only grow in future. It would be a pity if it became somewhat of a fad, with young journalists vying with each other to become 'greener-than-thou'. The environment is a subject that calls for deep investigation, preferably combined with field trips and on-the-spot surveys. Apart from technological knowledge, it calls for a lot of holism.

This review ought to demonstrate that an integral aspect of the environmental movement is the involvement of journalists, either as documenters or activists or as both. In other words, environmentalists in India are handicapped for a number of reasons: shortage of funds, a paucity of activists themselves, and lack of access to many avenues open in the West, like the courts, not to mention direct protest. This gives the media a heightened—one might even go so far as to say exaggerated—role in intervening in environmental controversies. Indeed, there is always the danger of the documenter mistaking her/himself, and being mistaken in the public eye, for the environmentalist.

At the same time, there is ample evidence that several committed individuals and institutions have lent a new edge to the very concept of environmental journalism. It is in this context that one must view the pioneering work of the CSE's *State of India's Environment* (SOE) reports, which have extended journalism to questioning the very basis of development and propounding an alternative philosophy, based on holism and social justice. In this case, the media have not merely reflected a reality but provided an alternative perspective, new insights.

A year after the CSE was established in New Delhi in 1980, its Director Anil Agarwal was returning from a meeting of the Consumers Association of Penang (CAP). On the flight home, he and K.P. Kannan of the Kerala Sastra Sahitya Parishad (KSSP) discussed the possibility of bringing out a report on India's environment similar to a brief monograph they had seen in the *State of Malaysian Environment*.

The problem was that India was a far bigger and more diverse country than Malaysia, with environmental movements and activists scattered over its length and breadth. People with information were not easily contactable face to face. Nevertheless, they agreed that the task of drawing up a document for India was long overdue. They identified individuals and institutions which could be asked to cooperate. Because of its very size, the Indian report necessarily had to have a much wider scope.

The difficulties of preparing such a report were compounded by the fact that Kannan was based in Thiruvananthapuram, at the southernmost tip of India. And in any case both he and Agarwal were already committed to completing several other projects. However, the CSE, which operates an information service on science, technology and development, was obviously the ideal headquarters for such a venture, since it could provide both with some writers as well as a minimal infrastructure. Agarwal and Kannan thought that the next World Environment Day (5 June, 1982) would be the best date to publish the report. As a bonus, Kannan offered to publish it in Malayalam as well.

In December 1981, Ravi Chopra, who had returned to India from the US, agreed to coordinate the effort. Quickly, three major objectives were set out by Anil Agarwal and Chopra:

1. The report should be a 'citizens' report'. Every year, the Government of India gives its version of the state of the nation: its economy, its industry and, beginning this year, the environment. There are no authoritative non-governmental publications which assess the state of our nation. To bring out a factual 'citizens report', a wide spectrum of individuals and

voluntary organisations, working among the people, would have to be involved.

2. The report should be published annually.

3. The manner in which the report is prepared should be in keeping with a desired set of values which are missing from professional and academic organisations (but are beginning to take roots in some voluntary groups). Thus, we would have to try to be self-reliant, 'non-hierarchical and non-sexist'.

As the editors of the first *State of India's Environment* report[2] mention in their introduction: 'None of us was exactly sure what all this would amount to in practice. But all the same we committed ourselves to trying to fulfil these objectives.'

Numerous individuals and organisations were contacted across the country. Their response was 'overwhelmingly positive'. The editors found that several voluntary groups engaged in the task of bringing development to the people had begun to focus on environmental issues. They realised that the very scope of ecology extended far beyond pretty trees, mountains, rivers and animals; in other words, beyond mere aesthetic values and scenic heritage. Many activists engaged in the development process were convinced that the conflict ahead concerned the control of natural resources. Thus, the realisation dawned that 'changes in environment had a direct impact on the lives of the people, particularly the poor, who were dependent on their immediate environment for their basic needs'.

The editors were candid enough to admit that the fog was beginning to lift for them. In other words, out of a seemingly disparate accumulation of facts and processes, a common thread was beginning to emerge: 'to explain how environmental changes were affecting the lives of the people'.

Since this was uncharted territory, no one had an idea of the plethora of people involved with the environment from various walks of life—activists, academics, officials and journalists. The task of collecting material began in real earnest. And each was able to complement the work of others. Agarwal, because of his extensive contacts and earlier work in India and abroad, was able to generate a tremendous amount of information. It was at

[2] Anil Agarwal, Ravi Chopra and Kalpana Sharma (eds), *The State of India's Environment 1982: A Citizen's Report* (New Delhi: CSE, 1982).

this stage that Kalpana Sharma, who, along with another Bombay-based journalist, had agreed to spend three weeks in the North-east, joined the team in Delhi as a co-editor.

The report helped to break fresh ground in several areas. The editors wrote:

A vital issue emerged from our many conversations: a significant section of India's population exists beyond the pale of the mainstream Indian society. Each time a major development project goes up, or there is a fresh inroad into the remote areas for untapped natural resources, a new ecological niche is destroyed and another lot of these marginal people are uprooted and pauperized. We needed knowledgeable people with a special sensitivity to these groups, to write about their lives.

As a matter of fact, the response was overwhelming and the CSE was literally flooded with more material than it could easily handle. The editors soon realised that the 100-page volume they had originally envisaged had doubled in size. This was also one of the reasons why it was delayed well beyond the original deadline. The report was a pathbreaker in several ways. For the first time, it did not just assemble facts and figures on various aspects of environmental degradation but also spelt out how this affected people's most basic daily activities—obtaining food, fuel, water and so on. In any other report on the national or global environment, this human dimension is generally missing in the welter of statistics.

Moreover, the media, the source of most urban people's knowledge of the deterioration of the environment, deal with problems in a piecemeal manner. It is only when a reader is presented with an overview of the nation's rivers, dams, forests, air, soil, plants, animals, towns, villages, health and energy problems that s/he is able to see a common thread running through them.

Cartoons and sketches were more telling than the words they displaced. In particular, the sketch depicting a fist damming a river and squeezing people and trees in its grasp at the same time has been widely reproduced in India (in the anti-Narmada dams protests, among others) and abroad. Ajit Ninan of *India Today* had a wasteland in the contours of the nation's map, which also made a telling comment on the degradation of the environment.

The contribution of media skills to the making of the two SOE reports should in no way be underestimated. Were it not for the professional expertise of its writers and editors, who were able to condense voluminous material, the report would have inevitably become incomprehensible to most. Two special features of the 1982 report are its excellent design and layout, contributed by Purnima Rao with Mukul Dube, and the use of pictures. A mound of material was often reduced to a single chart or diagram which brought home the point much more tellingly. The illustrations brightened up the text. Manjula Padmanabhan contributed much to the second report with her sketches.

The authors made a special effort to procure pictures from newspapers, photographers and international development agencies, which infused a great deal of life into the text. The well-worn cliché about a picture being worth a thousand words was brought out, for instance, by *The Hindu*'s photographs of the firewood special trains in Kurnool in Andhra Pradesh, which depicted how headloaders were responsible for bringing fuel to city residents from vast distances away.

The first SOE report was very well received by Indian official and non-official sources. The first print run of 3,500 copies sold out in a year, which amounts to 10 copies a day if one includes Sundays. By the time the second report was published in 1985, half the second print run of 2,500 was also sold. All newspapers and magazines in India reviewed it extremely favourably, as did the media abroad.

Eight months after the first report was published, in mid-1983, work started on the second. For this, Sunita Narain, who had worked with the first SOE team as a researcher, joined Agarwal as a co-editor. Just as the first SOE report was a revelation for its editors, the second provided a fresh set of surprises. The revelation for Agarwal and Narain, in their own words, was:

[*T*]he information that it provided on the linkages that operate on what can be called the interface areas: at the interfaces between different ecological spaces like croplands, grazing lands and forests; between the people and their environment; between economies of towns and villages, and so on. Very little is known about these relationships, especially as they relate to the people living at the margins of subsistence, and learning and writing about them has been extremely exciting for us. We have found that even many environmentalists lack knowledge of the relationships.[3]

Thus, the second SOE report became not merely an update, as many people erroneously imagined, but provided fresh information on a number of subjects to which little attention had been paid in the popular media. For instance, there was very little published on nomads and grazing lands. The second SOE report dealt with this subject in some detail. Similarly, while individual occupational diseases had been mentioned, no one had undertaken an overview of the subject, which in any case gained a new edge after the Bhopal catastrophe. Again, while the first report brought out the nexus between people and the environment, the second clearly and specifically drew out the connection with women.

The continuing feedback on the first report was almost invariably favourable, both at home and abroad. However, one of the criticisms, mainly from government officials but also from NGOs and individuals, was that it did not present alternatives or guidelines for action. How, for instance, would energy be provided from alternative sources, if nuclear, thermal and hydel power present environmental problems? While the authors do concede this point, they also state that the very activities of NGOs are themselves a documentation of alternative approaches to development, albeit on a micro scale.

With the accumulated knowledge generated in the first report and very widely garnered for the second, it became increasingly clear that the strength of CSE's initiative lay in the fact that it could take a holistic view of the interconnections between the various processes of environmental degradation. Thus the shrinking of grazing lands pointed to the acute shortage of fodder and put into perspective the official afforestation programmes, supported by forest departments as well as the World Bank,

---

[3] Anil Agarwal and Sunita Narain (eds), *The State of India's Environment 1984–85: The Second Citizen's Report* (New Delhi: CSE, 1985).

which emphasised the planting of non-browsable species of trees like the eucalyptus. The authors concluded by saying that:

So-called experts know extremely little about the lives of the people living at the margins of subsistence and how they are being squeezed by modernization and development. The major contribution that a report like this one, or ones in the future, can make is to increase this understanding so that truly sensible alternatives can be found. This report, for instance, makes it very clear that unless there is a holistic thinking about the management of India's environment and unless women become centrally involved in environmental management programmes, success will be impossible or short-lived or simply a fraudulent propaganda exercise.

This is why the CSE has very clearly recognised that information which leads to action amounts to the empowerment of people. Understandably, it wanted both reports to be as widely circulated as possible. Indeed, the remark opposite the table of contents in both reports to the effect that 'material from this publication may be used without prior permission if the source is properly acknowledged' has never failed to bemuse publishers and several individuals who sometimes believe that the word 'not' has been mistakenly omitted!

In the first SOE report, the authors wrote:

Our role has been to gather the material into a cohesive whole and turn it into a form which will encourage people to act. The sections on people's groups should be useful. It can put people in touch with one another, thus assisting in the current efforts to create a much-needed network of environmentalists.

For information to reach the masses of India's population, whose involvement is essential for any environmental movement, it must be presented in the local language using the local idiom. Grassroots workers are, therefore, encouraged to reshape this material to fit their own situation. We hope necessary alterations will be made by the translating groups.

Apart from the translations of both reports into Hindi by Anupam Mishra of the Gandhi Peace Foundation (many of the pictures in the Hindi versions are better!), Shivram Karanth, the notable Kannada writer, translated the nuclear energy chapter in the second report as a Kannada pamphlet in the early stages of the campaign against the Kaiga nuclear plant. He actually brought out both reports as paperbacks in Kannada, without any illustrations, each priced at a modest Rs 10.

Such was the people's response to the reports in other states that two persons from Chennai offered to translate them into Tamil if there was a publisher in sight. Unfortunately, there was not, and it failed to see the light of day. Later, efforts to translate the reports into Telugu and Bengali met the same fate. Even more tragically, manuscripts in Marathi and Malayalam, which had been translated at an enormous cost in terms of human labour, were stillborn. A combined report appeared in French, while West German groups indicated their readiness to translate them as well. However, as I told the groups in West Germany, it would help Indian environmentalists more if a similar document was brought out on that country's environmental problems!

As could easily be witnessed by the tremendous response to both reports, people throughout India are looking to the CSE not just as a source of information and networking, since it is in contact with activist groups throughout the country, but also as an organisation that could itself intervene in environmental conflicts. This additional role at times places the CSE in a quandary: if it is to turn activist, will its information invariably be treated as absolutely authentic? Or will its pronouncements be given less weight than those of environmental media organisations elsewhere in the world which do not play such an interventionist role?

The Worldwatch Institute in Washington, for instance, does not involve itself with NGOs but restricts itself solely to the business of disseminating information. Of course, it is in many ways easier to compile a global report, even annually, than a national one. The CSE has intervened in cases and become embroiled in a host of issues, often letting information gathering take a back seat, resulting in the third SOE being interminably delayed.[4] This ambiguity about the role of the organisation has

---

[4] Anil Agarwal and Sunita Narain (eds), *Floods, Flood Plains and Environmental Myths. State of India's Environment 3: A Citizen's Report* (New Delhi: CSE, 1991).

cost it dearly in terms of its lack of ability to retain researchers, as well as maintain productivity. On the other hand, had the CSE not intervened on a number of occasions, there is no telling which other organisation would have, and a grassroots group may well have lost its case as a consequence.

The peculiar blend of research and journalism developed in the reports combines academic vigour with contemporaneous comment, thus benefiting from both disciplines. All too often, those who conduct detailed research into ecological issues are appalled by the ignorance of the media; conversely, journalists find articles in scientific journals unreadable. The SOE reports were able to marry the two disciplines in a unique manner and thus satisfy a much larger number of readers than they would have otherwise.

In the final analysis, it is evident that the two reports came out at a time when interest in the degradation of the environment had been kindled. In true dialectical fashion, it was a product of people's concern even while it aroused that interest—in many cases, for the first time ever. If the 1970s could be seen as a decade when feminism came into its own worldwide, in the 1980s, it was the turn of environmentalism.

One price to be paid for this approach was that it became progressively more difficult with each report not only to come up with new information on land or water or forests, but with fresh insights as well. Not surprisingly, as Agarwal and Narain travelled extensively throughout the country and delved deeper into each subject, they found themselves hopelessly weighed down by sheer detail. At the same time, the expectations of readers (and contributors) had also grown apace, which meant that no amount of padding or fudging the issues would be tolerated. Ironically, therefore, the very decision to opt for a marriage of scholarship and journalism has proved to be its own stumbling block, and has caused indefinite delays in both subsequent SOE reports as well as the planned *State of India's Urban Environment,* on which years of hard labour have been spent. Of course, the work done will surface in some form eventually, but not in the shape or with the periodicity that the CSE had hoped for.

By the end of 1986, some 5,300 hardback copies of the second report and 750 paperbacks had been sold. This included a bulk order for 400 hardbacks from the Council for Promotion of Rural Technology, affiliated to the Rural Development Ministry. During the National Environment Awareness Month of 1986, the Environment Ministry also distributed copies as a source of material in teacher-training camps.

Questions are being raised about the prices of the hardback editions, which however can be countered by the fact that paperbacks are priced well below the reach of most individuals. The hardbacks are really meant for institutions and libraries.

The SOE reports should really be viewed as a unique cooperative effort in pooling small bits of information into an illuminating whole to serve as a sourcebook for government officials, activists, teachers, students and inquisitive laymen. There is probably no counterpart anywhere in the world where journalists collaborate with other providers of information in such a productive joint venture.

Perhaps the biggest tribute to the SOE report as an illustration of the media's involvement in environmental issues is that that can be used by various other agencies as a catalyst to generate new information. There have also been proposals to adapt the reports for children. But knowledge can be turned to power only if individuals adapt it for their own purposes, by way of education, training, journalism itself or activism. That, in the ultimate analysis, would be the biggest reward for the painstaking collective work that has gone into the making of the *State of Environment* reports.

In the early 1990s, the Earth Summit at Rio de Janeiro gave a fillip to environmental journalism in the country because of the heightened public interest in what was then the biggest assembly of world leaders ever. India played a leading part, not mincing its words of criticism against the US for failing to sign key environmental treaties, and the reports of the Summit made front-page news.

Subsequently, as is the case worldwide, there has been a steep decline of interest in the media regarding environmental issues, except when a disaster of some kind surfaces. Indeed, in the West, there has been a backlash of sorts with green issues disappearing off pages and screens. At the World Summit on Sustainable Development in Johannesburg in August 2002, much was made of a scurrilous book titled *The Skeptical Environmentalist* by Bjørn Lomborg, [5] which has since been savaged by critics. The Indian media too, since the economic liberalisation of the 1990s, have been more preoccupied with economic than environmental issues, and there is no saying whether green scribes will continue to flourish in future.

---

[5] Bjørn Lomborg, *The Skeptical Environmentalist: Measuring the Real State of the World* (New York: Cambridge University Press, 2001).

8

engendering the public sphere

pamela philipose

i t is now generally recognised that as the popular narrators of everyday happenings, the media play a pivotal role in democracies. They link individuals to the great and little events of their time and, indeed, with each other as members of a society. Not only do the media engender awareness at the broadest level, they help create an information society, a public sphere, in which the exchange of ideas and debate can take place. The unique power of the media, in fact, lies in their ownership of the right to select, highlight and interpret various developments as they occur.

This process of interpretation is not, however, without its biases and asymmetries. The ability of the media to provide an effective public sphere, in which all constituents of a society can engage equally, depends on the extent to which they are free from the influences of the dominant political and economic interests of the times, an aspect highlighted by social theorists like Jürgen Habermas. In this great sphere, numerous discourses do battle every day for newsprint and cyberspace; many are edged out or don't figure at all. Given the very real limits of space and time then, there occurs the privileging of some discourses over others and the manner in which this happens is itself a complex and multi-layered process.

It has been notoriously difficult to plot the connections between knowledge generation and human lives, but it can be said with some degree of certainty that the discourses that generally come to dominate the media are themselves closely linked to the power hierarchies and resurgent ideologies within a particular society and contribute, in turn, to perpetuating these very hierarchies and ideologies. American journalist Walter Lippmann termed it as the 'manufacturing of consent', a phrase that political philosopher and activist Noam Chomsky has used time and again to demonstrate how false representation in the media can become the reality for vast numbers of people.

Among the silences that have marked media coverage, gender has been one of the more conspicuous, reflecting the general blotting out of women's concerns in society. The last 58 years could be divided roughly into three phases: for 25 years or so after Independence, the visibility of gender-centric news in the media was negligible. This was followed by two decades of what could be seen as a period when the silence was broken to an extent, largely because of the impact of women's activism on urban society. The years that followed this phase could be termed as the 'backlash years', when factors like ownership patterns, the economics of running financially sustainable media houses and the twin processes of globalisation and liberalisation brought about a general dilution of emphasis on social issues, including those relating to gender.

Looking back on the early years of Independence, it was only when women-centric topics acquired a political dimension, for whatever reason, that they made it to the main space in Indian newspapers. Even a quick and random look at some of the newspapers of the 1950s and 1960s would reveal this. On 8 February 1953, for instance, the front pages of English-language newspapers featured a woman on the front page. The headlines that read 'Elizabeth proclaimed Queen', or words to that effect, captured the lingering afterglow of the colonial dispensation. Closer home, the fractious debate over the Hindu Code Bill that had led to B.R. Ambedkar's resignation as the Union Law Minister, was an issue that closely concerned the ruling establishment of the day and the tensions between various leaders within it. This was the aspect that the reporters seemed to have generally focused upon. The Bill, as it turned out, was never passed, or rather was diluted and enacted as a series of personal laws. When the Lok Sabha enacted the Hindu Succession Bill, the front pages of 9 May 1954 headlined the fact that now daughters were to get a share in their fathers' assets. While the reportage took specific note of the fact that Nehru had 'hailed the passage of the measure giving rights to women', the voices of women leaders who had anchored the legislation did not figure anywhere; nor were there any attempts to explain the social significance of such legislation. By the mid-1960s, one woman emerged as a front-page newsmaker in her own right, by becoming the Prime Minister of the country. Power gave Indira Gandhi a media presence that her female compatriots, being powerless, did not enjoy.

Things did change a little by the early 1970s, not because there was an intrinsic alteration in mindsets within the media but because of two significant and related developments that went toward creating what feminist academics sometimes term as the 'third wave' of the women's movement. The first was an international process, set in motion in 1967, when the UN General Assembly adopted the Declaration on the Elimination of Discrimination Against Women, which also earmarked 1975 as the International Women's Year. It was a formal acknowledgement on the part of the international community that it had failed women. The new theoretical articulation and secular activism ushered in by this project did raise popular awareness, albeit at a glacial pace, which, in turn, had a distant echo in the Indian media. The second development, set in motion by the first, was the setting up of the Status of Women Committee, constituted by the Indian government as part of its obligations as a signatory to the 1967 Declaration. Its report, 'Towards Equality', created a 'climate of expectation', as American scholar Leslie J. Calman has observed.[1]

'Towards Equality' observed that the status of women constituted a problem in almost all societies in the world, but it perceived the Indian situation as unique in that it was inherently linked to traditional social structures based on caste, community and class. The Committee recognised change in the status of women as a key indicator of the pattern and direction of social development. It noted:

'If the direction of that change is towards a more egalitarian distribution of roles between men and women, then the direction of change is a wholesome one. If, however, the

---

[1] Leslie J. Calman, *Toward Empowerment—Women and Movement Politics in India* (Boulder, CO: Westview Press, 1992).

various modernizing forces result in an intensification of inequalities, then we are moving away from the spirit of the Constitution."[2]

The Committee set out to measure the 'status' of Indian women rigorously in terms of demography, socio–cultural factors, legal entitlements, employment opportunities, educational development, political prospects and social welfare. Not only did it generate a great deal of data about women, it led to a heightened awareness in society about the innumerable ways in which they were being discriminated. Thus, women emerged not only as a definite social category worthy of focused attention, but their status was also recognised as a measure of national 'backwardness'.

These two broad processes—at the international and national level—ushered in a period of what may be termed as the activist phase of journalism with regard to gender. It helped to decisively transform the manner in which issues relating to women were portrayed within the information society. The 1990s were to mark something of a turning point in this trajectory, but we will come to that later. Plotting the links between feminist theorising and popular perceptions in the early 1970s as showcased by the media is a fascinating exercise. Take a concept like 'patriarchy', which emerged as part of the vocabulary of feminism. It was a concept that attempted to come up with a plausible explanation of why women have, throughout history, been socially peripheral and continue to be so in the present day. Radical feminists located women's oppression in patriarchy, which they perceived as a structured expression of male domination and control over women, and which had permeated all social, political and economic institutions.

When a construct like patriarchy is used to explain an everyday occurrence like rape, for instance, all kinds of doors are opened and shut. Rape thus could no longer be regarded as a random, unpremeditated act perpetrated by a few 'deviant' men, but as a great violence perpetrated by the powerful upon those who are powerless and socially and economically disadvantaged. In her 1970s feminist classic, *Against Our Will,* Susan Brownmiller spoke

---

[2] Government of India, *Towards Equality: Report of the Committee on the Status of Women* (New Delhi: GOI, 1974).

for many when she characterised rape as the 'conscious process of intimidation by which all men keep all women in a state of fear'.[3] There was something compelling about the way she dissected social responses to rape and exposed the ways in which a violated woman was further violated by society and the institutions of crime and justice.

This is not to say that the language of feminism translated seamlessly into the language of the media. Certainly the newsroom, the copydesk and the editorial desk in India reflected, for the most part, the general suspicion, prejudice and even hostility of the day against 'women libbers', usually regarded in the popular imagination as synonymous with 'bra burners'. As gatekeepers to public consciousness, the denizens of these spaces took their responsibilities seriously. Yet, despite them, the voices of change and the arguments for engagement could not completely be kept out, for the simple reason that the functioning of social and political institutions, like the judiciary and the legislature, were increasingly coming under the scanner of gender.

Noted editor B.G. Verghese also believes that post-Emergency India fostered a new kind of journalism because the Indira Gandhi government's attempts to shackle the press during that infamous interregnum made people more conscious of issues of freedom and equity and the need to protect such values. This in turn ushered in a trend, he maintains, that encouraged decentralisation, interventions of civil society actors and wider political participation. The press, he writes, was a major beneficiary of this new ethos. Perhaps what helped the process was the consciousness within the media fraternity that the press had not resisted the Emergency with the same passion and insistence as it had often displayed to the excesses of British rule during the nationalist movement.[4]

The Mathura rape case was certainly something of a watermark in terms of a civil society response to a particularly sensitive gender issue. In 1979, the Supreme Court reversed a verdict of the Bombay High Court convicting two policemen, accused of raping Mathura, a young tribal girl, in a Maharashtra police

[3] Susan Brownmiller, *Against Our Will: Men, Women and Rape* (New York: Ballantine Publishing Group, 1975).
[4] B.G. Verghese (ed.), *Breaking the Big Story—Great Moments in Indian Journalism* (New Delhi: Penguin, 2003).

station. The apex court chose to believe that the girl had willingly submitted to sexual intercourse since there was reason to doubt her character and since the 'alleged intercourse was a peaceful affair'. The ruling caused an uproar over what constituted 'consent' in a crime like custodial rape and whether a woman's previous sexual history could be regarded as a mitigating factor. The verdict caused four professors of law from Delhi University to write their now famous Open Letter to the Court, castigating the judgment, while women all over the country protested loudly the fact that the highest court in the land had turned, as one pamphlet of those turbulent days had put it, 'the accuser' into 'the accused'.

The mainstream media could not long remain insulated against the impact of such developments. For possibly the first time in the history of the press, the entire spectrum of violence against women, from sexual harassment to wife battery and from trafficking in women to dowry murders, made it to the front pages as well as the editorial page and became fit subjects for investigations, comment and analyses. Incidents that had, until that point, been dismissed as three-line reports tucked away in some corner of the newspaper or magazine, became front-page stories. Two cases, particularly, captured the shift in both popular perceptions and media coverage. In 1978, a Hyderabadi woman, Rameezabee, was brutally raped by four policemen. When her husband tried to intervene he was beaten so badly that he succumbed to his injuries. The incident roused such popular anger that the police station was stoned and set on fire. The public protest and media coverage of it forced the Andhra Pradesh government to appoint a committee to inquire into the incident. Similarly, the detailed reports on the 1980 attack on Maya Tyagi of Baghpat, who was first paraded naked and then raped by policemen, helped her immensely in her fight for justice. Eight years later, a lower court in 1980 awarded death sentences to her attackers. There were also efforts to be more proactive in such coverage. In April 1981, for instance, a newspaper even sent a correspondent out to 'buy' a woman and thus expose the connections between dire poverty and the degraded social status of women.

Cases like these forced changes in the language that was routinely deployed to define incidents of violence. A new linguistic subtlety came into play. For instance, since 'prostitution' often did not involve personal choice, terms like 'trafficking in women' came into currency. An expression like 'eve-teasing', which tamps down the gravity of sexual harassment, was found wanting. As were the ubiquitous 'stove deaths' and 'domestic accidents' that surfaced as brief news reports in the city pages, and which were discovered in many cases to be nothing but cold-blooded 'dowry murders'.

Here again, it was women's activism that prompted changes in news coverage and, in fact, even the anti-dowry campaigns of specific groups and coalitions—like the Dahej Virodhi Manch in Delhi or Vimochana in Bangalore—received fairly significant press coverage. What contributed to this process were two distinct developments. First, a brief mushrooming of the 'alternative media' like magazines, newsletters, pamphlets, journals that focused on subjects of this kind. Second, the presence of women professionals in mainstream media who had themselves been influenced by feminism and who now tried to bring their perspectives to their work. Some of them formed groups to foster a more sympathetic approach to women and to analyse existing media coverage. To cite one instance, Mumbai's Women and Media group sent a team to Deorala to study the media's treatment of the Roop Kanwar *sati* case of 1987. The report it produced highlighted ways in which some sections of the local media actively glamorised the incident and contributed towards a popular perception of *sati* as an ancient, hallowed and honourable practice.

Interestingly, women activists were quick to acknowledge the help they received from the media during this period of sustained activism. Nandita Gandhi and Nandita Shah, in their book, *The Issues at Stake,* observed that the initial demonstrations and protests of the 1980s received very sympathetic media coverage: 'The print media recreated the poignancy of women's suffering, and their anger and struggles reached hundreds of readers. The importance of the role played by the media in propagating women's issues was not lost to the new women's groups.' But the authors went on to state that as the

... topicality of women's protests began to fade, women's organisations found it more difficult to persuade mainstream newspapers and magazines to publish their articles. Coverage, too, became quite arbitrary. To warrant news space,

women's issues had not only to be topical but 'descriptive
and juicy' (read titillating). Analytical articles had no place
here.[5]

They also decried the 'peculiar sense of humour when it comes to
women' and noted that women politicians too are 'usually portrayed in subtle and not-so-subtle discriminatory colours. What
makes news is how they dress and behave, not how they think or
act.' They quoted media analyst, Vimal Balasubramanyan, who
in her 1988 work on women and the media had remarked that
even while generous space and coverage is given to women's issues, the general media subvert the women's question.[6]

The very fact that such subversion could take place possibly
points to the incomplete and often flawed media mainstreaming
of gender concerns. Certainly some changes of perception were
effected during that brave interregnum when women's activism
of the 1970s and 1980s attempted to influence not just media
coverage but scholarship and the generation of knowledge. There
were, during this period, serious interventions made to interpret the realities of women's lives and the links between
macro processes of the political economy and their own
marginalised status.

This, in turn, forced the state to legislate and evolve policies
and programmes in response. In 1988, for instance, the Central
government came up with a National Perspective Plan for
Women. In 1993, the Panchayati Raj Act, providing for 33 per
cent representation of women in local bodies, was passed. But
while there was a growing 'official' recognition of political norms
like equality, social—especially gender—justice and democratic
rights vis-à-vis the official discourse, there was very little
commensurate transformation in terms of social and political
practice.

Since there has always been a fairly close association between
efficacious activism and media sensitivity, it may be useful to
digress just a bit and look at the peculiar dilemmas that the

---

[5] Nandita Gandhi and Nandita Shah, *The Issues at Stake: Theory and Practice in the Contemporary Women's Movement in India* (New Delhi: Kali for
Women, 1992).
[6] Vimal Balasubramanyan, *Mirror Image: The Question of Women and Media* (Bombay: CED Publications, 1988).

women's movement increasingly faced as the 1990s—in Joseph Stiglitz's characterisation of the decade—roared. Indian feminists now recognise that the decade had brought formidable challenges that they were ill equipped to respond to, including growing communalism, economic liberalisation and globalisation, and the rising tide of violence in society. Maithreyi Krishnaraj, in an *Economic and Political Weekly* commentary, has pointed out how past strategies suddenly seemed to reach a dead-end during this period and how the recourse to legal remedies was clearly unable to bring changes in entrenched attitudes and values in society.

For one, the 'pale, amorphous secularism' of the women's movement could not really counter the aggressive ethno-privileging attempted by a resurgent Hindutva ideology, which often coopted the language of feminism for different ends. Similarly, the discrete efforts of NGOs, supported by international agencies, to push for change in niche areas came to replace the 'visible, broad assertive struggles' of an earlier era, undermining in the process the energy and autonomy the women's movement had displayed in the 1980s. All this, Krishnaraj points out, impacted on the very language of communication. As she put it:

> With the arrival of the new language of empowerment, the more explicit concern for equality is underplayed. Other linguistic changes hide shifts in discourse that postpone and dilute feminist agendas. We now talk of bargaining, of negotiation at individual household levels rather than at a collective level. Though we speak of class/caste/religious intersection, the emphasis in discourse is on individual identification, how a woman negotiates barriers of poverty, of class or caste.[7]

The 1990s was a period of immense change at a rate previously not experienced and imagined. Plotting the links between these changes and the nature of the media of the day would be a difficult task but certain leitmotifs could be plucked out to gain a broad perspective. It may be useful to remember that it was in this decade that the country's ruling elite con-

---

[7] Maithreyi Krishnaraj, 'Challenges before the Women's Movement in the Changing Context', *Economic and Political Weekly*, 25 October 2003.

sciously sloughed off its 'socialist' skin. Economic restructuring, domestically, brought with it the forces of globalisation,
deregulation and privatisation. Over time, the impact these
powerful phenomena had on the media and the dominant elite
led to a discernible shift in emphasis from the broad social and
political obligations and preoccupations of the earlier period to
a narrower focus that valorised individual success and the pursuit of profits.

Perhaps no one better personified this trend at an international level than media baron Rupert Murdoch, whose empire
grew in a manifest way during the 1990s. The pattern of media
ownership and content focus he promoted the world over was so
widely replicated by other powerful media houses that some commentators termed the phenomenon as the 'Murdochisation' of
the media. 'Murdochisation' combined business practices like
strategic pricing policies with predatory takeovers and amal-
gamations with the complete suborning of editorial independence
to management control and interests. This resulted in two developments. First, the new economies of scale made it tougher
for independent, small-circulation media operations to survive
and triggered significant changes in ownership patterns. Second, media content underwent a transformation. Not only did it
increasingly reflect the interests of the politico-military establishment, it should have come as no surprise that the coverage
of the Iraq war beamed on Murdoch's Fox News came wrapped
in Stars and Stripes, which seriously impacted on information
flows as editors consciously 'lightened' the content of their publications and channels and strove to reflect the preoccupations
of the dominant elite.

The new market-driven focus erased the distinction between
reader/viewer on the one hand, and the consumer on the other.
The pressure to attain higher profit levels led to a conscious
blending of news with entertainment as a strategy to gain higher
readership/viewership ratings. Indeed, the new emphasis on
ratings is itself comment enough. Perhaps the most debilitating
consequence of these developments was the general homo-
genisation of news that tended to squeeze out more serious,
more nuanced coverage. Daya Thussu, a teacher in the Media
and Communications Department of Goldsmiths College, University of London, cited a major study conducted by the Project

for Excellence in Journalism,[8] which examined the US mass media over a span of 25 years. According to it, there has been a distinct shift toward lifestyle, celebrity, entertainment and celebrity crime/scandal in the news.

In many ways, this was the global pattern and India by no means bucked the trend. The neglect of journalism in the public interest had serious repercussions on the coverage of gender issues. Old stereotypes came to be replaced by new ones and, interestingly, the earlier language of women's liberation and independence was successfully coopted to serve the requirements of the market. The advertising industry was, as usual, the first to reflect the changed media culture, crucially influencing it in the process. Slowly, such resilient icons of yore like the 'Rin' housewife transmogrified into the 'Rin' manager. The self-confident, urbanised woman professional, unrepresentative though she was of the women in the country, came to be hailed as the symbol of the 'liberated' Indian woman who flaunted her disposable income and sexuality with equal élan. She now figured in advertisements for scooters, computers, holiday packages. Simultaneously, the demands of infotainment also renewed the appeal of women as sex symbols that fed in turn the notorious 'Food & Fornication' formula of city-smart supplements.

As news coverage got more event-driven rather than process-driven, when—as in the memorable words of a senior British editor Karl Miller—the duty to inform deferred cravenly to the duty to entertain, 'women as victims' occasionally figured in the news if the incident involving them was sensational enough, but 'women as marginalised category' no longer excited even the weak concern of the 1980s. Sonia Bathla[9] points to how coverage of violent crime against women, which was a media focus in the early 1980s, declined sharply since then, with editors citing 'reader fatigue' over atrocity-related stories as an excuse for no longer focusing on them, even though there was no cessation of such violence in everyday life.

[8] Daya Thussu and Des Freedman (eds), *War and Media: Reporting Conflict 24/7* (London: Sage Publications, 2003).
[9] Sonia Bathla, *Women, Democracy and the Media: Cultural and Political Representation in the Indian Press* (New Delhi and Thousand Oaks, CA: Sage Publications, 1999).

The impatience with complex analysis meant that there were few attempts to situate oppression in broader social phenomena, leading, in turn, to oversimplification and a serious lack of contextualising. The premium given to form over content, the emphasis placed on 'smart writing' and 'smart visual' rather than substance, meant that younger professionals concentrated more on stylish usage and facile expression rather than on boning up on valuable background information and analyses in order to understand complex social processes. This resulted in what can be usefully termed as the dumbing down spiral. For women, specifically, it resulted in 'symbolic annihilation', as a media analyst Gail Tuchman puts it, through a combination of 'condemnation, trivialisation and erasure'.

It may be difficult to anticipate how these trends play out in the long term. But given the clear nexus between power, the exercise of power and the media, it is unlikely that the broad mass of women will ever inhabit the favoured main space in the foreseeable future. This is not just because of their low social visibility, their lack of economic resources and political leverage, but because of the nature of the media, which are more homogenised, more focused on the sphere of power than ever before. The pressure to make profits and garner advertising in an increasingly globalised world will ensure that the serious coverage of ordinary lives, including those of women, will continue to fight a losing battle against hype, the privileging of commercial information and infotainment masquerading as news.

The dissipation of diversity in a country as heterogeneous as India is particularly alarming because, as several media commentators have observed, it is pluralism that provides a modicum of space for those committed to serious and professional journalism and allows them to not just take on the powerful lobbies working to manipulate news and opinion but to further and deepen Indian democracy through their work.

9

gender, identity and the
tamil popular press

v. geetha

*i*n the 1980s, when women's groups and feminists discussed media representations of femininity and issues relating to gender, we invariably used words such as 'objectification', 'downgrading' and 'humiliating' to define and plot our discursive field. These words remain with us, but the media have since engaged with gender in such complex ways that it is not very useful or illuminating to sift media content using these concepts as our only measure. Tamil (print) media, for instance, continue to print and publish images of half-clad women, usually actresses or stills from films, has its quota of misogynistic jokes and snippets and diffuses patriarchal commonsense as it has always done. But there is a difference. Whether it is the brash, sensational *Kumudam*, the more sedate *Kalki*, the commercially sagacious *Ananda Vikatan*, or newsweeklies such as *Nakkeeran* or the relatively new *Kumudam Reporter*, they are open to tales of female oppression and woe. There appears to be an implicit recognition that, by and large, women are victims of a system that uses them ill and that they suffer rights violations, which may not be condoned.

There are two immediate reasons for this making of space for female victim stories. For one, women-centred stories of woe are inherently newsworthy. They are always already dramatic, and the narrative invariably hints at and promises an exciting or at least horrifying denouement. Besides, there is the visual interest: the photographs of women, as they talk, expostulate, show off their wounds or express an emotion make excellent copy.

But this is not all. Today, women's groups, at least some of them, invite media attention. They hold press conferences, write press notices and keep in touch with particular journalists, whose goodwill and confidence they enjoy. This means that they 'feed' stories to the media, and the latter, especially reporters and correspondents in smaller towns, who are hungry for news, respond enthusiastically. It is also obviously useful to have the media at the site of demonstrations and protests: the cause in question gets reported widely and if there is the possibility of state displeasure, the media can be expected to cover it. More recently, there has been another development: the presence of the lone feminist or at least sensitive female reporter who deliberately sets out to report on victim stories.

Clearly, there is a tacit compact here, between the individual journalist or magazine and a rights group, and, unwittingly enough, this relationship precludes mindless and habitual objectification, especially representations of the victimised body that otherwise can end up being as titillating as the alluring female body. However, this cannot be taken to mean that the one affects the other—that victim stories impinge upon editorial decisions to such an extent that the routinely semi-clad images, which belong to the centre spreads of Tamil weeklies, are replaced, diminish in number or that there are attempts to make them disappear.

What we have here is a new reporting grammar: the reporting voice is invariably low and subdued as it mimics the cautious yet curious tone of the as yet innocent observer who asks the most innocuous questions of an event and ends up telling the tale as he has understood it. In some instances, individual journalists or the paper or magazine they write for create their own lexicon, a semantic shorthand that lets them tell the story in a manner that is peculiarly theirs and which helps them control the twists and turns of the narrative. (The exceptions to this general rule are stories filed by sensitive female reporters that invariably foreground the relationships of power, which are central to any narrative of oppression, and the voices of the women themselves.) For instance, when reporting the protracted and infamous Premananda case (August–November 1996), which involved a godman who had set up an ashram in the vicinity of Pudukkottai town in Tamil Nadu and was charged with the sexual assault of minor girls, most news story writers referred to the godman as 'Prems', and to the young women who had fled his ashram as 'the beauties'. (This was the case not only with newsweeklies such as *Junior Vikatan*, but also local editions of dailies and eveningers such as *Tamizh Murasu*.) It was as if the reporter in question was on familiar, even intimate terms with the characters caught up in this ugly drama and therefore privy to untold secrets that he might yet share with his readers.

Besides, the deploying of these terms and an entire vocabulary that played into the associative meanings they invoked, helped to keep alive reader interest—the godman became an almost likeable character, whose villainy evoked both horror and fascination, and the girls, however pathetic and shocking their current state of existence, exuded seductive prowess. In other words, the reporter played a voyeur who could peep into shows that are not on view for the rest of the world and used this privileged position to 'see' and to 'warn' those who could not, of the horrors to which he had been witness. Playing the gossip and moralist by turn, he responded rather brilliantly to his readers' hunger for the forbidden: he crossed limits they would not, but returned to reassure them of the validity and rightness of these limiting lines that separated the everyday from whatever lay beyond it.

This genre of journalistic writing is what enables the telling of female victim tales. Part-sensational, part-sincere and possessed of a will to 'tell the truth', 'to report the unreported', this mode of writing has come to stay in the Tamil media. Embarrassingly sentimental and brash, it betrays a political energy that is volatile and ephemeral, anarchic and flippant.

The question is, what does this telling amount to? What is its sense of the horrors it narrates? (I have in mind conventional news stories, and not ones filed by feminist reporters.) At one level, it is clear that Tamil newsweeklies, reporting on the underside of the civic world, manage to accommodate female victim tales within a more general critique they offer, often unintentionally, of power and its abuses. This obsession with power and its doings is a staple of popular culture: crimes of trust and betrayal involving men and women in responsible positions of authority are central to Tamil movie plots and television serials. This fascination with the abuses of power is seldom recompensed by a strong sense of the moral or the political—power is

its own source of interest and portrayals of its deployment are
avidly consumed. In the case of news stories, power is always
understood in its details and it is because of the attention paid to
the various elements that make up a drama that power emerges
in all its garishness. In the instance of female victim tales, a
generalised picture of female subordination and patriarchal power
seldom emerges from the dense narratives that are served to
the reader. Nor is there an editorial or authorial voice that frames
these tales for us, often, they remain just so many stories that
bear periodic witness to the unredeemed criminality of men and
society in matters concerning women.

Significantly, victim tales have a counterpart: tales of achievers.
The Tamil media in general, and not merely the newsweeklies,
report enthusiastically on instances of female success, of whatever
sort. Such women are praised for their heroism, self-sacrifice,
courage, honesty, as the case may be. Again, there is no defined
basis to assessing success; just as the fact of being female and in
trouble marks out a victim's tale as newsworthy in particular
ways, so does a success tale qualify for being so, simply because
the achiever is female.

This reductive reasoning though is not entirely insensitive to
context or conjuncture. That is, 'femaleness', whether invoked
in the cause of suffering or success, is always marked. Given the
manner in which issues of identity and gender intersect, whether
this has to do with caste or community, it is not at all surprising
that Tamil news media hyphenate the identities of women who
are dalits or Muslims or Christians. Only rarely is this done for
women belonging to other castes and, of course, Hindu women
are seldom referred to as such—they remain, for the most part,
unmarked, unless of course they figure in a tale where their
religious identity is primary to the telling of the tale.

The question arises: what does this mean in the larger context of Tamil journalism? Does the bearer of a hyphenated identity immediately attract a different register of reporting and
analysis? Or is this a formal rather than a substantive marking,
with no further implications for representation and understanding, both for the journalist and the reader? One could take up a
particular instance, say, the portrayal of Muslim women in the
Tamil media, to address the issues at stake here.

It would be useful to consider, at this point, the historical
conjuncture that has rendered Muslim women visible in the

national media, including the English-language press. Beginning with the Shah Bano case, and later the communal riots of the mid-1980s, and through the 1990s decade of the Masjid riots and into our immediate present (2005), Muslim women have 'become' subjects of media attention in particular ways. They are almost always shown as victims, either of riots or unjust community laws, or as brave loners fighting a recalcitrant and stubborn community. Since the Gujarat riots and killings of 2002, this picture has come to stay with us, only now it is more poignant and tragic than ever before in our recent history. Visually, this has meant that the camera plays with the veil, either dramatically foregrounding it, or suggesting that beyond the veil there are secrets that stand to be revealed, that might yet shock and surprise readers and viewers.

This deliberate construction of the Muslim woman as a mystery to be probed, understood and helped, in spite of her self and her community, is one that the mainstream press seldom interrogates, even when it means well by its subject. Part of the reason for this generous condescension on the part of the secular press must be located in the fact that there are very few Muslim women journalists, and even fewer feminists, who are active in the media. Such voices as we hear from Gujarat and Kashmir address issues of survival for the most part, and gender concerns figure, if at all, in a marginal fashion. The absence of critical, feminist-insiders in the media has meant that gender concerns with respect to the Muslim community are often articulated as arguments in abstraction, without the stain of history and the present, and without a sense of what Muslim women think and what they might want to express in a civic context.

Interestingly, the Tamil press, in particular the newsweeklies, do not appear to take note of this larger context which frames media representations of Muslim life. There have been several news stories about Muslim women over the last few years in mainstream newsweeklies, and most of them are, invariably, about local lives and situations, successes and sufferings (in *Kumudam Reporter*, *Nakkeeran*, *Ananda Vikatan*, *Kalki*, from 2001 up to the present). The stories unfold in the usual manner of victim tales, with the identity of the victim marked only by her wearing a veil, and by the fact of her name. At least three of the stories raise questions that are yet to be clearly debated or resolved at the national level: of a gender-just civil code for all women and personal law reform. Two of these stories are news reports of conferences held by Muslim women, in which they had resolved that they would like representation in local *jamaat*s that hear cases relating to marriage, divorce and inheritance. Another resolution had to do with stricter enforcement of personal laws to regulate male behaviour, with respect to dowry, drinking and usury, all of which, the women resolved, were patently un-Islamic practices. The third story had to do with a demand raised by some Muslim women that if they are not allowed representation in *jamaat*s, they would go ahead and build their own mosque and constitute their own *jamaat*.

While these concerns were reported widely in local editions of Tamil dailies and in some weeklies, they neither referred to larger national debates on these matters, nor did they seek to raise questions for their readers about the implications of some of the issues raised by Muslim women. In the matter of the mosque, for instance, the demand for a women's mosque was criticised by a well-known Muslim woman and activist. *Ananda Vikatan* carried both sets of arguments, for and against the mosque, but refrained from editorial comment.

It must be noted here that the Tamil press is not entirely innocent of the politics of Hindutva. The daily *Dinamalar* is blatantly supportive of the Hindu right and has been in the forefront of campaigns against so-called local Muslim militant groups and 'terrorists'. In their uncritical acceptance and articulation of 'Hindu' tolerance and the space they provide to Hindu religious leaders, the Kanchi Shankaracharya, for one, most Tamil weeklies may be said to adhere to a 'soft' Hindutva option: the sort that exists as a diffuse, shadowy 'commonsense', with the potential to turn aggressive and xenophobic. But given the marvellous inconsistencies that riddle the commercially hungry world of the Tamil media, stories count for the attention they evoke, and for the excitement they generate for the moment, and ideological argument is rarely sustained for its own sake. Besides, there is at least a section of the media that did take a principled position on Gujarat, even while insisting that justice be done to the Godhra victims (*Kalki*, for example argued thus).

One rather unusual reason for what appears to be routine reporting of Muslim women's tales in the Tamil news media has, perhaps, to do with the fact that almost all these stories refer back to an individual activist, D. Sharifa, whose organisation, STEPS has been active in Pudukkottai for over a decade. Sharifa has often been featured in newsweeklies on account of the rather unusual instances of violence against women that she has had to deal with—for instance, the Premananda case, where she was entrusted by the Tamil Nadu government with the responsibility of protecting the witnesses against the godman's misdeeds, by granting them temporary shelter in her short-stay home. In all the years that Sharifa has been active (since 1989), the media have been attentive to her work, also because she took the local press into her confidence and used whatever publicity she garnered to the advantage of the women that came to her centre soliciting help. Therefore, when she started working closely with women in the Muslim community, the media did not see anything particularly unusual in the stories that she brought to them. Her identity as a Muslim woman had never really been primary to the media's sense of her work and concerns. Therefore, even when Muslim women constituted the subject of what she had to narrate to them, they did not appear to have granted this fact undue emphasis.

On the other hand, though, Sharifa has been maligned for her mosque demand in the Muslim community press and accused of being insensitive to community needs and, predictably enough, un-Islamic. Clearly, the community press, at least the Tamil papers and magazines with a recognisably Muslim identity, is far more sensitive and aware of the context within which Sharifa and her group's demands would be viewed and understood. For one, there is the anxiety that matters that are bound to stir dissension and alarm within the community might well be utilised by ideologists and parties inimical to Muslim lives and welfare, in this instance, by the Hindu right. Second, and this is a far more complicated reason, Muslim intellectual opinion in Tamil Nadu for the past decade and more has concerned itself with coming to terms with Hindutva and its implications. Radical Muslim groups and organisations have emerged during this period: the Tamil Nadu *Muslim Munnetra Kazhagam*, for example, and these have worked hard to forge links with what they see as Catholic secular initiatives, including those launched by dalit parties and even the far left. In the event, issues pertaining to the community-in-itself, if one might call it that, especially issues relating to gender justice, have not been addressed or perhaps not even recognised as pertinent.

More important to the context of this discussion, gender concerns, however understood by newly emergent articulate groups, have become subsumed or rendered further invisible by the imperatives of anti-Hindutva discourses. It is not surprising, therefore, that community magazines have been sharp with Sharifa's arguments for a separate mosque for women, since they see her raising of such issues as rendering an already beleaguered community even more vulnerable. Significantly, Muslim women, are not part of these intellectual debates, but they are allowed a voice if they air strictly conventional interpretations of women's rights. It is not that women are quiet. On issues such as the triple *talaq*, the high incidence of dowry in the community and the manner of settling disputes by referring to the *jamaat*, women have spoken out strongly in various meetings held over the last five years in Tamil Nadu. The debates at these meetings are highly revealing: very few women see the question of their rights as actively conflicting with their identity as Muslims. In their understanding, they are claiming rights granted to them by their faith, but which are being denied to them by unscrupulous and opportunistic interpretations of Islam. Further, they are not particularly interested in the formal acknowledgement of these rights, in the interests of presenting to the world an image of Islam as a quintessentially liberal faith— for them, these rights have to work, realised in their lived contexts. This is in sharp contrast to the attitudes of Muslim male intellectuals who, as a rule, are defensive and anxious about the public identity of Islam and what it stands for.

There is a rather curious media story that is pertinent to our argument at this point. Debates regarding Hindutva and its meanings in the Tamil context have been legion in what is known as the 'little magazine' circuit. Little magazines are small, literary journals, which chiefly address each other. There are at least over 50 of these, and often the same set of people write in them. Some have devoted readers and writers who defend the editorial and other positions of the magazine in question zealously. This last decade, most of the little magazines have been critical of Hindutva, with some leading intellectuals associated with some of the more stridently anti-caste and anti-Hindutva magazines (for instance, *Pudiya Tadam* and the more catholic *Pudiya Kattru*) supporting and endorsing minority rights.

Muslim community magazines are also involved in these debates, in as much as they answer to their specific needs. They have been gratified by the support extended to the cause of minority rights and to the critical voices raised against Hindutva by those who are not Muslims, but who are sensitive to the general crisis that has beset the community in a local as well as global sense.

On the other hand, neither the critics of Hindutva, nor their Muslim colleagues have raised the vexed question of gender justice in the context of community rights and identity. For example, the questions raised by Sharifa and women like her from within the community have not been seriously examined. Neither has the inextricable link between Hindutva, the violence in Gujarat and the horrors visited upon Muslim women there been written about in the little magazines—though women's groups in the state have addressed this issue in fairly precise terms.

In the absence of protocols for discussions on gender justice, except those allowed by a formal praise of Islam's generous granting of rights to women, there exists either a vacuous silence or loud, acrimonious argument. In one instance, a female columnist in *Dalit Murasu*, a magazine, uneasily poised between the little magazine culture of intense and almost incestuous debate and the larger expansive world of popular critical politics, wrote scathingly of gender issues, pertaining to notions of female modesty, as these had been raised and resolved in *Unnarvu*, a Tamil Muslim magazine. A protracted debate followed, with the *Dalit Murasu* columnist refusing to surrender, what appeared to her, a feminist perspective to the imperatives of a secularism that did not interrogate minority arguments on gender. For its part, *Unnarvu* refused to engage her concerns, since its columnists were not used to debating gender, except in a defensive sense and as part of a larger argument about community identity.

It is in this context that we might have to reconsider the manner in which Tamil magazines report on gender: do they normalise complex problems through their unique mode of representation, by submitting all tales to a genre of writing that is devoted to the event, the details of it and not to the argument?

Is their relative ease with reporting Muslim women's issues an instance of a majority press being 'liberal' in the manner that all privileged individuals and institutions can afford to be liberal, because they are not beset with crises of identity that are fundamental and constitutive? Or is this liberalism really an effect of the commercial logic that governs Tamil media, where stories have to compel attention and offer entertainment above all else?

These are important questions that await answers. Meanwhile, we have no choice but to accept that the popular press in Tamil does possess an infectious energy that keeps it alive, if only in a limited commercial, garish sense. Our only consolation is that the papers and weeklies, by and large, are not actively peddling hatred and lies.

10

sports journalism: going against the grain

nirmal shekar

*t*here is journalism, and then there is sports journalism: so much a part of it, yet so different from it. A hybrid and a maverick, it is an island that revels in its isolation, constantly celebrating its independence by skilfully violating all time-tested norms of sound journalism.

It sounds and behaves like a gifted child that has been given that extra bit of freedom by its doting parents to rebel, to misbehave and ignore the widely accepted rules in the game of life. It draws its strength from being a part of the big family unit— journalism, media, whatever you want to call it—yet prides itself in the fact that it is so different from the rest.

Look at the major newspapers. Listen to radio commentaries on sports events. Watch sports on television. What strikes you immediately? Then again, if you are a sports lover and someone used to reading reports and hearing TV commentary, perhaps what should strike you first won't strike you at all.

But a student of journalism will surely notice immediately that the sports pages and the sports coverage on TV are very different from other branches of journalism/media. For, every other 'report' on sports tends to violate the widely understood and accepted norms of good reporting with a fair bit of comment thrown in. On the other hand, take away the opinions, comments, the flowery imagery and wordplay, as well as the emotions that are poured into the coverage of sports events, both in the print and broadcast media, and sports reporting will turn out to be rather dull and prosaic.

In the event, sports journalism draws its life-blood from going against the grain, so to say. Its chief claim to glamour and glory lies in its capacity to ignore the rules of the game. And this is precisely why, as an arm of journalism, sports journalism is a game within a game with its own set of rules.

Once looked down upon condescendingly by other branches of journalism—an American writer famously described the sports department of a newspaper as the 'toyshop'—sports journalism has seen exponential growth in the last three decades, matching strides with an industry (sports) that has enjoyed a long, unbroken boom period. As an amateur activity turned into a professional business, with many leading sports recording an annual turnover of tens of millions of dollars in several nations around the world, the obscure toyshop in the distant corner has taken centre stage.

Sports journalism has indeed come a long way from its early days when a few pioneers put pen to paper for the sheer love of cricket or football or boxing or athletics. Few branches of journalism have grown as fast as sports in the last three or four decades. There was a time, in the pre-Independence era, when even the major English-language papers of the country devoted no more than a few columns to sports coverage. One or at the most two journalists ran the whole show. Today, the leading national newspapers in India pay so much attention to sports coverage that a good slice of their annual budget for news coverage goes towards sports.

From the time that a sports journalist was considered a poor country cousin of the more famous practitioners in the profession, the political scribe or the general news reporter, my colleagues in the sports writing business have today come to occupy a special position. Fifty years ago, few newspaper readers would have been familiar with names of sportswriters unless the person happened to have the word-spinning skills of the late Neville Cardus, a man whose contribution to cricket journalism was much the same as Michelangelo's to the Sistine Chapel. There was the odd cricket scribe or football writer from England, a handful of boxing reporters/critics from the United States, but overall the number of people who were household names among newspaper readers could be counted on the fingers of our two hands.

Fast-forward to 2005, and in every sports-loving nation anywhere in the world newspaper readers and television viewers are as familiar with the names of men and women reporting major sports in leading newspapers and on television as they are with the political columnists and commentators. This is hardly a surprise in an era when the name Sachin Tendulkar is as readily recognisable as Prime Minister Manmohan Singh! And in this country itself, if we take away the preening and pouting celluloid stars of Kollywood or Bollywood or any other 'wood' we can think of, our cricketers and the odd tennis star are India's pop icons, equal to the Bryan Adamses, Bonos and Michael Jacksons.

A bit of that glamour is bound to rub off on the men and women whose job it is to recapture the heroics of the megastars in words and pictures, although when I say glamour I don't mean the literal variety, scantily clad, on display these days on cricket commentary teams. On the other hand, the point is that when one writes and talks about people who are worshipped by millions, one does get noticed. To set the record straight, people who need to spend two hours in front of a mirror and then wonder when the last time was that they wore the outfit they had chosen for the day before attending a sports event, are still in a very, very thin minority in the sports media in India.

Yet, in the larger context, there can be no doubt at all that television has turned sports journalism on its head. Every major sport anywhere in the world owes its financial strength to that little box which many of us cannot do without in our drawing rooms. In an overcrowded world that is forever on the fast-forward mode, sports are made for television and television is made for sports. It is more than a marriage of convenience. Neither can do without the other. For TV has turned sports into instant theatre. 'Have remote, will watch' is the sports lover's comforting and predominant thought in an era when sporting fireworks are no more than a remote-click away.

'Unquestionably, TV is saving sports, although I'm not sure if sports is worth saving,' said Howard Cosell, the father of television sports journalism in the United States and as big a legend in his lifetime (Cosell died in 1995) as any of the superstars whose heroics he described to the viewers. Then again, if TV saved sports, what now can save television, especially sports television? 'Can the torrent of silly words from the sportscasters be reduced to a bearable trickle?' asked the *New York Times*'s TV critic John O'Connor a quarter of a century ago. Today, we can proudly say that we Indians can ask that question of our sportscasters too!

Television has not only presided over a dumbing-down process in sports journalism but it has also led to boosterism, jingoism and blind hero worship. The victim is not merely objectivity as sports presenters run out of adjectives at an amazing speed. The line between fair and objective journalism and brazen promotion of people and events has become blurred, making it difficult to present viewers with a thoroughly professional, sound entertainment package using sports as a medium. There is so much hype on television that one sometimes wonders if some of the things we hear are said by trained media professionals or by clever marketing pros with one eye on the balance sheet.

This apart, there are the evils of saturation coverage, where one sport (cricket is a good example in India) is followed and boosted to such an extent that all the others languish in the obscure hinterland with no hope of catching the eye of sports fans. In essence, the minority sports are put in deep freeze. Saturation coverage also leads to 'formula' coverage of events, so much so that every show looks and sounds the same and we are thankful to the athletes themselves for providing us the variety that the presenting teams find elusive in the commentary box.

Then there is the issue of bias. Most sportscasters who love their job find themselves having to slant stories/events in favour of the home team or, in some cases, in favour of the teams that matter in any given sport. Marketing logic dictates that the money-spinning athletes and teams cannot be criticised to the extent that their image might suffer. Everything else follows suit.

If I have dwelt as long as I have on television and its impact on sports journalism, it is only because many of the changes in the sports media, print included, have been triggered by the influence of TV. While TV has turned sports stars, promoters and agents into millionaires many times over, it has also had its destructive effects on sports at the grassroots level. For it is the unbroken television coverage of major international events that has ruined the party for the men, women and even children who play sports at the local, regional or even national level. Before the advent of TV, in the 1950s, 1960s and for the most part of the 1970s, interstate or inter-club matches in many sports used to command on-site audiences running to thousands. A Ranji Trophy championship final would often see more than 10,000 spectators attend every single day of the match. A national football championship final would bring in three or four times that number. Today, if a few hundred turn up for a Ranji final the organiser would consider himself lucky.

This apart, for a sportswriter, another great loss because of the television revolution is the fact that he does not get to know the sports heroes of his era as well as his predecessors in the 1950s or 1960s or even the 1970s did theirs. One would think that the opposite would be true; but not really. In an era when fans who worship cult icons such as a David Beckham or an Anna Kournikova want to know everything, one would think that the all-seeing TV cameras and tabloid newshounds would give them everything they want. Of course they do. But then, the more we think we know about the superstars, the less we actually do. Television has brought them closer to us but has taken them far away from us too. And so, in a way, have the newspapers and magazines that employ inventive methods to bring news about the superstars (especially their private lives) to readers. What this phenomenon has achieved is to bring closer the image of the superstar; what it has removed from our grasp is the real person.

As professionals in the business, we may have met a Pete Sampras or a David Beckham or a Sachin Tendulkar several times in the course of our work. But, at the end of the day, we will never perhaps know them as well as the sportswriters of the 1950s and 1960s knew the heroic performers of their more leisurely and far more romantic era. My predecessors would have been able, week after week, to join a Rod Laver or Ken Rosewall, tennis legends of the 1960s, for a few beers in the pub after a long day at the Wimbledon championship. They would have been able to go out to dinner now and again with the late M.L. Jaisimha or Mansur Ali Khan Pataudi, former Indian Test cricketers, and get to know them in the flesh, so to say, stripped of all the gaudy attire forced on them by the image makers. But, if today, I tried to do that with a Beckham or a Kournikova or even a Tendulkar, I would first have to get past the sort of security that George Bush would find suffocating on a visit to

Baghdad. And, even if I did manage to pull off the impossible, it would still be tough to get under the layers and layers of popular myth to try and get to know the person (the megastar), warts and all, before setting out to tell the readers the truth, and nothing but the truth.

In the event, however tough the job, it is indeed the duty of sportswriting professionals in the print media today to debunk the myths created by television and the image makers who always lurk behind the cameras. This, of course, is one of many challenges that sports journalists in the print media face as a result of the TV revolution. Television is only interested in stars and superstars and seldom, if ever, turns its attention to the grassroots level. So long as the Tendulkars, Rahul Dravids and Sourav Gangulys are big enough only for a single-column item and headline, playing school cricket, television has no interest in them. It may reveal a passing interest when they show promise and are mentioned in bigger headlines. But the moment they are good enough for banner headlines, TV takes over.

This is precisely why it is important for the print media in this country to continue to support local/regional/school/college level sports. While many of the broadsheets in this country certainly do this, the demands made by the superstars and the super-events in a year-round sports calendar on space in the newspapers make it very tough for a sports editor to juggle with his priorities.

Twenty-five years ago, when I joined *The Hindu* in Chennai as a sportswriter, I could, on a daily basis, hope to write at least 500 words on local events, whether it was a football league game or a cricket match. Today, the priorities have changed so much—and the international sports programme is so crowded and coverage so readily available thanks to the information revolution—that a young sportswriter will be lucky to get 100 or 200 words into print on a local assignment. Television is killing local sports and while it is on life-support, it has fallen upon print media professionals to do their bit to see that an important pillar of the sporting edifice does not crash.

While doing this, it has also become necessary for sports journalists in the print media to evolve with the times as reporters/writers/columnists. With cable television bringing home live coverage of almost all major sports events anywhere in the world, sportswriters will have to work that much harder to simply find enough readers the next morning. This is especially true of popular sports. When a sports scribe writes from a Test match involving India or from Wimbledon or the US Open tennis championship, he will have realised that a good 50 per cent of his readers might have watched the action live. Why would they want to read his story then?

The challenge lies here. To get readers, whose time is precious each morning, to read reports of events they have already witnessed on the small screen takes some doing. And the ones who manage to hold the readers' attention are often the sports journalists who write well and who add to what has already been seen on TV.

We live in the age of opinion. On TV, in bars, in schools and colleges, in drawing rooms ... everywhere we are bombarded with opinions, particularly on sports and politics and cinema. And an experienced sportswriter who doubles as a columnist can carry the readers with him if he has the correct perspective and writes with passion and energy. The more innovative and creative he is, the more thorough his research is, the more analytical and evocative the prose is, the surer he can be that readers will enjoy what he has written, no matter that the event has already been seen live on television.

Then again, the sports writing professional in the Indian print media today not only has to adapt quickly and deal with the challenges thrown at him by television, he also has to stand up to competition from former players who attend matches and write columns for newspapers and magazines. Obviously, a professional sportswriter cannot compare himself with a former great when it comes to name value and on-the-playing-field experience. Where he can score is in the quality of his writing, although there are a handful of former players who write like a dream, the principal example being Peter Roebuck, the former Somerset cricket captain who, today, is the finest living cricket writer, word for word.

'Sportswriting is easy. You sit in front of a typewriter until little drops of blood run down your forehead', said the late Red Smith, one of the greatest English-language sports writers of all time and a legend in the American sportswriting community. Smith's lean, athletic prose was a thing of beauty. I grew up reading his boxing reports in *The New York Times* and his was a huge influence on my career choice. Some of his breed are still around amongst us today, for sports provides a wonderful platform for the better writers to showcase their talents.

From the days of Arthur Conan Doyle, Albert Camus and Ernest Hemingway, some of the finest writers of all time have been drawn to sports, which provides a wonderful theatre for observation. Yet, those were days when television had not robbed sporting events of their mystery by beaming them live. But, then, a good sportswriter will always get read, no matter what television has done. And it is all the more important now for sportswriters to avoid clichés and meaningless adjectives and instead concentrate on vivid writing that brings to the reader the sight, sounds and scents of whatever event he is writing about.

This is where print journalism in India lags behind its counterpart in England or the United States. While in some ways, English-language sportswriting in India is superior to what we can find in places like Australia and some parts of the US, by and large the quality of journalism is much superior in Britain and the United States compared to India. And I am not talking about the vernacular dailies and magazines. There are patches of excellence here and there and above-average stuff does appear now and again; but in terms of consistency—word for word, sentence for sentence, report for report, column for column— sportswriting in India has some way to go before it can match what can be read in the broadsheets in England.

While this comparison may not be entirely fair, because English is not the mother tongue for almost every single Indian sportswriter, what is more significant is that few sportswriters in Indian newspapers have adapted to the times in terms of the style and content of their reports in the high noon of the Internet era. While reporters working for publications that are basically newspapers of record have to necessarily bring in the relevant information in their reports, no matter that the result is already known to the reader, even within this limitation they can work to provide readers vibrant copy.

Without sacrificing the age-old cardinal rules of good sports journalism, the scribe can still move with the times if only he cares to remember that information, in itself, may be of little value to the reader at a time when almost everything anyone may want is a mouse-click away or even an SMS away on the cell phone.

It is this flexibility, this ability to change with the times and give the readers everything they want, and some more, that may be the lack in the Indian sports media, which, as days go by, will have to find more and more novel ways—quite apart from in-depth analyses, investigative reports, timely comments, personality-oriented features and attractive graphics as well as outstanding pictures—in which to present news to readers who will have less and less time for newspapers and its sports pages.

It is a huge challenge. But the final whistle has not yet been blown on sports journalism in India. And it never will be. For this is a game without an end. And as an optimist for whom the romance of words will never fade, I am confident that sports journalism in India will rise up to the challenge and come out a winner.

11

agriculture: the missing dimension

devinder sharma

*i*n 1994, the then Indian Prime Minister, P.V. Narasimha Rao visited the United States. Like any other visiting head of state, the Prime Minister was expected to figure prominently in the news columns of the American newspapers. After all, he was the Prime Minister of the world's biggest democracy.

During his visit, Mr Narasimha Rao addressed the US Congress, and on behalf of India, co-sponsored a resolution of the Comprehensive Test Ban Treaty (CTBT) with the United States. The American media, however, completely blacked him out. There was not even a single line on the Indian Prime Minister's visit. For the media managers, this was a nightmare. All their efforts had fallen flat. To show the presence of the Indian Prime Minister on American soil, the media planners had no alternative, except the following: they bought a full-page advertisement in *The New York Times* announcing the Prime Minister's visit.

Ten years later, in 2003 to be precise, the American media went berserk over the news of a genetically modified (GM) potato, with a higher protein content, that had been developed by Indian scientists. The transgenic potato was projected as the probable answer to India's gnawing crisis of malnutrition. Within hours of the breaking of this news, the international news wires were abuzz with excitement. Dailies like *The New York Times*, *The Washington Post*, *The Financial Times*, *The Wall Street Journal* and almost all the Indian newspapers for that matter, had played up the story. The television channels had broadcast the report in prime bulletins, and suddenly for the media, the transgenic potato became a hot potato.

bending it from beckham

I was taken by surprise. The BBC Radio presenter, who was busy talking about the football star David Beckham, suddenly shifted gear to the genetically modified potato, and told his listeners that he had a food policy analyst on line from New Delhi. And before I could respond to his greeting, he fired the first *googly:* 'When will you stop treating the multinational corporations as wicked?'

Knowing that it was a live and a popular breakfast programme, I had little time to react. 'I think this question should be directed to the multinationals,' I replied, adding, 'as far as I am concerned, I would stop treating them as wicked the day they stop acting wickedly.' While I was still drawing the link between multinational corporations and the GM potato being researched in India, the commentator asked: 'Why are you opposed to the GM potato which is reported to contain 40 per cent more proteins and could be the answer to India's mounting problem of malnutrition?'

'Who gave you these fake protein figures?' I asked. 'The GM potato that is undergoing research contains no more than 2.8 per cent protein, a mere increase of 0.6 to 0.8 per cent protein than what exists in the normal potato.'

'Well, this is what has been claimed by the Secretary of the Department of Biotechnology,' he quipped, adding, 'but don't you think that even a little increase in proteins would help?'

'What a shame. Those who talk of addressing the acute malnutrition crisis by feeding GM potatoes containing 2.8 per cent proteins must be living in a fool's paradise,' I reacted angrily. 'If they are really sincere about fighting malnutrition, they should ensure that the 50 million tonnes of food grain that are rotting in the open are first fed to the hungry. And before you ask me why, let me tell you that the over 25 million tonnes of food that is stocked and rotting comprises wheat, which contains four times more proteins than potatoes.'

A couple of more questions, and the live interview ended. The BBC presenter turned back to more juicy stuff on Beckham, his interest in India's hunger and malnutrition being as superficial as that of the biotechnologists.

But no sooner was I back in my office, than another reporter was on the line, this time from Paris. He too was seeking my reaction to the claims made by Mrs Manju Sharma, Secretary, Department of Biotechnology. In the three days after Mrs Sharma had made the tall (but false) claims at an international conference in France, the global print and electronic media had literally chased the story as if it was likely to lead the way to unearthing the 'weapons of mass destruction'.

And that reminds me of another obtuse research claim that had adroned the front pages of newspapers in the early 1980s. Scientists had succeeded in crossing the potato with the tomato, and they called it *pomato,* hoping that it would increase the shelf life of tomatoes. The skin of the tomato would become thicker and that would mean that housewives would not have to throw out overripe tomatoes every other day. Many newspapers had come out with editorials, probably meant to make for light reading, praising the effort of the scientists. Mercifully, we did not hear of this 'scientific' feat again.

The scientific world has certainly come a long way since the days of the *pomato.* In these days of genetic engineering, when all kinds of permutations and combinations are being ruthlessly tried by the neo-breed of biotechnologists, and with the multi-billion dollar biotechnology industry waiting for a miracle to rescue its flagging reputation, the *protato*—as the GM potato is called—is being promoted as the magic bullet. Scientists are giving the impression that they finally have the technological remedy to fight the scourge of mankind, silent hunger.

'Hidden hunger' or 'silent hunger', as it is called, is the new buzzword in the scientific echelons. For 30 years after the advent of green revolution technology, scientists are rediscovering the importance of nutritional security for the masses. The desperation is not in reality aimed at addressing the problems of 'hidden hunger', but more tuned to according public acceptance to the controversial science and technology of genetic engineering. It would make terrible economic sense if the biotechnologists were for once to forget the 'novel' foods under preparation and urge the government to speed up food distribution among the hungry masses.

The potato, on an average, contains 1.98 per cent protein. Even if its availability has been enhanced by a third, the protein percentage would be 2.8. per cent. How would this 'protein-rich' potato help solve malnutrition in the country? How would the country's nutritional security be addressed? The media never asked these questions. Nor did they allow news columns to provide space for a critical assessment of the technology.

the engineered media

Politics is important, but perhaps more important is the role that the corporate houses play to woo the political powers in a desperate effort to bring in a genetically engineered food product or technology. The prime minister of a major country does not make news, as far as the media are concerned. However, the same media become excited at any and every development in genetic engineering. In reality, it is not because of their new-found love for agriculture and food security that the genetically modified potato has captured media attention. It is because multinational corporations are developing the genetically altered crops.

Times have changed. Agriculture only makes news when the commercial interests of multinationals are involved. In the age of globalisation, the media realise that the progress in biotechnology is essentially being targeted at the agriculture and food industry; but only for promoting agribusiness and trade opportunities for the private companies. Agriculture is otherwise despised and is dubbed a 'down-market' subject.

'Isn't it like sending a soldier to the battle front and then asking him not to use the latest sophisticated assault rifle?' a British radio journalist asked me the other day. He was referring to the Indian government's initial decision to burn down the illegally grown, genetically modified cotton on some 10,000 acres of farmland in Gujarat.

It will certainly be tragic to deprive a soldier of the latest weapon. But it will be more sinister and criminal to provide the soldier with an AK-47 gun and then deliberately make him step into a 'booby' trap,' I replied, adding that Bt cotton, containing a gene from a soil-borne bacterium, *Bacillus thuringiensis* (Bt), is an attractive biological trap, more potent than the toxin it produces that kills the dreaded bollworm pest. Experience has

conclusively shown that, over the past few decades, gullible cotton
growers have been continuously pushed into 'a vicious circle of
poisoning'. The only difference is that the 'chemical treadmill' is
now being replaced by a more dangerous and hitherto unknown
'biological treadmill'.

'But then a majority of cotton growers are happy with the
standing crop even if the seed was clandestinely supplied', claimed
the journalist, stating that there is a growing demand that the
genetically modified crop, which has proved to be effective against
the bollworm insects, should not be destroyed. 'Yes, you are
very right', I replied. 'This is exactly what had happened when
the fourth generation pesticides *synthetic pyrethroids* were introduced in the country less than 20 years ago. And since then,
over 10,000 cotton growers have committed suicide.'

Who will be responsible if and when thousands of cotton growers again take the fatal route once the insect develops resistance to the Bt gene? Will the Agriculture Minister and the Secretary of the Department of Biotechnology, who appear to be
more than eager to hasten the process of commercialisation, be
held responsible for the resulting deaths? After all, are not the
suicides by thousands of farmers 'collateral' damage in the lethal process of the targeted pest developing immunity against
the chemical or the gene? It is a heavy price that the Indian
farmers have paid and will very likely continue to pay in the
future with the introduction of the Bt varieties.

Welcome to the world of modern electronic media. In an age
of information technology where news and entertainment have
merged to keep you glued to the television screen for the most
part of the day (and night), it is becoming increasingly difficult
to tell the difference between a soap opera and the dramatic
happenings in the field of biotechnology and genetic engineering. For most viewers, genetic engineering is another term for
science fiction. For others, it is a brave new world in the offing.
And for journalists and media persons, genetic engineering provides good copy, often on the front page.

But at a time when the 'corporatisation' of the media all over
the world has turned news into a marketable commodity,
multinational corporations have tied with the media
conglomerates to blacken out alternative viewpoints. Even

though these conglomerates may have different names and external appearances, they share the same values for earning more profits. The resulting paradigm shift in news presentation has also brought about a simultaneous change in the public perception of journalists and media personnel. And in the process, the media have abdicated their civic role and become only a vehicle for making money.

Instead of introspecting its own propagandist role, the bio-technology industry has often asked: 'Who is engineering the media to report negatively on a promising technology?' It is the spate of 'negative' reporting in the Western media that has forced the industry to tread cautiously. Such has been the media uproar in the United Kingdom and in other parts of Europe that 1999 will go down in the history of journalism as a year when media returned to take on their role as a mirror of society. There was a return to the old journalism rules of professional and intelligent reporting that we had forgotten in this age of market economy.

The British media had stood up to the industrial onslaught to protect the interests of the consumers, farmers and the environment. In India and in other developing countries, on the other hand, the media continue to eclipse the voice of caution and reasoning. It is not, therefore, unusual to see that press releases by the multinational biotechnology companies are reproduced in entirety, whereas any questioning of the technology in the context of its socio-economic implications is censored. This is true not only for the news columns but also for the letters column in almost all the major newspapers.

Ever since the process of economic liberalisation and globalisation was ushered in, the media, too, have quietly given a go-by to agriculture, food security and hunger issues. The Confederation of Indian Industry (CII) and the Federation of Indian Chambers of Commerce and Industry (FICCI) have, in the bargain, turned into prized reporting beats. Only a decade back, the CII and FICCI were beats that were assigned to cub reporters. No senior journalist felt comfortable even visiting the headquarters of the industry lobby groups. But in this changed scenario, where commerce reigns supreme, the media, too, have begun to follow the money.

following the rich,
following the poor

It was in the early 1980s. I had just joined *The Indian Express* at Chandigarh as its agriculture correspondent. My intrepid journalist colleague, Sanjeev Gaur, who was later stabbed outside the Golden Temple in Amritsar at the height of the Punjab terrorism, was visibly upset. He had filed a disturbing news report, which occupied a significant portion of the front page of the newspaper. The report and its follow-up still haunt me.

A mentally retarded beggar, who was quite a familiar figure to those who frequented the central shopping-cum-office plaza in Sector 17, had picked up a bottle of toned milk from outside a shop owing to acute hunger. No sooner had he gulped it down than he was rounded up by the shop owner and thrashed, and then handed over to the police. He was put in jail. His crime: he had 'stolen' a bottle of milk that probably cost no more than Rs 3. A week later, he died in police custody.

Twenty years later, I am amazed that the country's elite and educated are not even remotely outraged when told that a few hundred of the rich and beautiful people have actually defaulted the nationalised banks (they call it *non-performing assets*) of Rs 120,000 crore. Not many people have stood up to question of why the defaulters are not in jail. Not many are aware that just 10 per cent of the defaulted sum, amounting to Rs 10,000 crore, is what the nation needs to feed its 320 million people who go to bed hungry. Not many would even care to know that India's population of the hungry and malnourished is almost equal to the combined population of the European Union.

Invariably, at the time of the presentation of the annual budget, you see the members of the elite class lined up in the CII or FICCI headquarters, despising and criticising the government for pampering the farmers. They frown at the nominal subsidies received by the country's 550 million farmers, with an average landholding size of 1.47 hectares. They applaud the finance minister if he succeeds in opening up the government's limited treasure chest for the sake of the industry. They are visibly upset if the finance minister fails to oblige them. After all, the elite class is the symbol of growth.

The budget has become a subsidy bazaar for the rich and the elite. If the finance minister opens up the state treasury for India's industrial houses, it is dubbed as a 'dream budget', and if he announces sops for the farmers, the small-scale units and the poorer sections, the media call it a move of 'political compulsion' in the light of the ensuing elections. No wonder, a budget that is soft on the average citizens of the country comes only at the time of elections. Agriculture therefore gets lip-service in the post-budget analysis, as the focus is on business and industry. The media have rarely complained about this phenomenon.

Look at another disturbing scenario. At a time when the country is galvanising the masses into the artificial spirit of 'feel good', no one noticed the cries of a one-month-old baby who was sold by her mother for a mere Rs 10—less than the price of a bottle of mineral water—in December 2003. For Sumitra Behera, 35, a resident of Badibahal village in Angul district of Orissa, selling her one-month-old daughter was perhaps the only way to feed her two other daughters: Urbashi, 10, and Banbasi, 2. In the same month, three other families grappling with hunger in Angul, Puri and Keonjhar, respectively, in Orissa, had reportedly sold their children. This report was buried on page 7 of a New Delhi-based newspaper.

Two decades earlier, the nation had felt outraged when a major newspaper 'bought' a woman for Rs 2,000. The intrepid reporter, who risked his life to investigate the shoddy and inhuman trade, wrote in his columns that even a pair of shoes would cost more. It does not require the investigating skills of Ashwini Sarin anymore to lift the veil of India Shining behind which lies the hidden face of 'Truth'. You can now buy a child for less than what you pay for a bottle of mineral water.

As abject poverty remained buried behind the façade of the feel-good factor, there was excitement in the air. The German luxury car maker, DaimlerChrysler, announced the launch in India of the most luxurious car in the world. At Rs 50 million a piece, the upwardly mobile classes had quickly begun to queue up for the treat. This came at a time when Sachin Tendulkar had recovered his old style, when Team India was back from Pakistan, when Amitabh Bachchan had been named as the brand ambassador for Uttar Pradesh. Selling dreams was no longer the prerogative of Bollywood. The media have probably overtaken Bollywood when it comes to creating fantasies.

Despite the Planning Commission bringing down the percentage of the poverty-stricken in its showpiece documents, the magic trick of playing with numbers on paper has not made any difference to the growing disparities in the real world. Amidst the need to grapple with political elections, and the resultant marketing hype to sell fantasies of growth and development, the shameful paradox of hunger in times of plenty is quietly buried by the government in collusion with the media under the mountains of grain that continue to rot in the open warehouses. That 7.5 million people, more than the population of Switzerland, had applied for a mere 38,000 lowly-paid jobs in the Indian Railways in November 2003, is no longer a matter of concern at a time when the country is on a fast-track information highway.

pushing the trade agenda

The day the World Trade Organisation (WTO) came into existence on 1 January 1995, *The Indian Express* had carried a pocket cartoon on its front page. It showed two people walking amidst highrise buildings with huge billboards for popular multinational brands like Pepsi Cola, Coke, Philips and McDonalds. The cartoon depicted one of the persons walking down the street, asking: 'What does WTO stand for?' The other man replied: 'We Take Over'.

In 2005, the message that the cartoonist conveyed emerged true. Perhaps cartoonists have a better idea of what is happening in society than most journalists. For over a decade now, ever since the Dunkel Draft (Arthur Dunkel was the first chief of WTO) became a controversial issue in India, the media had tried in vain to give the impression that globalisation would lead to tremendous opportunities for the Indian farmers. Through editorials, news reports and analyses and panel discussions (with protagonists of globalisation), a very clever effort was made to swing public opinion in favour of trade.

Simply to help the business and industry, the media refrained from analysing the true implications of the trade regime. They refused to take a peep into the destruction wrought by the 'disagreement' on agriculture. They refused to see that every day, thousands of farmers and the rural people in the majority world without land or adequate livelihoods constituting a reservoir of frustration and disaffection, trudge to the cities, their abject poverty contrasting vividly with the affluence of the urban centres. These are the victims—in fact, the first generation of the affected—of the great trade robbery that is being enacted through the process of opening up for international trade. These are the hapless sufferers who are being fed a daily dose of empty promises. Increase in poverty in the short run is a price that has to be paid for long-term economic growth, we are told.

The full impact on human lives, women and children in particular, and the resulting loss in livelihood security and thereby the accelerated march towards hunger and destitution cannot be easily quantified. Surging food imports have hit farm incomes and had severe effects on employment levels in many developing countries. Unable to compete with cheap food imports, and in the absence of any adequate protection measures, income and livelihood losses have hurt women and poor farmers the most. Farmers in the developing world have suddenly become the children of a lesser god. They are the neo-poor.

It has not been easy to articulate a critical analysis of the negative implications of the trade regime. There is hardly any space made available for alternative viewpoint and analysis. Except for the vernacular media, which are increasingly following the popular trend initiated by the English-language newspapers, agricultural reporting and analysis have remained confined to the official releases and the claims of the agribusiness industry. The exploitation being inflicted through the opening up of trade and liberalisation of economy remains buried under the propaganda unleashed by the business lobby groups and the mainstream economists.

This is in complete contrast to the way agriculture was handled by the media in the 1980s. When I began my career as an agriculture correspondent with *The Indian Express* in 1981, there was no restraint on analytical reports and news analysis that examined scientific achievements in relation to their utility for the farmers and the ecological footprint that the technology would leave behind. In fact, the newspaper encouraged reporting that was based on reflections from the grassroots. Let me illustrate this with an example.

Following the then Prime Minister Mrs Indira Gandhi's policy thrust on dryland agriculture, which extended to roughly 70 per cent of the country's cultivable lands, *The Indian Express* had deputed me to travel into the rain-fed regions, visit agricultural institutes, and then come out with a series of news reports. The three-part series that I wrote started with the introductory line: 'There is little hope for millions of farmers languishing in the dryland regions of the country ....' This was in 1985. Twenty years later, I am dismayed to see that the dryland farmers continue to struggle for survival against all odds. They are the victims of technology bias (in favour of farmers in irrigated areas) and of the apathy of the policy-makers and planners.

Nearly 400 million farmers live in the rain-fed areas of the country. The media have little concern for their children. The poor, hungry and the marginalised do not make any news except at times of a disaster. Agriculture and other social issues have been blanked out from the pages of mainline print media. Business reporters have been clearly told to refrain from carrying anything related to social issues. Agriculture only makes news when a business and industrial house makes a foray into the rural areas. Dryland farmers appear in the pages of *The New York Times* when a private company launches e-*chaupals*, a network of computers providing information to the villagers.

Globalisation has trivialised such analyses. In an era of economic liberalisation, the biggest casualty is the way the popular media have been manipulated to serve the interests of business and industry. The ability of journalists to stand up and question policy decisions has been successfully thwarted. With the media becoming instruments to maximise profits for the company owning it, finding space for news on agriculture has become the biggest challenge for any discerning reporter.

globalisation: stifling voices

Just before the failed WTO Cancun Ministerial conference in September 2003, President Toure of Mali co-authored a letter to *The New York Times* condemning the cotton subsidies in America that have been devastating for West African countries like Burkina Faso, Mali, Chad and Benin. His colleague, President Compaore of Burkina Faso, spoke to the Trade Negotiating Committee of the WTO in June 2003. Both leaders voiced their concern at the way direct financial assistance, to the tune of 73 per cent of the world's cotton production, by a number of exporting countries, including the US, the European Union and China, destroyed millions of livelihoods in West African countries. As a result, African cotton producers realise only 60 per cent of their costs, although their cost of production is less than half of what is reaped in the developed countries.

Unrelenting, the WTO has delivered its verdict. The text of the Draft Cancun Ministerial document says:

> The Director-General is instructed to consult with the relevant international organizations including the Bretton Woods Institutions, the Food and Agriculture Organisation and the International Trade Centre to effectively direct existing programmes and resources towards diversification of the economies where cotton accounts for a major share of their GDP.

In other words, there is nothing wrong with the highly subsidised cotton farming in the US, EU and China; the fault rests with millions of small and marginal farmers in West Africa. The Cancun Ministerial had instructed (the draft obviously remains rejected with the Cancun failure) the WTO Director-general, the Food and Agriculture Organisation (FAO) and the World Bank/International Monetary Fund (IMF) to make available adequate investments for suitable programmes that would enable these farmers to diversify from cotton to other crops. The WTO says the West African farmers should stop growing cotton.

The lesson for the rest of the world is crystal clear. The developing world should stop growing crops that are being negatively impacted by the monumental subsidies provided by the rich and industrialised countries. For the G-21, that created a lot of noise and dust over the US $ 311 billion in farm subsidies that the richest trading block, the Organisation for Economic Cooperation and Development (OECD), provides for its agriculture, the writing is on the wall. And this is exactly what I have been warning against all these years. The process of shifting the production of staple foods and major commercial commodities to the OECD had in fact begun much earlier. The WTO is merely legitimising the new farming system approach. Such an analysis could have shifted the focus of the entire free trade debate to the ground realities. But the media have remained more or less silent.

The World Bank and the IMF have, under the Structural Adjustment Programmes (SAP), very clearly tied up credit to crop diversification. They continue to force developing countries to shift from staple foods (crucial for food security needs) to cash crops that meet the luxury requirements of the Western countries. These institutions have been forcing developing countries to dismantle state support to food procurement, withdraw price support to farmers and relax land ceiling laws, and hence enable corporate houses to move into agriculture. For some strange reason, the media refuse to examine the negative implications of these moves. In fact, the media think otherwise. Farmers need to be left at the mercy of the market forces. Since they are 'inefficient' producers, they need to be replaced by the industrial and corporate houses.

The same prescription for farming has never been suggested for the rich and industrialised countries. Let us be very clear. The one part of the world that needs to go in for immediate crop diversification is the industrial world. These are the countries that produce mounting surpluses of wheat, rice, corn, soybean, sugar beet and cotton, and that too under environmentally unsound conditions leading to an ecological catastrophe. These are the countries that inflict double the damage—first by destroying the land with highly intensive crop practices, polluting the ground water and contaminating the environment, and then receiving massive subsidies to keep these unsustainable practices artificially viable. These are the countries that are faced with the tragic consequences of massive farm displacements, and are in the grip of food calamities arising from industrial farming.

If the WTO has its way, and the developing countries fail to understand the prevailing politics that drives the agriculture trade agenda, the world will soon have two kinds of agriculture systems: the rich countries will produce staple foods for the world's six billion plus people, and developing countries will grow cash crops like tomatoes, cut flowers, peas, sunflowers, strawberries and vegetables. The dollars that developing countries earn from exporting these crops will eventually be used to buy food grains from the developed nations—in reality, back to the days of 'ship-to-mouth' existence. Unfortunately, the media had little role in building up the debate and discussion that led to the developing countries' opposing stand at the failed WTO Ministerial at Cancun in September 2003. Some developing countries, led by Brazil, India and China, refused to accept the doctrine of free trade in agriculture because of pressure from their own domestic constituencies.

Ever since economic liberalisation became the buzzword in mid-1991, agriculture has for all practical purposes disappeared from the national radar screen. In a country like India where farmers form the backbone of the economy, with 60 per cent of the workforce and 27 per cent of the GDP, farmers have been very conveniently sacrificed at the altar of economic growth and development. Agriculture has been gradually pushed into the category of untouchable subjects from which the media must keep away. Consequently, the media no longer remain the reflection of society. Today's media, as Noam Chomsky says, have adopted the role of missionaries of the corporate world.

12

urban reporting: citizens and 'others'

kalpana sharma

C ities are a reporter's dream. They represent the variety, the excitement, the drama and the complexity that can yield end-less stories. Some cities are more interesting than others. But all cities have common elements of wealth and poverty, of in-dustry and vagrancy, of beauty and degradation, of philanthropy and philandering.

Little of this range is evident in the urban reporting in the majority of English-language newspapers in India since the 1990s. Instead, urban reporting has come to consist of the interests of the consuming classes, those who have benefited most from the post-liberalisation economy in India, from the growth of the con-sumer culture, from globalisation.

In a sense, this is inevitable. The media have been a part of the changes in the Indian economy, changes that have brought benefits to a small, upwardly mobile urban population while leav-ing out the majority living in rural India or the people who con-stitute the growing number of the urban poor. English-language newspapers, in particular, have chosen to cater only to the class that reads them and to promote their interests. Gone are the days when newspapers felt they were responsible for recording contemporary history by reporting events that touched all of so-ciety. A glance at any English-language newspaper in India illus-trates the nature of this shift of focus, from one that is inclusive to one that is exclusive. Thus, city stories are dominated by cov-erage of the celebrity brigade—film stars, models, industrialists, socialites and the party set of the rich and the idle. Page after page is devoted to what these individuals wear, eat and even think on a variety of subjects about which they know very little.

There are also routine articles on crime, education, fitness and diet fads, some local politics, the police and perhaps on local festivals. But the preponderance of reports concentrates on the activities of a very small elite set of people.

This narrowing down of the areas of interest has meant that the concerns of the large bulk of the urban population remain unaddressed, particularly by the English-language media. This was not the case in the 1970s and 1980s when a city beat consisted of covering the police and crime, the municipality, health, labour, civic issues and the lower courts. Besides these, there was the world of art, culture, entertainment and business as well as issues specific to certain cities.

In principle, the beats remain the same, but the emphasis has changed. For instance, the civic beat does entail a certain amount of reporting on the state of the roads, water shortages, lack of sanitation, etc. But more often that not, it consists of reports of the beautification efforts in the more elite neighbourhoods. During the monsoons in Mumbai, for instance, when some predictable areas get flooded, there are photographs and reports on this. But there is hardly anything locating the real source of the problem—the fact that poor people inevitably land up living in the low-lying, flood-prone areas and by virtue of the fact that these areas are inhabited by the poor, civic services and improvements are minimal. Thus, no long-term effort is made to drain such areas to prevent flooding in the future. Newspapers continue to report the flooding and people continue to live with the annual phenomenon. Nothing changes.

On the other hand, campaigns by citizens' groups living in the better-off part of the city on beautification, or segregating garbage, or complaining about the 'hawker menace' receive a lot of coverage in the press. Some newspapers lend a hand to the campaigns. The people behind them are profiled and the problems are highlighted. City authorities are known to respond to such pressure from the media.

Similarly, in the past the health beat consisted of regular assessment of the state of public hospitals. Such scrutiny by the media put necessary pressure on these public institutions that are the lifeline for the poor in particular. Without the glare of media publicity, such institutions could literally get away with murder. Today, you find little about public hospitals. Instead, there are endless pieces on the new super-speciality hospitals, part of the growing, private health care sector. Such articles are usually prompted by public relations agencies hired by the hospitals to raise their profile in the city. And the press falls in line and virtually provides uncritical free publicity to them. If there are mishaps, as there must be in any health institution, the PR machinery swiftly covers these up and ensures that very little gets out to the media.

Health has also come to mean not the common and deadly diseases that continue to kill millions of men, women and children in India, but either lifestyle diseases like hypertension and diabetes, or articles on fitness and diets or donor-led concerns such as the stream of articles on HIV/AIDS. The fact that even in a city like Mumbai, thousands of women die during childbirth, millions of children are afflicted with gastro–intestinal diseases that could lead to dehydration and even death, that every year people contract falciparum malaria, TB, cholera and typhoid, and that almost everyone suffers from acute respiratory diseases, are subjects that rarely find space in the newspapers. But if new drugs or new technology related to heart disease are available, even outside India, such news will be splashed all over the papers, often on the front page.

The one area of coverage that has almost entirely disappeared from the pages of newspapers is labour. This is not entirely surprising, given that the role of trade unions and collective bargaining has also been greatly diminished in the post-liberalisation period. Workers were an integral part of a city like Mumbai with its central districts dominated by textile mills. With the gradual closure of these mills, and the move away from manufacturing to services, the nature of labour and the working classes has also changed. From permanent employment, people have increasingly accepted working on contract. As a result, the role of unions to negotiate rights of workers has almost disappeared as terms of employment are individually negotiated.

In most cities, including Mumbai, the growth of the informal sector has coincided with the decline of the formal industrial sector. Those forced out by the closure of industries have inevitably landed up finding jobs, often temporary ones, in the informal sector. Such jobs include working in hazardous industries, without any job security, at abysmally low wages. These issues

do not find their way into the pages of newspapers partly because no one is assigned the labour beat anymore. Even if newspapers were interested, the very nature of the informal sector
forces workers, who have no right to organise into unions, to
keep their problems to themselves.

While the low end of the informal sector fails to gain media
scrutiny, very little is written about the conditions of work in
the new service industries that are beginning to dominate many
cities. Outsourcing jobs are more visible, more glamourous. But
access to the people who work there is tightly controlled. Once
again, the nature of the employment ensures that the workers
in such jobs do not speak out for fear of losing their jobs. And
the free trade zones, where workers are not allowed to unionise
and the media are not given access, are yet one more area of
'labour' that escapes media scrutiny. If labour had been considered a legitimate beat, some of this could still have found its
way into the media and the many areas of exploitation that continue to hide behind the glitz and glamour of these new sectors
of work could have been exposed.

The agencies that appear to determine much of what goes
into newspapers are, in fact, public relations companies. Celebrity journalism, or 'Page Three journalism', as it has come to be
known, is now entirely decided by the effectiveness of the individual celebrity's PR. Indeed, in some newspapers, editorial space
is sold on the society pages. There are rates set for photographs
and items that appear on these pages.

What all this has done is to erase entire aspects of cities,
particularly the urban poor. They appear on the horizon if there
is a riot, if a fire destroys some slums, if slums have to be cleared
for a highway, a railway line or a building, if an epidemic kills or
affects them, if floods or rains drown and destroy their homes.
As all such events are deemed 'news' by the event-driven media,
there is momentary recognition of the existence of another city,
another set of people. But then it disappears just as rapidly.
There is no before and no after. We do not understand why the
poor always live in low-lying areas that get flooded each year.
Such fragmented and piecemeal reporting guarantees the invis-
ibility of the urban poor. It also ensures that their issues and
concerns are never addressed because those in power do not
face any pressure from the media on these concerns.

The concept of citizenry promoted by such reporting is another fallout of the new type of urban reporting. The upwardly mobile consuming classes, those who apparently pay their dues and thus deserve the services offered by the state, are deemed 'citizens'. Not so the poor. There is an assumption that the poor drain the State's resources and contribute nothing in return. Thus you find newspaper reports referring to 'citizens and slum dwellers', as if the latter are deprived of their citizenship by virtue of their economic misfortune.

Finally, it is the very nature and structure of the Indian media that seems to work against sound and insightful urban reporting. The most important newspapers in cities are also those considered 'national' newspapers as they have simultaneous editions from many different centres. To maintain a 'national' profile, these newspapers tend to pay less attention to purely 'local' issues. Yet, if they did, they would have an impact on policy-makers who do take what appears in such newspapers seriously. On the other hand, the purely 'local' papers that are far more responsive to civic concerns are considered too 'local' to be heeded by the decision-makers. This is a strange anomaly, one that seems peculiar to the Indian media. The so-called 'national' newspapers are now relegating city issues to separate supplements. But even these are becoming celebrity and lifestyle oriented, with only a token gesture towards the concerns of the majority of city dwellers.

Can this, or will this, change? In the near future, it is unlikely. The circulation of newspapers seems to be increasingly dependent on their ability to brand themselves as fun and frivolous. Such a branding has no space for serious reporting on urban issues.

PART III
The Constraints of Practice

13

porous legalities and the dilemmas of contemporary media

lawrence liang

*m*ore often than not, the media story of copyright piracy narrates itself through the language of statistics, figures and the narrative strategy of excess, designed to induce a 'shock-and-awe' response at the alarming rate of piracy and illegality that exists, especially in non-Western countries. As with any journalistic story that seeks an international audience, the choice of narrative strategy is the key. And for the story to be understood and have appeal, it will have to transcend the cultural specificity under which certain stories come to be appreciated. This is especially true when one is trying one's hand in the genre of horror stories and in the present case, the horror story of piracy just does not work in terms of inducing a sense of anxiety and fear in countries like India.

One must, however, provide reasons for why these media stories do not work in some contexts, and for that we will have to travel to 'distant' cities like Delhi and Sao Paulo—and perhaps even walk through the more unfamiliar by-lanes of 'familiar' cities like New York. After urban studies, the idea of an illegal city is familiar to us. One reads for instance that an average of 40 per cent and in some cases 70 per cent of the population of major cities live in illegal conditions. Furthermore, 70 to 95 per cent of all new housing is built illegally.[1] The primary reason for this state of illegality arises from the nature of land tenure forms

---

[1] A. Durand-Lasserve and V. Clerc, 'Regularization and Integration of Irregular Settlements: Lessons from Experience', *Urban Management Program* (Working Paper 6), Nairobi: UNDP/UNCHS/The World Bank, 1996.

in cities, where the twin tropes of ownership and title are clearly unable to account for the myriad ways through which people assert a claim on land and to the city more generally. The people who live in this perpetual state of illegality also engage in other networks of illegality, such as stealing electricity and water, and bribing their way through the Kafkaesque bureaucratic structures to access civic amenities that the legal city takes for granted. A first glance at the official responses to this older illegal city reveals the familiar face of anonymous statistics and 'shock and awe' figures. Thus, when we cut back to the piracy story, and we are told that over 70 per cent of the software used in India is illegal, we encounter this figure with a sense of familiarity and not anxiety.

Clearly, any simplistic account of the widespread illegality in terms of efficiency, morality, disorder or corruption would only perform an epistemic violence, which does little to aid the journalist's understanding of urban experience, and the ways in which people create avenues of participation and make claims to the city. The contribution of urban studies has been to provide a more nuanced sense of the phenomenon of the illegal city.

In a city like Bangalore, for instance, the urban planning authority, the Bangalore Development Authority (BDA), provides for approximately 15–20 per cent of the housing requirements, while private developers meet another 12–15 per cent. The rest of the city emerges outside of planned development and is hence outside the law. Most urban citizens have no choice but to build, buy or rent illegal dwellings, since they either cannot afford the cheapest legal accommodation or there is not enough supply to meet the demands of a growing city marked by high migration as a result of the new information technology dreams that also spur the imagination of the city's official residents.

A liberal understanding of land tenure forms is limited because its interest in land relies too heavily on how ownership and legitimate claims are narrated through the title deed and other legal documents. Any attempt to understand the ways in which people make a claim to land in the city would have to take into account the multiple and complex forms of networks and relationships that constitute a land tenure claim. Thus we have the hawker who has a designated place even though he is not entitled to the place in any formal manner, the squatter who pays a rent to the local policeman, the illegal slum that begs, borrows and steals electricity and water from the rest of the productive city, the unauthorised revenue layout that gets regularised or legalised near election time on the basis of their strength as a vote bank.

Writing about the modernist project of planning, James Holston claims:

> Modernist planning does not admit or develop productively the paradoxes of its imagined futures. Instead it attempts to be a plan without contradictions or conflict. It assumes a rational domination of the future in which its total and totalizing plan dissolves any conflict between the imagined and existing society in the enforced coherence of its order. This assumption is false and arrogant as it fails to include as its constituent element, the conflict, ambiguity and indeterminacy characteristic of actual social life.[2]

While the older illegal city has been in existence for a while, over the past 10 years there has been another layer that has been integrated into the experience and narration of this illegal city. The proliferation of non-legal media practices ranging from pirated VCDs, DVDs, and MP3s to grey-market mobile phones, informs the practices and imagination of the illegal city. This essay attempts to understand this new layer of illegality and the manner in which it integrates into the older city by questioning how the older and the newer forms integrate or intertwine to collectively interrogate our liberal assumptions of legality and highlight the limitations of any report based on a strictly legal understanding of contemporary urban practices. I do this by examining the cassette revolution that took place in India in the 1980s, and the sphere of illegality in which it emerged. Building on some significant attempts to provide entry points into understanding this aspect of the city, I would also like to posit the idea that porous legalities are often the only modes through which people can access and create avenues of participation in the new economy.

---

[2] James Holston, 'Spaces of Insurgent Citizenship', in James Holston (ed.), *Cities and Citizenship* (London: Duke University Press, 1999), pp. 165–66.

The information era props up a master plan, similar to that of modernist planning. The institutional imagination of the era relies on the World Trade Organisation (WTO) as chief architect and planner, copyright lawyers as the executive managers of this new plan and the only people who retain their jobs from the old city as the executors of the old plan, the police force and the demolition squad. Just as one cannot understand land tenure through the prism of liberal legality alone, any attempt to understand the complex networks of economic and social relations that underlie the phenomenon of piracy will have to engage with the conflict of control over the means of technological and cultural production in the contemporary moment of globalisation. The ways in which the illegal media city emerges and co-exists alongside the vibrant, innovative and productive debris of the older city, and the schizoid relationship between legality and illegality in post-colonial cities suggest that the crisis may not lie in these relations, and we may need to turn the gaze of the law away from the usual suspects of legality to legality itself and the relations that underlie its existence. Jacques Derrida has said very poignantly that the admiring fascination for the rebel can be understood not merely as the fascination for someone who commits a particular crime but for someone, who, in defying the law, bares the violence of the legal system or the juridical order.[3]

the creation of the new media city

Before we begin to signal the different entry points through which we can understand this new, illegal city, it would be useful for us to take a trip to the 1980s to understand the developments that preceded the formation of this new city in India. I believe that it is critical for us to understand this period to get a sense of why non-State, non-elite electronic cultures have always had a problematic relationship with law and legality.

Peter Manuel provides us with an excellent history of the emergence of new media in India, tracing the cassette revolution that

---

[3] Jacques Derrida,' The Mystical Foundation of Authority', in Drucilla Cornell, Michel Rosenfeld and David G. Carlson (eds), *Deconstruction and the Possibility of Justice* (New York: Routledge, 1992).

took place from the mid-1980s onwards. This revolution, he claims, created a new aesthetic of media production and consumption that escapes the totalising imagination of old media in the form of national television, radio and cinema. According to him, new media challenge the one-way, monopolistic, homogenising tendencies of old media as they tend to be decentralised in ownership, control and consumption patterns and hence offer greater potential for consumer input and interaction. I shall briefly summarise Manuel's account of the emergence of cassette culture in India.[4]

In 1908, the British-owned GCI (Gramophone Company of India) had established its factory in Calcutta, and through exclusive distribution agreements, it came to dominate the market in an absolute manner. The monopoly had a profound cultural impact in terms of the local genres and languages, which it appropriated, ignored or reduced into a single dialect. The necessity of an all-India market to make great profits ensured the emergence of an all-India aesthetic form in film music. The dominance of Hindi film music and the monopoly of GCI continued till well past the post-colonial period.

The development model adopted by the Nehruvian state emphasised public investment in large-scale infrastructure projects like dams, mines and factories while discouraging luxury consumption through high import tariffs. These policies of overtaxation and cumbersome licensing inhibited the consumer electronics and related industries. Manuel reports that by the late 1970s, however, large numbers of immigrant workers to the Gulf countries had begun to bring back cassette players into India (these were Japanese two-in-ones) and the ubiquitous cassette player soon became a symbol of affluence and object of modern desire. This is also the period that saw the emergence of a nascent market for pirated cassettes of film music, feeding off the growth of cassette players and also contributing to the expansion of the grey market where such 'luxury' items could be purchased by the relatively well off.

The liberalisation policy of the state in the late 1970s, designed to stimulate growth, demand, exports and product quality, saw

---

[4] See, generally, Peter Manuel, *Cassette Culture: Popular Music and Technology in North India* (New Delhi: Oxford University Press, 2001).

an easing up of many import restrictions. The burgeoning middle class stimulated the electronic industry, and while a few were willing to pay the high import duties on foreign electronic goods, a larger number were content to buy them off the grey market.

Certain significant developments in this period helped to create a mature market for the consumer electronics industry:

- Reduction of duties enabled Indian manufacturers to import selected components for local manufacture of cassette players.
- New policies encouraged foreign collaborations in the field of consumer electronics including magnetic tape production.
- Tape coating became big in India and from the period 1982 to 1985, record dealers switched to cassettes and by the mid-1980s, cassettes came to account for 95 per cent of the market.

Sales of cassettes went up from $1.2 million in 1980 to $12 million in 1986 and $21 million in 1990. Export of Indian-made records jumped from 1.65 million rupees in 1983 to 99.75 million in 1987. By the end of the 1980s, Indian consumers were buying around 2.5 million cassette players. This is also the period that saw the swift decline of GCI or HMV (His Master's Voice) as the dominant/sole player in the industry, and the emergence of a handful of large players and over 500 small music-producing companies. In a period of a few years, India had become the world's second largest manufacturer of cassettes and was marketing 217 million cassettes. This period also saw the decline of film music as the dominant aesthetic form and its market dropped from 90 per cent to 40 per cent. A whole new range of forms, from devotional music to local-language songs and other kinds of music, began to emerge.[5]

This period of tremendous growth was, however, marked clearly by its troubled relationship with legality, with various practices that often straddled both the worlds—sometimes making it difficult to distinguish one from the other. In its initial boom period, most of the music companies were a part of the informal but well networked sector. They often worked with illegally obtained components to ensure the cost effectiveness of their product. These ranged from smuggled goods to indigenously

---

[5] Peter Manuel, *Cassette Culture.*

manufactured but unlicensed products, components and magnetic tapes.

It is in this context that we can evaluate the story of one such maverick entrepreneur, who with a combination of dynamic business skills, ruthless tactics and an elastic idea of legality, came to shape the music industry. In 1979, two brothers, Gulshan and Gopal Arora, who ran a fruit juice shop in Delhi and were also electronic buffs, began a small studio where they recorded Garhwali, Punjabi and Bhojpuri songs. After borrowing money, they visited Japan, Hong Kong and Korea to study cassette technology and the industry. They returned to set up a factory in India to produce magnetic tapes, and also started producing cassettes and silicon paper and finally built a complete manufacturing plant where they offered duplication services to the smaller regional cassette producers. By the late 1980s, T-Series emerged as the clear market leader and currently they have a set-up worth over $ 120 million, having diversified into manufacturing video tapes, televisions, VCD players, MP3 players, washing machines and even detergents.

The elastic legality of Gulshan Kumar's world translated itself in the following manner:[6]

- Using a provision in the fair use clause of the Indian Copyright Act which allows for version recording, T-Series issued thousands of cover versions of GCI's classic film songs, particularly those which HMV itself found to be infeasible for release. T-Series also changed the rules of distribution by targeting neighbourhood shops, grocery shops, *paan wallahs* and tea stalls, to literally convert the cassette into a bazaar product.
- T-Series was also involved in straightforward copyright infringement in the form of pirate releases of popular hits, relying on the loose enforcement of copyright laws.
- The company illegally obtained film scores even before the release of the film to ensure that their recordings were the first to hit the market.
- It inserted huge amounts of inferior tape into the established brands to discredit the well-established names.

---

[6] This is a summary of Manuel's overall argument. See ibid.

While one could easily dismiss these practices as unscrupulous, unethical or clearly illegal, we also need to keep in mind the overall impact that T-Series had on the music industry in India and on cassette culture itself. T-Series created a new cassette-consuming public by focusing on various genres and languages, which were completely ignored by HMV. HMV had promoted Hindi at the cost of many other languages, owing to the infeasibility in economic terms given the scale of their operations. T-Series, by changing the rules of the game and introducing for the first time the idea of networked production, where it would offer its duplication services to a number of the small players, revived smaller traditions of music. Finally, the reduction of the price of the cassette by T-Series created a mass commodity.

Clearly, no straightforward account of legality and business ethics can capture the dynamics and the network of interests that fuelled the cassette revolution. For instance, in an interview with Peter Manuel, one of the employees of T-Series stated: 'What the people say about our activities in the early years—it is mostly true. But I tell you that back then, the big *ghazal* singers would come to us and ask us to market pirated versions of their own cassettes, for their own publicity, since HMV wasn't really able to keep up with the demand.'[7] Similarly, in the past, even major players like HMV dealt with the pirates. For instance, when HMV found that it could not meet the demand for one of their biggest hits, *Maine Pyar Kiya,* they are reported to have entered into an agreement with the pirates, whereby the pirates would raise their price from Rs 11 to Rs 13 and pay HMV half a rupee for every unit that they sold, on condition that HMV did not sue them or raid their businesses. Other producers are also known to have colluded with pirates in production and marketing so that they could minimise their costs, taxes and royalties by hiding the extent of their sales.

The role played by piracy in the building up of a market, in the process of creating a lock-in period and also in the reduction of price, has been most obvious in the software and film industries. (The price of a VCD has come down to Rs 99, even lower than the pirated copy's price of Rs 100.) Similarly, the Free School

---

[7] Peter Manuel, *Cassette Culture.*

Street phenomenon of Kolkata created a sub-cultural market for large amounts of 1960s rock, before these tapes were available in the Indian markets. Without such a niche elite public, it is highly debatable whether Magnasound could have emerged in the early 1990s as the most important player in the English music industry in India.

I would like to conclude this segment with two ironical stories that can then lead us to the contemporary scene. The first is that after its rather chequered history with copyright law, T-Series is now one of the most aggressive enforcers of their copyright in India. They have a battery of professionals, generally retired police officials, who monitor copyright and trademark infringement cases. The second story is an extract from Peter Manuel's conclusion to the history of cassette cultures in India. After providing us with a fascinating look at the ad hoc world of innovation based on very porous ideas of legality, Manuel speculates on the possible developments in the future, where he says:

> In India a pre-recorded CD costs as much as Rs 250 or twelve times the price of a tape. CD players themselves are anywhere between Rs 5000 upwards, which would constitute a fortune for most Indians. As a result, CDs naturally remain confined to the upper class. For the music producer, the growth of the CD market is seen as a possible weapon against piracy, as the CDs cannot be duplicated (onto other CDs).[8]

entering the new city

We can now return to the contemporary urban landscape where the prevailing model of piracy is precisely through the form that was intended to guard against piracy. With the absolute collapse of the costs of CD writers and CDs, every computer owner is a potential producer and redistributor. The logical transition of the older inhabitants of the world of pirated cassette cultures, like video library owners, into the world of CDs, then, appears as a natural progression. I have outlined the two central histories

---

[8] Ibid.

that we need to narrate to understand the present moment. The first attempt was to problematise and contextualise the idea of illegality vis-à-vis claiming a space in the city, and the manner in which these claims challenge the liberal premise of law, citizenship and democratic institutions. The second move was to provide a brief history of the emergence of cassette culture, and of the reasons why it emerged in a context of illegality, and of the central role that it plays in the creation of a public that is not based on the print or broadcast medium's imagined sense of the public sphere. It also narrates a world of innovation and discovery, which treats any monopolistic claims, be it legality or economic participation, with a sense of irreverence.

I would now like to examine some of the ways in which a critical dialogue around International Patents (IP) may take place. At the moment there exists a rich body of work in the US that seeks to challenge some of the developments in IP law. These are generally posited within literary theory inspired critiques of the assumption of authorship, that is, they argue that copyright endangers the free flow of information within the public domain. Implicit within this critique, however, is an assumption of a vibrant public sphere, where constitutionally guaranteed rights, such as freedom of speech and expression, should dictate IP policy.

The challenge of having an intercontinental dialogue is really to push the limits of thinking through the problem of understanding the publics, which lie outside the assumptions of the liberal public sphere. It involves an understanding of the complex spatial logic of globalisation and of the unfolding of highly unequal division of labour within the sphere of cultural production— a bootlegged version of the Nike t-shirt in India surely has a very different tale to tell as it circulates as a fake, compared to the circulation of a copy in Los Angeles, or even in Thailand, which is one of the largest hosts of the various sweatshops of the world. To understand the difference between the cultural politics of content and appropriation, is also to comprehend a world where content may fit into the larger politics of the cultural hegemony of Hollywood, while at the same time enabling diverse entry points into the global modern for a range of people ordinarily left out of the imagination of the nationalist project of modernity.

The social of the remix in India may have little to do with the romantic assumptions of cultural appropriation and re-significa-tion, as expressed in the Campbell versus Acuff Rose[9] case and more to do with the impact of the structural transformation of industry practices and monopolies, as articulated in the Sega versus Accolade case.[10]

The avenues I suggest below offer an entry point into under-standing the challenges posed by different media practices to an IP regime that insists on the creation of a global regime of own-ership and control on which there is a containment of all social conflict and an assumed social cohesion that there will be no dispute over the forms of property that emerge and expand.

The first and most simplistic account of the phenomenon of piracy is that of unequal access between the developing and the developed countries. The argument is that the price differential forces people in developing countries to buy pirated goods since they would not be able to buy the original goods. While there is truth in this proposition of the price factor, the inherent prob-lem of such an entry point is that it relies on a model of piety (the poor, Third-World figure) and is fundamentally dependent on 'development', catching up with the West's account of global relations. The global contemporary is far more complex and one would have to provide an account of the complex logic of cul-tural production in the era of globalisation. The pirate in devel-oping countries is not a figure of piety and this account divests him of any agential role as s/he navigates through the mediascape of globalisation that frames her/his experience.

The second entry point emerges from writers like Jeremy Rifkin who would argue that there is a fundamental shift in our understanding of the logic of production, distribution and con-sumption. Rifkin argues that we live in an age of access. The

---

[9] 510 U.S. 569 (1994).

[10] 24 U.S.P.Q.2d 1561. In Campbell, the Supreme Court had to deal with whether a parody falls under the fair use defence, and it held that it does, on account of the fact that the parody involves transformative authorship and creates a new work in itself. I would broadly characterise this as a content-related issue. In India, if we were to ask the content question of remixes, it would probably be found wanting, as it would not satisfy the requirement of transformative authorship. Instead, we need to look at it in terms of what it does to media monopolies and the creation of entry points for smaller media players, and the larger social benefit of having diverse players within a vertical industry.

culture of the Internet, for instance, is predicated on a culture of networked distribution and circulation. In this new era, there is a transition from the idea of the market in the older senses of the term to the idea of networks. His account of the nature of the networked economy would render futile any notion of piety, as his account is not configured on differential access or privilege alone. He sees the culture of the networked economy as fundamentally shaping the way people think about production, distribution and collaboration. The older form of regulation and structuring of economic transactions will then just not be feasible within this framework.

According to Rifkin:

> The young people of the new 'protean' generation are far more comfortable conducting business and engaging in social activity in the worlds of electronic commerce and cyberspace, and they adapt easily to the many simulated worlds that make up the cultural economy. Theirs is a world that is more theatrical than ideological and oriented more to a play ethos, than to a work ethos. For them, access is already a way of life, and while property is important, being connected is even more important. The people of the twenty-first century are likely to see themselves as nodes in embedded networks of shared interests as they are to perceive themselves as autonomous agents in a Darwinian world of competitive survival. For them, personal freedom has less to do with the right of possession and the ability to exclude others, than with the right to be included in webs of mutual relationships. They are the first generation of the Age of Access.[11]

In such an account, copyright would emerge as a slightly archaic mode of regulation that is culturally embedded in the technology pf paper. This is also a world which transforms the older worlds of legal imaginaries, using the language of exclusive rights to generate a world of access. The GNU General Public License, which acts as the main license for most free software, is a classic instance of such a use.

---

[11] Jeremy Rifkin, *The Age of Access, The New Culture of Hypercapitalism Where All of Life is a Paid-for Experience* (New York: Penguin, 2001), p. 17.

Our third entry point is through an examination of the intertwined histories of postcolonial nationalist aspirations of modernity and a particular relationship to the public sphere. Ravi
Sundaram, in a series of articles, has been theorising the phenomenon of piracy and illegal media cultures in the new media
city.[12] According to him, this world of non-legal media in a number of South Asian cities, marked by its rather ad hoc
innovativeness and its various strategies of survival, is the world
of recycled modernity. It exists in the quotidian spaces of the
everyday and cannot be understood within the terms of the earlier publics (the nationalist public and the elite public sphere).
Fuelled by aspirations of upward mobility, it is an account of the
claims to modernity made by a class of people otherwise unac-
counted for by the meta-narrative of the nationalist project of
modernity. These cultures of recycling do not, however, exhibit
any of the characteristic valour or romance of counter publics.
Beginning with the audio cassette revolution that we examined,
and moving rapidly into the worlds of computers and digital entertainment, this world has been based on a dispersed logic of
production and consumption, and marked by its preponderant
illegality. This rearticulated entry point into the modern is also
contemporaneous with the emergence of the global moment.
The arrival of the global via media, new forms of labour like call
centres, and the software industry in India, replaces the earlier
configuration of national/modern with the global/modern. While
understanding the issue of entry points that one makes into
the modern, it now becomes critically important for us to
recognise the shifts in registers of imagination that the global
brings upon the national/modern configuration.

Our fourth entry point into understanding these practices
comes from a metaphorically rich account of the role of networks and seepages provided by Raqs Media Collective. Looking
at five figures of transgressions in the contemporary context

---

[12] See, for example, Ravi Sundaram, 'Recycling Modernity: Pirate Electronic
Cultures in India', *Sarai Reader 01: The Public Domain* (New Delhi: Sarai,
2001); *Beyond the Nationalist Panopticon: The Experience of Cyberpublics
in India*, http://Amsterdam.nettime.org/Lists-Archives/nettime-1-96 11/msg
00018.html, 10 November 1996; and *Electronic Marginality or Alternative
Cyberfutures in the Third World*, www.1judmila.org/nettime/zk4/08.htm,
7 May 1997.

(the migrant, the hacker, the pirate, the alien and the squatter), Raqs discusses the modes through which these transgressors of law emerge as residues in the gigantic movement of capital:

> Capital transforms older forms of labour and ways of life into those that are either useful for it at present, or those that have no function and so must be made redundant. Thus you have the paradox of a new factory, which instead of creating new jobs often renders the people who live around 'unemployable'. A new dam, that instead of providing irrigation, renders a million displaced, a new highway that destroys common paths, making movement more, not less difficult for the people and the communities it cuts through.[13]

The question posed by Raqs is: How does one begin to understand what happens to these people who fall off the official maps, official plans and official histories? The argument is that these people travel with the histories of the networks that they are a part of and are able at any point to deploy the insistent, ubiquitous insider knowledge of today's networked world. They then introduce the powerful metaphor of seepage and how it may help us to think through these acts of transgressions:

> How does this network act, and how does it make itself known in our consciousness? We like to think about this in terms of 'seepage'. By seepage, we mean the action of many currents of fluid material leaching on to a stable structure, entering and spreading through it by way of pores, until it becomes a part of the structure ... in terms of its surface, and at the same time continues to act on its core, to gradually disaggregate its solidity, and to crumble it over time with moisture. In a wider sense, seepage can be conceived as those acts that ooze through the pores of the outer surfaces of structures into available pores within the structure, and result in a weakening of the structure itself. Initially the process is invisible, and then it slowly starts causing mould and settles into a

---

[13] Raqs Media Collective, 'X Notes on Practice: Stubborn Structures and Insistent Seepage in a Networked World', in Marina Vishmidt and Melanie gilligan (eds) *Immaterial Labour: Work, Research and Art* (London/New York: Black Dog Publishing, forthcoming).

disfiguration—and this produces an anxiety about the strength and durability of the structure.[14]

By itself, seepage is not an alternative form; it even needs the structure to become what it is, but it creates new conditions in which structures become fragile and are rendered difficult to sustain. It enables the play of an alternative imagination, and so we begin seeing faces and patterns on the wall that change as the seepage ebbs and flows.

In a networked world, there are many acts of seepage, some of which we have already described. They destabilise the structure, without making any claims. So the encroacher redefines the city, even as she needs the city to survive. The trespasser alters the border by crossing it, rendering it meaningless and yet making it present everywhere, even in the heart of the capital city, so that every citizen becomes a suspect alien and the compact of citizenship that sustains the state is quietly eroded. The pirate renders impossible the difference between the authorised and the unauthorised copy, spreading information and culture, and devaluing intellectual property at the same time. Seepage complicates the norm by inducing invisible structural changes that accumulate over time.[15]

It is crucial to the concept of seepage that individual acts of insubordination not be uprooted from the original experience. They have to remain embedded in the wider context to make any sense. And this wider context is a networked context, a context in which incessant movement between nodes is critical.

porous legalities and avenues of participation

Finally, I would like to identify another entry point building on those that I have outlined thus far. What seems to weave the stories of the inhabitants of the older city with the denizens of the new city is the umbilical cord of illegality that defines the ways

[14] Ibid.
[15] Ibid.

through which they create for themselves avenues of participation. Building on the seepage metaphor of Raqs, I would like to add another trope, which helps us to understand what allows these seepages to take place, namely, the idea of porous legalities. Porous legalities are created through different forms and materials, but primarily through a profound distrust of the self-narrated life of law and law enforcers. The slum dweller with a desperate instinct for survival has little choice but to ignore the law in order to carry on with the rather difficult task of surviving a hostile city, challenging the idea that it is the natural role of law to ensure the public good. At other times, you follow the pores created to benefit the elite few who know how to enter into the legal machinery in their favour, and entering these pores use the same routes to secure yourself. In this avenue, the idea of corruption, especially within the police force, acts like a self-fulfilling prophecy that works at different levels/hierarchies for different kinds of claims. The music company paying the police to conduct raids also has to deal with the policeman who will pass the information of the raid to the pirates. A few pores exist as a part of the structure and design of the legal order itself. Thus, the ability to produce cover versions available in the Copyright Act becomes the basis of the creation of a new set of media practices that, in turn, create an anxiety of regulation all over again.

One could understand these porous legalities as inevitable reproductions of social relations of power, but social struggles, whether they constellate around power, law or knowledge, also have an internal logic of their own where they tend to be performative, as they actively produce (rather than merely reproducing) the forms of power, law or knowledge that best suit their horizons of expectations. The tragedy would be to examine a practice of illegality, especially around media, within its own horizons of expectations. We need instead to uncover the various constellations of fantasy, mobility and innovations that mark the realities of these social worlds. Santos states: 'Though for different reasons, maps, poems and laws distort social realities, traditions or territories, and all according to certain rules. Maps distort reality in order to establish orientations; poems distort reality to establish originality and laws distort reality to establish exclusivity.'[16]

---

[16] Boaventura de Sousa Santos, *Towards a New Common Sense* (New York: Routledge, 1995), p. 182.

The figures of illegality pose fundamental questions to our neat categories of the liberal public sphere where citizens interact through constitutionally guaranteed rights, as the exclusive mode of understanding the world of law and legality. The status of these transgressors as the 'not quite' and yet 'not quiet' citizens, creating their own avenues of participation in the multiple worlds of media, modernity and globalisation, demands that journalists ask fundamentally different questions of the relationship between law, legality and property (tangible and intangible), on the one hand, and that which we call the public domain, on the other.

14

covering caste:
visible dalit, invisible brahmin

s. anand

The Untouchables have no Press. The Congress Press is closed to them and is determined not to give them the slightest publicity. They cannot have their own Press and for obvious reasons .... The staff of the Associated Press in India, which is the main news distributing agency in India, is entirely drawn from Madras Brahmins—indeed the whole of the Press in India is in their hands and they, for well-known reasons, are entirely pro-Congress and will not allow any news hostile to the Congress to get publicity. These are reasons beyond the control of the Untouchables.[1]

The fact that no Dalit men or women worked in minor editorial jobs on Indian-language dailies meant that aspects of the life of Dalits were neglected. And the fact that no sizeable daily in India was owned or edited by Dalits meant that stories about them were unlikely to receive the constant, sympathetic coverage of stories about, for example, the urban, consuming middle class.[2]

C overage of caste in the Indian media has been equated with reporting on issues that concern the 'lower castes'—the dalits and other backward classes (shudras). The mostly urbanised

---

[1] B.R.Ambedkar, 'Plea to the Foreigner' (from *What Congress and Gandhi have done to the Untouchables*), in Vasant Moon (ed.), *Dr. Babasaheb Ambedkar: Writing and Speeches*, Vol. 9 (Bombay: Department of Education, Government of Maharashtra, 1945 [reprinted 1991]).

[2] Robin Jeffrey, *India's Newspaper Revolution: Capitalism, Politics and the Indian-language Press* (New Delhi: Oxford University Press, 2003).

media reflects the common sense of the brahminical upper middle class that caste has always something to do with others and not the *dwija* ('twice-born', non-dalit, non-shudra) self. That almost one-fourth of the Indian population has never been allowed to participate in the mainstream press—the largest media in the world's largest democracy[3] both in the English and Indian languages,—has never become an issue for media managers, despite recent attempts by dalits to point out this ugly, shameful anomaly.[4] This essay examines the connections between the absence of dalits in the print media and the structure and nature of 'coverage of caste issues'[5] by such exclusionist media.

the 'nationalist' press

In the period immediately after Independence, in the field of conflict reporting, the print media were primarily concerned with the violence that followed the India–Pakistan partition on religious lines, and 'communalism' came to be (and continues to be) a major issue. In mainstream journalistic accounts, the phrase 'communal violence/riots' was always used to describe clashes between the two principal religious blocs. In such a scenario, caste violence, that is, violence that resulted from a conflict between castes within the Hindu community, almost never

---

[3] India has 43,828 publications, including 4,890 dailies. Newspapers are published in 18 principal languages and over 81 small languages and dialects. The total circulation of the Indian press reached nearly 127 million in 1998 (the most recent figure available). Daily newspapers had a circulation of three million in 2000, while non-dailies accounted for just under eight million copies (UNESCO, http://www.unesco.org/courier/2001_06/uk/medias.htm).

[4] See, for instance, the memorandum submitted to the Editors' Guild and the Press Council by Chandra Bhan Prasad and Sheoraj Singh Bechain, 'End Apartheid from Indian Media: Democratise Nation's Opinion', (New Delhi: Authors, n.d [1998]). The pamphlet was dedicated to senior Delhi-based journalist B.N.Uniyal, who in 1996 wrote an edit-page comment, 'In Search of a Dalit Journalist' in *The Pioneer* (16 November 1996). Uniyal's piece was reproduced in the 'Dalit Millennium' special supplement of *The Pioneer* (30 January 2000). However, no mainstream editor has responded to this situation.

[5] I shall not, however, discuss elections-related coverage, where caste is an analytical category to understand 'vote-bank' and 'vote-share'.

qualified as 'communal'. That column size in centimetres devoted to reporting caste violence was far less than what was devoted to 'communal' Hindu–Muslim violence owes to the perception that caste violence was somehow internal to Hinduism and hence not 'communal'. Such reasoning was premised on the brahminical–nationalist consensus and belief that the dalits (earlier labelled variously as the depressed classes, harijans and scheduled castes) were very much a part of 'Hindu society'. Though the post-1947 state did bestow formal recognition on the caste divisions within Hindu society, these differences came to be disavowed by the brahminical elite that embraced only the material aspects of modernity and was sceptical about the philosophical aspects of modernity (the values of liberty, equality, fraternity). This could be understood as part of the Nehruvian approach to modernity, appearing aggressively 'modern' at the institutional, surface level (parliament, dams, industries) but retaining the comforts and disadvantages of the premodern baggage of caste and patriarchy.

Well before Bhimrao Ambedkar assumed the role of stewarding the Indian Constitution, he had been concerned about this skewed understanding of what constituted 'communalism' for both the colonial administrators and the largely brahminical Congress nationalists. As early as in 1918, Ambedkar gave evidence before the Southborough Committee, and argued that the dalits were a separate element as much as the Muslims.[6] In fact, following the submissions of Ambedkar and other dalits, the Constitution of 1919 had recognised the 'Depressed Classes' as statutory minorities and provisions relating to their safety and security were embodied in it. For the colonialists, it would appear, both the Muslim and Depressed Classes 'questions' figured as 'communal' in a sense in which the 'women's question' did not. But this sense of 'communal' (as that which concerns a distinct community) has given way to a negative usage which has exclusively religious-fundamentalist significance, not only in journalism, but also in academic debates on 'communalism'.

That the dalits were a separate element in Indian society, a separate community, was a position Ambedkar argued in every forum available to him—the Simon Commission (1928), the two

---

[6] See Vasant Moon (ed.) *Dr. Babasaheb Ambedkar*, p. 250.

Round Table conferences (1930 and 1931), his various scholarly and polemical writings—in his effort to correct the perceptions of the Cabinet Mission Plan (1946), etc. In the making of the Constitution, Ambedkar was hamstrung by the caste Hindu majority in the Constituent Assembly, but in 1956 he decided that if recognition that the dalits were a separate element was not being granted politically, he would win such recognition religiously (at least for a section of dalits) by conversion to Buddhism. In sharp contrast, M.K. Gandhi, a non-dalit *baniya* who fought with Ambedkar over the question of representing the 'untouchables',[7] sought to argue in various forums that the 'untouchables' were part of the Hindu fold. In his submission before the Second Round Table Conference in 1931, Gandhi argued for the political recognition of only three communities—Hindus, Muslims and Sikhs. For Ambedkar, and the dalits in general, the ground reality was that in most of India the untouchables were ghettoised and forced to live in separate settlements at a distance from the main village. Their separateness was not desired but enforced on them. It was this social reality that Gandhi and the Congress sought to subvert at an international forum, the price for which continues to be paid by dalits today as they battle it out at forums such as the World Conference against Racism in Durban, 2001.

However, when Ramsay MacDonald recognised the 'untouchables' as a separate element and issued the Communal Award, Gandhi went on a fast-unto-death. This resulted in the Poona Pact of 1932 which withdrew the separate recognition of, and joint electorates for, the dalits. It is this hypocritical Gandhian common sense of socially treating the dalits as a separate element but politically demarcating them as one with 'Hindus', that also informs the understanding and approach of the mainstream media that have been beholden to Gandhian nationalist values (at least in print). The deliberate neglect and suppression of the

[7] For the full debate between Ambedkar and Gandhi on the issue of separate electorates at the Second Round Table Conference, see Ambedkar's 'What Congress and Gandhi have done to the Untouchables', in Vasant Moon (ed.), *Dr. Babasaheb Ambedkar: Writing and Speeches*, Vol. 9 (Bombay: Department of Education, Government of Maharashtra, 1945 [reprinted 1991], pp. 40–125 and pp. 181–98; and also Gail Omvedt, *Dalits and the Democratic Revolution: Dr Ambedkar and the Dalit Movement in Colonial India* (New Delhi: Sage Publications, 1994).

Ambedkarite point of view in the mainstream 'nationalist' press is epitomised by an editorial in *The Hindu* following the Poona Pact, which shockingly does not make a single reference to Ambedkar, but heaps adulation on Gandhi and his struggles.[8] Such attitudes of wishing away caste reality resurface even to-day in what is regarded as India's most 'progressive' English-language newspaper, which in its commemorative 125-year anniversary issue (13 September 2003) did not discuss Ambedkar once, used his picture nowhere, but issued an entire special supplement devoted to M.K. Gandhi.

If the 'nationalist' *The Hindu* practised, and continues to prac-tise, casteism by omission, the Uttar Pradesh press during the immediate post-Independence period was vehemently against Ambedkar and the political moves of the Scheduled Caste Fed-eration (SCF). Ramnarayan Rawat has, in a recent research ar-ticle, demonstrated how the SCF created the space for an alter-native to Congress-type 'nationalist' politics in post-1947 Uttar Pradesh. At the fifth conference of the Uttar Pradesh SCF in Lucknow on 24 and 25 April 1948, 'Ambedkar denied the rumours that he had joined the Congress'. According to Rawat, he report-edly said:

What I want is power—political power for my people, for if we have power we will have social status' .... He particularly em-phasized the significance of their separate identity and the need to transform it into a potent political force, under one banner, one slogan, one leader, one party and one programme .... Notions of 'independence' and 'citizenship' were meaningless for the Dalits unless they had a share in political power, he argued.[9]

[8] See Editorial, 'The Poona Pact', *The Hindu,* 26 September 1936. The edito-rial even mentions Tej Bahadur Sapru, but not Ambedkar. Perhaps there is an oblique uncharitable reference in the words 'those who do not look with favour on India's aspirations'. I thank Ravikumar for drawing my attention to this point.
[9] Ramnarayan S. Rawat, 'Partition Politics and Achhut Identity: A Study of the Scheduled Castes Federation and Dalit Politics in U.P., 1946–48', in Suvir Kaul (ed.), *The Partitions of Memory: The Afterlife of the Division of India* (New Delhi: Permanent Black, 2001).

Rawat then documents the reactions of the UP press which dismissed Ambedkar's speech as a 'frustrated outburst':

> With Partition fresh in collective memory, the editorial in the *Leader* commented, 'Dr. Ambedkar has chosen precisely at this moment to tell the Scheduled Castes, "a united nation is all rot". Dr. Ambedkar wants the Scheduled Castes to form a third nation'. Ambedkar's criticism of the Congress was also considered unacceptable. An editorial in the *National Herald* described his speech as a cynical outburst lacking in wisdom and foresight. The editorial in *Vartman* described the speech as 'reactionary and against the ideals of Indian nationalism. Any hopes of change in the ideas of Ambedkar, when he joined the Cabinet, have been quashed by his speech'. The editorial presented him with two choices: either submit to nationalism or resign from the Cabinet. These newspapers, indeed the UP press in general, were clear that their loyalty lay with the Congress. For the press, the Congress symbolized nationalism and national unity; editors were clear about what constituted nationalism; consequently, they were equally clear about 'Indian' politics, and what was 'anti-national' or 'communal' politics. Ambedkar was described as a potential Qaid-e-Azam, and this despite the fact that he did not raise the SCF's demand for a separate electorate, always the bane of Ambedkarite politics for the nationalist.[10]

During the anti-colonial 'nationalist' period, it was the temple-entry efforts by brahmins and other powerful caste Hindus that were given more mainstream coverage than similar, and other more militant, dalit-initiated efforts. A study contrasting the reporting of the Ambedkar-led Mahad Chavdar Tank satyagraha (1927) and the Kalaram temple entry struggle in Nasik (1930) with the Vaidyanatha Iyer-led temple entry of *panchamas* (fifth castes) in Madurai in 1939, would throw up interesting findings. Such an exercise, however, is beyond the scope of this essay.

---

[12] Ibid.

the caste composition of media

Crucial to any discussion on the 'coverage of caste issues' in the Indian media is the caste composition of the media themselves. With the exception of researcher Robin Jeffrey's tangential effort that documents the absence of dalits in the Indian-language print media, there has been no attempt made to seriously examine or address this issue.[11] Jeffrey's sub-chapter of 10 pages in a book of 234 pages again focuses on absolute dalit *exclusion* and does not throw much light on the predominant *inclusion* of others.[12] Jeffrey does not probe the caste/communal composition of non-dalit journalists—how many brahmins, jats, yadavs, Muslims, nadars? Such a task was casually attempted by Uniyal in *The Pioneer*, who looked up the 'Accreditation Index 1996' of the Press Information Bureau (PIB) in New Delhi:

> Of the 686 accredited correspondents listed in it, as many as 454 bore their caste surnames, and of them as many as 240 turned out to be Brahmins, 70 Punjabi Khatris, 44 Kayasthas, 26 Muslims with as many Baniyas, 19 Christians, 12 Jains and 9 (Bengali) Baidyas. I checked out the caste affiliation of 47 of the remaining 232 correspondents at random. None of them turned out to be a dalit either.[13]

Since no one has staked claim to being a dalit journalist from the remaining 232 even after Uniyal's article was reproduced in January 2000, we may presume that a dalit working journalist does not exist in the national capital, at least on the PIB records. And Jeffrey, despite his extensive interviews with journalists, owners and editors in the 1990s, did not find a dalit journalist in the Indian-language press either.[14] If we are to risk deriving

---

[11] Robin Jeffrey, *India's Newspaper Revolution*.
[12] Ibid., pp. 160–70.
[13] B.N. Uniyal, 'In Search of a Dalit Journalist', *The Pioneer*, 16 November 2003.
[14] One mainstream dalit working journalist has stood up to be counted. An English-language little magazine published from Chennai, *The Dalit*, which in its inaugural issue (January–February 2001) addressed the question of absence of dalits in the media, featured an account 'On being a Dalit Journalist' by Dara Gopi, a senior correspondent with *Deccan Chronicle* in Vijayawada. *Vaartha*, the second largest selling Telugu daily, had an outspoken dalit journalist, Malleypally Laxmaiah, on its rolls till recently. He quit in 2002 to be a freelancer.

larger conclusions with this scant available data, we see that more than 35 per cent of the PIB-accredited Delhi journalists are brahmins, a community estimated to constitute a little over three per cent of the Indian population, whereas dalits, who constitute 16.48 per cent of the Indian population (according to the 1991 census), go virtually unrepresented. (We may assume that the same holds true for the non-representation of the 8.08 per cent adivasi population of the nation.) The percentage of brahmin journalists will doubtless be higher in brahmin-owned establishments such as *The Hindu*, as will be the percentage of nadar journalists in nadar-owned newspapers such as *Dinathanthi* and *Dinakaran* in the Tamil language. In both cases, however, the absence of dalits does not become an issue.

Given that the *chatur-varna* (four varnas) system and its various mutations, the caste system in general, has held the subcontinent under its thrall for more than two millennia, and that such a worldview sanctioned and legitimised the exclusive dominance of brahmins, especially in the realm of knowledge-production and dissemination, it may be pointed out that such statistical aberrations need not be exaggerated. However, if 56 years after the nation formally decided to control its own destiny and entered into a tryst with democracy under the guidance of a dalit, the Indian journalistic fraternity cannot own up to a single accredited dalit journalist, it reflects rather poorly on the true state of democracy in the media, and by extension, in Indian society. While the constitutional guarantee of representation in the form of reservation ensured the presence of dalits and *adivasis* (tribals) in various state–controlled institutions —parliament, assemblies, public sector undertakings, educational institutions— this did not result in civil society as such accepting the logic of affirmative action and ensuring the presence of social and political minorities in its midst. As a result, the private sector never believed in voluntarily extending reservation and trying to reflect the diversity of the population. The media institutions in the country, being privately owned and controlled, mostly by extended families, partook of this logic. So dalits, had to *incidentally,* if at all, make it as journalists in a *Times of India* or as engineers in the TVS chain of companies. As civil society in India largely continues to be in the hold of the brahminical caste system, and not so much in that of the Constitution, dalits and adivasis seem to be absent from those realms of the public sphere that are not under state control. Chandra Bhan Prasad, perhaps India's only dalit writing a weekly column in a mainstream English-language newspaper for over four years (in *The Pioneer*, ironically known for its sympathies to the Hindutva world-view and the RSS),[15] points out that the evolution of India into a republic in 1950 was a moment of 'rupture'.

> ... where the state was directed to end the age-old system of exclusion, and reconstruct society along democratic lines. Bound by the verdict of the Constitution, the state has given some space in institutions under its direct control. But society, by and large, has been refusing to internalize that verdict to the hilt, and therefore dalits remain excluded from institutions outside the command of the state.[16]

The commercial print media in India do fall outside the command of the state and therefore can remain oblivious to the fundamental neglect of dalits in its midst. This, according to Jeffrey, was precisely the point made by the Press Council of India when asked to respond to the memorandum, 'End Apartheid from Indian Media: Democratise Nation's Opinion', submitted in the late 1990s by Chandra Bhan Prasad and Sheoraj Singh 'Bechain'. The action of the kind demanded in the memorandum, ensuring a minimal dalit presence among reporters— was beyond the powers of the Council because 'the print media is run entirely by the private sector'.[17]

The truth is that the media in India practice, more effectively than other institutions, a doctrine of exclusion. As Prasad argues:

> Contrary to the popular perception that untouchability is a 'social evil', it is in essence a doctrine of exclusion .... [I]f there is not a single dalit who is an editor of a national daily,

[15] A selection of articles (April 1999 to April 2003) from Chandra Bhan Prasad's Sunday column, 'Dalit Diary' in *The Pioneer* has been published in *Dalit Diary 1999–2003: Reflections on Apartheid in India* (Pondicherry: Navayana, 2004).
[16] Chandra Bhan Prasad, 'Untouchability and Its "Hidden" Agenda', *The Pioneer*, 9 April 2000.
[17] Jeffrey, *India's Newspaper Revolution*, p. 169.

an anchor on TV channels, or a member of the FICCI (Federation of Indian Chambers of Commerce and Industry) or CII (Confederation of Indian Industry), it is not by accident, but because of the doctrine of untouchability.[18]

Now that we have established that the media, like the rest of the uncivil society in India, practice untouchability, it becomes a little easier to deal with the question of how 'caste' is covered by such media. But we shall stay with Prasad and his concerns awhile. Beginning 4 February 2001, Prasad produced a series of articles in his column 'Dalit Diary', comparing racism-torn USA and casteism-ridden India with reference to the representational status of social minorities—Blacks, Hispanics and Native Americans in the US, and dalits and adivasis in India. Black presence in Hollywood was compared with the near-absence of dalits in Bollywood; Delhi University's and Jawaharlal University's abysmal record in implementing the policy of reservation was contrasted with the minority presence in Harvard University; Black presence in Microsoft Corp and IBM was empirically contrasted with the dalit absence in Indian info-tech companies; and the series culminated on 8 April that year by presenting data that contrasted the situations in the Indian and American print media.[19] Prasad argues that the 1922-founded ASNE or the American Society of Newspaper Editors (the equivalent of the Editors' Guild of India) acknowledged and accepted that there was racism by omission in the American print media in 1975 when Blacks and other social minorities comprised only 3.5 per cent of the journalistic workforce. In 1978, ASNE set itself a 'Year 2000' goal to have proportionate representation of Blacks and other minorities and resolved that (a) newspapers open a diversity department, (b) offer special scholarships to train Black/other candidates in journalism, (c) organise job fairs to recruit them, and (d) participate in annual newsroom racial/ethnic census. Prasad reports that of the 1,446 American newspapers, 950 decided to abide by ASNE's resolutions, and in 20 years, Blacks and journalists of ethnic origin would 'comprise 11.64 of [the] total journalists in America'. Two tables based on ASNE's 2001

---

[18] Prasad, 'Untouchability and Its "Hidden" Agenda'.
[19] Chandra Bhan Prasad, 'Blacks in US Media and Blackout in India', *The Pioneer*, 8 April 2001.

survey provided by Prasad are worth reproducing here (see
Tables 14.1 and 14.2).

Table 14.1: Presence of Minorities among Journalists in the US

Newspaper	Daily Circulation (in millions)	Blacks/Other Minorities (in per cent)
Wall Street Journal	1.75	17.1
USA Today	1.76	18.7
New York Times	11.32	16.2
Los Angeles Times	10.80	18.7
Washington Post	07.75	19.5

Source: Chandra Bhan Prasad, 'Dalit Diary', The Pioneer, 8 April 2001.

The second table, also sourced from ASNE documents by Prasad,
gives a break-up in terms of the specific occupations of these
journalists.

Table 14.2: Occupational Break-up of Minority Journalists in the US

Professional Category	Total Employees	Blacks/Other Minorities (%)
Supervisors	13728	1254 (9.1)
Copy/Layout Editors	10901	1113 (10.2)
Reporters	25593	3244 (12.7)
Photographers	06171	0951 (15.4)
Grand Total	56393	6563 (11.63)

Source: Chandra Bhan Prasad, 'Dalit Diary', The Pioneer, 8 April 2001.

seeing caste only in dalits

If there are no dalits in the media, and if the owners and editors
of newspapers and magazines do not wish to respond to this
apartheid despite their attention being drawn to it,[20] how does
this reflect on the manner in which caste is 'covered/ reported'

[20] It is not as if there is hope for dalit journalists to emerge from India's leading
journalism institues. The self-admittedly 'elite' Asian College of Journalism
based in Chennai, which offers a sought-after one-year post-graduate diploma
programme in journalism, allocates special seats for students nominated from
SAARC countries, but has no provision to ensure the presence of dalit and
adivasi students—yet another case of a 'progressive' institution outside state
control not effecting affirmative action in faculty and student intake.

in the print media? The first anomaly created by this social imbalance in the media world is the tendency, even among progressive, well-minded journalists, to unwittingly equate the issue of covering caste to writing stories about the conditions of
dalits. Such reports invariably tend to be about dalits caught in
caste conflict, dalits subjected to atrocities, dalits facing grave
social problems, dalits denied constitutional rights, dalits being
murdered, raped, maimed, brutalised. These stories are located
mostly in rural India and when filed by an urban, well-connected,
non-dalit journalist writing for the English language press, they
pass for both 'developmental journalism' and 'rural reporting',
and sometimes even fetch awards. A typical example of such
reporting would be P. Sainath's piece captioned, 'A Dalit goes to
Court', which won him the Amnesty International award in 2000.
His report begins thus:

> On average in the State of Rajasthan, a dalit woman is raped
> every sixty hours. One dalit is murdered about every nine
> days. Some dalit is the victim of grievous hurt every 64 hours.
> A dalit house or property suffers an arson attack every five
> days. The guilty are rarely punished. Conviction rates range
> between two and three per cent. And many offences commit-
> ted against dalits never even reach the courtroom stage. Genu-
> ine and serious cases are often scuttled.[21]

Most of Sainath's reportage on the condition of dalits in contemporary India has a similar ring.[22] Sainath, in fact, has become a role model for several aspiring journalists committed to
probing socially relevant developmental issues.[23] But for his series on the situation of dalits across India that appeared in *The
Hindu*'s Sunday Magazine section for weeks, even the little exposure that the issue of dalit oppression and marginalisation

[21] See *The Hindu*, 13 June 1999.
[22] S. Viswanathan, a Chennai-based correspondent of *Frontline*, has also
regularly and extensively reported on violence against dalits in Tamil Nadu
between 1993 and 2003. In his reportage, too the usual stereotypes apply.
[23] After reading Sainath's *Everybody Loves a Good Drought: Stories from
India's Poorest Districts* (New Delhi: Penguin, 1996) while on my first job
with *Deccan Chronicle* in Hyderabad, I too felt inspired by the scope for such
journalism.

received in the mainstream press would not have been possible. Sainath's reports, many of which have become part of the syllabi of journalism courses and are provided as reading material for young bureaucrats being trained in Shimla, represent both the possibilities and limitations of 'coverage of caste issues' in the Indian media. It is easier in sections of the dalit-free, 'secular', English-language media to discuss the state of dalits in the rural countryside (where, incidentally, the equally rural OBC-shudras are their oppressors) than to discuss the issue of brahminism and brahmin hegemony in the urban public sphere. Sainath's style of 'rural reporting' and 'developmental journalism' does mention the occasional brahmin block development officer, but precludes the scope of discussing the preponderance of brahmins and other *savarna*s (similar-ranked castes) in, say, Jawaharlal Nehru University's (JNU) history or economics department or on the editorial staff of *The Hindu, The Hindustan Times* or *The Times of India*. Such journalism does not see caste discrimination when historian Romila Thapar or economist Prabhat Patnaik does not find a single 'competent' dalit or adivasi candidate to fill the constitutionally stipulated quota of 22.5 per cent in their respective departments, but points us merely to caste discrimination in rural panchayats where dalits are not allowed to contest for democratically elected posts or are not allowed to function freely even if elected.

The question Prasad asks is: is not the exclusion practised by the 'progressive', 'secular' Thapars and Patnaiks more appalling and unforgivable than the exclusion practised by feudal casteist fanatics in rural Bihar or rural Tamil Nadu?[24] The self-styled progressive, secular intellectuals have at least some pretence to equality and morality, whereas the Ranvir Sena, RSS or Thevar fanatics make no such claims. The urbanised, 'secular' brahminic self does not have to account for caste as much as the rural-feudal other is made to account for it, though it is obvious that the former's crimes are graver than the latter's.

---

[24] See 'An Interview with Chandra Bhan Prasad', by S. Anand, http://www.ambedkar.org/chandrabhan/interview.htm, where Prasad says: 'The Department of History in JNU grew under the shadow of Bipan [Chandra] and Romila [Thapar]. But, they did not allow a single Dalit to become a teacher. They threw constitutional provisions into the dustbin. Today, the same Romila Thapar talks of defending the Constitution.'

Nor does such journalism deal adequately with what could be termed success stories of dalits, rural or urban. Such issues are best left for Prasad to deal with in his 'Dalit Diary'—a little-read column that in the world of media apartheid is the only 'separate settlement' dalits have managed in recent times. This is perhaps what Jeffrey means when he points out that the absence of dalit journalists would mean 'aspects of the life of Dalits [are] neglected'. [25]

However, it must be emphasised that even if violence against dalits is the only kind of reporting we see in terms of 'coverage of caste issues', this, too, is grossly under-reported. Statistics compiled by the National Crime Records Bureau for 2000 indicate that 25,455 crimes were committed against dalits. Every hour two dalits are assaulted; every day three dalit women are raped, two dalits are murdered, and two dalit homes are torched. [26] According to Ramkumar, a dalit rights activist in Uttar Pradesh, 'the stories that appear in the press are just a minuscule proportion of the atrocities that Dalits face every day ... and those recorded by the police as formal complaints are "less than 5 per cent of the actual number of cases"'. [27] According to another newspaper article, 'About three million Dalit women have been raped and around one million Dalits killed from the time of Independence. This is 25 times more than [the] number of soldiers killed during the wars fought after Independence.'[28] Such statistics should make us feel the need for a hundred Sainaths, but we must also bear in mind that, if such violence has to abate, at least 20 of these journalists need to be dalits.

Let us now travel with the reporters and stringers based in small towns who file stories that deal with caste. These reports, again, invariably, involve dalits in some kind of distress or conflict. These reports are usually of single-column length and are used only in local edition pages, and how they are placed on the page would depend on a non-dalit news editor/subeditor's prejudice and mood. The reports would gain in prominence if the violence is of some magnitude and involves the death of dalits or

---

[25] Jeffrey, *India's Newspaper Revolution*, p. 178.
[26] See 'India's "Untouchables" Face Violence, Discrimination', *National Geographic*, 2 June 2003.
[27] 'Their Tomorrow Never Comes', *The Hindu*, 29 December 2002.
[28] Tulsiram, *The Pioneer*, 30 January 2000.

non-dalits in conflict. For instance, the lynching of five dalits in
Jhajjar, Haryana, on 15 October 2002 for allegedly slaughtering a
cow generated a lot of media interest. Earlier in the same year,
on 21 May, when two dalits in Thinniyam, a remote village in
Tamil Nadu's Tiruchi district, were forced to consume dried human excreta, it did not become an issue for the 'national media'.
The Hindu reported it, but only in its Tamil Nadu edition pages.[29]

caste and the newspaper's public sphere

Given the largely dalit-free press, a dalit-non-dalit conflict is almost always reported, if at all, by non-dalits. Commenting on
the situation that obtains in the Tamil press, activist-theoreti-
cian of the dalit movement, Ravikumar observes that the OBC
nadar-owned *Dinathanthi*, Tamil Nadu's largest circulated and
read daily, employs mostly nadars as reporters/news gatherers
in the small towns and villages of northern Tamil Nadu. In the
context of communal strife between dalits and non-dalits, the
news gatherer, who often also doubles up as the newspaper's
advertisement agent, invariably reports with bias against dalits.[30]
Dinamalar, the second largest selling Tamil daily, also employs
mostly OBC news gatherers in non-metropolitan centres, and
here again the non-dalit prejudice flourishes in reporting. This,
argues Ravikumar, can be very debilitating for dalits since the
state machinery draws its conclusions about a conflict situation
based on newspaper reports.

Jeffrey celebrates the 'capitalistic expansion' of Indian-language newspapers of mass circulation such as *Dinathanthi* (Tamil)
and *Eenadu* (Telugu). One of the important arguments in his

[29] As *Outlook* newsmagazine's correspondent in Chennai, when I suggested
a report on Thinniyam, it was turned down. I subsequently wrote an essay-
length piece for *Himal*, a Kathmandu-based monthly, discussing Thinniyam
in the context of the Hindutva valourisation of the cow and its urine ("Holy"
Cow and "Unholy" Dalit', September 2002, http://www.himalmag.com/2002/
november).
[30] See Ravikumar's article, *'Ezhudhaa ezhuththu: Dalitthugalum,
Patrikaikalum'* ('Unwritten Writing: Dalits and Print Media') in the Tamil
bimonthly, *Dalit,* January–February 2004.

pioneering study is that in the last 20 years, the tremendous growth of newspapers has 'created' a 'public sphere'. Jeffrey, though critical of German social theorist Jurgen Habermas's reading of the emergence of the 'public sphere' in Europe, finds this category useful to 'conceptualize the effects of India's newspaper revolution on society and politics'. [31] In a more recent essay, reproduced in this book, he begins on a note of hope:

> India is transforming itself, and the print revolution—and especially the daily newspaper revolution—of the past twenty years is helping to propel that transformation. 'A million mutinies now' was the best thing about V. S. Naipaul's book of that title. Millions of mutinies are, indeed, going on, and the fact that people now read about them in their newspapers, and read about *themselves* in their newspapers, helps to explain the mutinous environment. [32]

For Jeffrey,

> [t]he 'public sphere' is that 'space' between family life and the State or government where people in modern times carry on debate about how their world is going and how it ought to go. The public sphere and newspapers grow up together. One can't have Habermas' public sphere without the presence of the newspaper. [33]

And how do people in modern times 'carry on debate about how their world is going and how it ought to go'? Jeffrey offers as illustration an innocuous-seeming, single-column report in *Punjab Kesari* in 1998:

Telephone Pole: May Fall Down at Any Time
Jalandhar, 4 June (Rajendra). The residents of the Laksmipura area have demanded the removal of Telephone Pole No. 2219 because it is half uprooted and might fall down any moment

---

[31] Jeffrey, *India's Newspaper Revolution*, p.12

[32] Jeffrey, 'Breaking News', *The Little Magazine*, 4 (2), 2003. Parts of this article are reproduced in this volume as 'The Public Sphere of Print Journalism' (http://www.littlemag.com/viamedia/robinjeffery.html).

[33] Ibid.

and cause an accident. It is noteworthy that it is tied up
with rope.

He then explains what this means for the 'creation of public
sphere':

> This is the most basic sort of village-*ghat* journalism. What
> did the residents of Laksmipura do *before* there were newspa-
> pers to proclaim the danger of Telephone Pole No. 2219? Such
> stories are repeated every day wherever local dailies are pro-
> duced. Because of the indignation they can breed, and the
> fact that such reports endure—they are part of the *public*
> record—citizens relish them, buy the newspapers to read
> about them, and officials are forced to take note of them. If
> Telephone Pole No. 2219 falls down and injures someone in
> three months' time, angry citizens will point out that it was a
> *public* issue long before. Heads may be expected to roll. There-
> fore, before that, the mills of the administrative gods may be
> expected to grind, and Telephone Pole No. 2219 may get re-
> paired. That's how a 'public sphere' can work. To be sure,
> these are not nation-shaking debates; but in thousands of small
> ways, they are nation-building and citizen-empowering (all
> emphases in original).[34]

What does not, and would not, get reported with equal zeal
for 'nation-building' and 'citizen-empowerment' is an incident of
dalits staking claim to fishing rights in the common village pond
or lake; dalits complaining about funds from the panchayat cor-
pus being used to lay roads or water pipelines only for the caste
Hindu part of the village, leaving their ghetto untouched; or an
instance of an oppressor caste landlord refusing to pay the minimum wage for his mostly-dalit agricultural labourers. The invariably non-dalit rural reporter will also not eagerly report the
fact of a chargesheet or a First Information Report (FIR) not
being filed by the local police station under the Scheduled Caste/
Scheduled Tribe Prevention of Atrocities Act if a caste Hindu
had abused a dalit in a punishable offence. If the reporter for
Dinathanthi, Eenadu or *Punjab Kesari* were also the advertise-

---

[34] Ibid.

ment agent for the daily, he would be even more wary of bringing such an incident into the public sphere. He would gain nothing in terms of ad revenue from the economically poor dalits,
and lose the faith of the powerful caste Hindu community which
rewards him in many ways, and to which he could well belong. If
by staging *dharnas* and using political pressure a dalit comes
close to getting an FIR filed, the rural 'news agent' is more likely
to report that some 'misguided' dalits, in order to get compensa-
tion from the government under the Scheduled Caste/Sched-
uled Tribe Act, have been harassing a respectable citizen of the
local community.

Ambedkar's observation about a Hindu's notion of the 'public'
would be useful here: '[T]he effect of Caste on the ethics of the
Hindus is simply deplorable. Caste has killed public spirit. Caste
has destroyed the sense of public charity. Caste has made public
opinion impossible. A Hindu's public is his Caste.' [35] In 2003, not
much has changed. Ravikumar reflects on what the public-pri-
vate binary means for the dalit:

> The public has come to connote things and spaces which are
> inaccessible for the dalits. Common wells, public roads and
> cremation grounds are spaces denied to dalits .... The pur-
> pose of Hindu politics has been to restrict and relegate dalits
> to the 'reserved' sectors. The dalits have to defy such social
> strictures to enter the public sphere.[36]

It is the unfolding of the process of claiming the right to access the public sphere since 1989, when the Scheduled Castes,
Scheduled Tribes Prevention of Atrocities Act was passed, the
Mandal Commission recommendations were implemented, and
the Ambedkar birth centenary celebrations were held, which
resulted in a surge of dalit political consciousness across the
nation, the rise and growth of the Bahujan Samajwadi Party
(BSP) and other dalit political outfits, as well as increased violence against dalits and the subsequent scanty reporting of the

[35] B.R. Ambedkar, 'Annihilation of Caste', in Vasant Moon (ed.), *Dr. Babasaheb
Ambedkar: Writings and Speeches'*, Vol. 1, p. 56.
[36] Ravikumar, 'Introduction', *Ambedkar: Autobiographical Notes* (Pondicherry:
Navayana, 2003), p. 2.

same by the media. And in the struggle of the dalits claiming their rightful space in civil society, the dalit-free press in India has failed badly.

In the metropolitan centres, caste is shut out of the public sphere in different ways. If an educated dalit working woman in Chennai were to walk into newspaper offices and tell them that she was repeatedly denied house for rent on grounds of her caste, reporters would not spring into action. If an odd dalit reporter did work there, s/he would not risk insisting that such a story be carried lest her own caste identity become an issue at the work-place (if it was not already one). In contrast, if a caste-unmarked middle-class consumer walked in with a bottle of an aerated drink with a cockroach in it, or a chocolate bar with worms in it, or a soap purchased from the nearby store with a postdated manufacturing label on it, such news would be carried without much ado. I am not merely abstracting here. These instances of 'vigilante journalism', dealing with dangerously leaning electric poles or open manholes, insects in chocolates or soft drinks, are what I have witnessed over the years as a journalist with *Deccan Chronicle, The Hindu* and *Outlook*.[37] They become news because they do not pose serious problems for newspaper managements.

However, the instance of dalits denied housing, [38] though a fit case for news, seeks an open acknowledgement of the existence of casteism in the urban public sphere, and this the newspapers would be loathe to do. Pictures of open, overflowing sewers and manholes are routinely splashed in the 'city pages' of newspapers to draw the attention of the civic authorities; however, the fact that a specific dalit subcaste has to physically handle the collective scum of millions of defecating urban masses does not inspire journalism which would explore the casteism inherent in certain 'unclean' castes being forced to clean the city. Such

[37] The following news reports of worms found in Cadbury India's cocoa powder boxes in October 2003: *Outlook*, which claims to sell to the best among the 'SEC-A readers', ran a cover story 'Are MNC Products to be Trusted? Villains or Victims?' (3 November 2003), A gloss, upper-class version of the village-*ghat* journalism that Jeffrey points us to. (The National Readership Survey data uses the category SEC-A to refer to the elite 'socio-economic class'.)

[38] It is not just dalits who are denied housing in 'decent' localities of Chennai where I live. Most brahmin house-owners deny housing to non-brahmin tenants and sometimes say this in as many words in the classified sections of newspapers.

sights anger neither the journalists, nor the uncivil society to which they belong.[39] In the urbanised space of the newsroom, then, where 'beats' are allotted to reporters to cover crime, political parties, education, power, health, environment, gender issues, cinema, foreign affairs, information technology, the stock market, different kinds of sport, etc; none is allotted to 'caste', though indeed caste as a category has the potential to operate in almost all the 'beats' I have listed.

This denial of space, or rather the selective manner of offering space for 'caste issues', by the dalit-free media owes a great deal to the tendency to treat caste as a pre-modern category. The urbanised, 'secular' upper classes in India—the English-speaking intellectuals and other elite groups—have come to believe that caste does not exist within them, or amidst them. This, in spite of the fact that caste has a marked role in both the 'private' (marriage, food habits, life and death rituals) and 'public' (networking for jobs, caste composition of the workplace, social lives) spheres of their lives. While Bhanwari Devi's dalit identity and Roop Kanwar' feudal-rural-Rajput identity become crucial for media reports, [40] the caste of Nisha Sharma (a brahmin?), who became a 'newsmaker' in 2003 for walking out of a marriage over excessive dowry demands, is never mentioned. Nisha Sharma became an anti-dowry poster girl for the media, but she did not make so much news when she later wedded Ashwin Sharma to become 'Nishita' Sharma (since her mother-in-law gave her a new name). Not much had changed, since the father continued to see his daughter as a burden. 'Getting his daughter married is the primary duty of a father', Nishi's 'relieved' father said after she wedded Ashwin Sharma, 'chosen' by

[39] *Dalit Murasu* (Dalit Voice), a monthly Tamil newsmagazine of some seven years standing brought out from Chennai, which offers one of the feeble signs of hope for independent dalit-controlled media, recently ran a cover story titled 'Vekkankkatta Naadu' (A Shameless Society) (October 2003) splashing a picture of a woman collecting faeces from a track in a railway station. A subcaste among dalits is forced to perform its 'traditional' village role of 'scavenging' even in a metropolitan setting.

[40] Bhanwari Devi, a dalit, was gang-raped in 1992 in Bhateri village, Rajasthan. Two years later, a judge in a lower court concluded that since she was a dalit, her rapists, 'upper caste' men, could not have possibly raped her. Roop Kanwar was a 17-year-old Rajput widow who on 4 September 1987 allegedly committed *sati* or self-immolation on her husband's funeral pyre at Deorala in Rajasthan.

192 Practising Journalism

her parents.[41] After becoming an anti-dowry poster girl, it was
reported that Nisha, 21, received hundreds of dowry-free proposals cutting across caste, religion and even nationalities. But
Nisha chose to marry a fellow-Sharma. Nisha Sharma's caste,
and the connections between the menace of dowry and educated/
employed urban brahmin or baniya women trying to find grooms
from within the community, was never explored by the media.

But sometimes caste has a nasty way of taking 'secular' journalists—'varna' journalists as Chandra Bhan Prasad refers to
them—by shock and surprise. Then president K.R. Narayanan,
while on an official tour of France in April 2000, was accompanied by a large media delegation from India. Three French newspapers—*Le Figaro*, *Le Monde*, and *France Soir*—referred to
Narayanan as an 'untouchable' in bold headlines. K.K. Katyal,
reporting for *The Hindu*, wrote angrily in his leader-page column, 'Which Indian's blood would not boil on reading the *Le
Figaro* headline: 'An Untouchable at Elysee Palace'?'[42] To prevent a diplomatic row, the editor of *Le Figaro*, Michael Schifres,
soon offered a personal apology to Narayanan for unintentionally having hurt him. Seema Mustafa, another senior journalist, reporting for *The Asian Age* and *Deccan Chronicle*, noted
self-congratulatorily that 'the apology comes after the media
accompanying the president reported extensively on the matter. The official reaction initially was to downplay the incident
lest it mar the final message of the presidential visit.'[43] Mustafa
also reported how Indian mediapersons asked the French if the
Western media would have responded kindly to a reference to a
Black as 'negro/nigger'. The thrust was that the French papers
should have used the politically correct 'dalit', to which the
French journalists replied that such a term would not have made
sense to their readers; and understandably so. For Mustafa, and
perhaps the Indian media delegation, what was the moral of this
story? '[C]learly, the foreign office has to work extensively to

---

[41] See 'Anti-dowry Icon, Nisha Sharma, ties the Knot, http//www.rediff.com/
news/2003/nov/19delhi.htm.

[42] 'The President and the Press' *The Hindu*, 24 April 2000. For an analysis of
the Indian media's reporting on this incident and their fear of
internationalisation of the dalit issue, see 'Untouchability is no "Internal Matter"'
by S. Anand (http://www.ambedkar.org.News/hl/Untouchability%20Is.htm).

[43] Seema Mustafa, *Deccan Chronicle* (20 April 2000).

correct French perception of India.' Katyal wrote of how it must be ensured that 'such perceptions of India abroad' are corrected, and how 'the Paris episode would serve a useful purpose if it sensitises the foreign office to the need for a close look at the state of press relations abroad and to undertake an overhaul.' It did not, however, occur to either Katyal, Mustafa or other upper-class/*savarna* journalists that such 'episodes' demand that both Indian society and the state take stronger measures to tackle caste and untouchability practices in India.

Had there been a sensitised dalit journalist accompanying the president to France, we could have seen a different kind of reaction—not one of panic, guilt and embarrassment—to what the French media had reported. On his return to India, Narayanan, who had not responded while in France, upbraided the Indian mediapersons for assuming a moral high ground, pointing out that the French newspapers' description of him as an untouchable was only a reflection of what the Indian media had been writing about him. Narayanan referred to how in the three years since he became president the Indian press has been keeping the issue alive by writing about it 'day in and day out'. 'I am used to this for a long time. I am used to this kind of publicity in the Indian media, of being an untouchable in Rashtrapati Bhavan.'[44] The Indian media did not ever report about Shankar Dayal Sharma as a brahmin president despite his regular pilgrimages to Tirupati and other 'high holy' shrines at the expense of the state exchequer; the media did not refer to president S. Radhakrishnan or V.V. Giri as brahmins; but Narayanan's caste identity was invoked by the media when they deemed necessary and suppressed in an international context.

my non-secular caste self

I would like to conclude on a personal note by sharing my experience of reporting caste, and by first making visible my own brahmin identity in a media world where dalits seem to be the only bearers of caste, despite being invisible within the media. I was born a Tamil brahmin and had my upbringing mostly in

---

[44] *Deccan Chronicle,* 23 April 2000.

Hyderabad and other parts of Andhra Pradesh. My early upbringing was under the totalising spell of the Tamil-brahmin subcul-
ture, in terms of language, food, circle of friends, aesthetics, so
much so that my access to other social worlds was cut off by sheer
prejudice nurtured by the family. An extended spell of hostel life
since graduation helped me escape familial colonialism, but I carried with me all the unearned privileges and the earned prejudices of a brahmin birth. College and university life (1990–97)
exposed me to a burgeoning student dalit movement in the post-
Ambedkar centenary phase, though I did not make immediate
sense of Mandal or the Ambedkarite movement. While working
on my MPhil with the English Department of University of
Hyderabad, I took up my first journalistic job as a subeditor with
Deccan Chronicle, Hyderabad, in 1996. I literally walked into the
job, unalive to the fact of how brahmin privilege works in un-
stated ways. While on my first job, I acquired some political and
cultural perspective on the several 'caste issues' I faced in university life, and in my own life, on reading Kancha Ilaiah's *Why I am
Not a Hindu.* [45] I wrote a full-page review of the work in *Deccan
Chronicle,* which I began by introducing myself as a brahmin,
quite like Ilaiah who foregrounds his shudra-OBC identity. I then
discovered the writings of Ambedkar. Around the time, my marriage to my non-brahmin partner also caused a rupture in my
caste self, and forced a rethink of my own undying brahminism. I
began writing occasionally on caste in the *Deccan Chronicle,* and
also commissioned others to write, and this did not necessarily
mean writing about dalits. The fact that I was a born-brahmin
enabled me to express a few anti-brahmin ideas with ease. I moved
to Chennai in 1998 and exposure to the mostly debrahminised
(yet, strangely, anti-dalit) Tamil political and intellectual cultures
heightened my brahminical guilt and pressured me to seriously
rescript my sense of the 'personal'— this was almost a conversion
sans a formal change of religion. I was with the copydesk of *The
Indian Express* for a year where I did manage a few analytical
pieces on caste against several odds. I was still not a reporter.

In 1999, I joined the brahmin-dominated desk of *The Hindu.* I
had always considered *The Hindu* as my last option since my

---

[45] Kancha Ilaiah, *Why I am Not a Hindu: A Sudra Critique of Hindutva,
Philosophy, Culture and Political Economy* (Calcutta: Samya, 1996).

grandmother used to say after I completed my MA, 'Wear a *namam* (a caste mark worn on the forehead), and tell them you belong to such and such Iyengar subcaste; who knows, we may be related to *The Hindu* editors! They will certainly give you a job.' I was utterly embarrassed by this frank advice, but also knew that there was truth in this claim, since *The Hindu* had a fair share of *namam* journalists. After circumstances forced me to quit *The (New) Indian Express*,[46] when I did seek employment with *The Hindu* I did not use the caste card like my grandmother would have wanted me to, but I do realise one's brahmin-ness is not necessarily or always inscribed on one's forehead or caste tag (which I did not bear). The advantages of being born in the 'right caste', I think, equally helped me with my other jobs, as also in other spheres in my life, sometimes without my even being aware of these advantages.

Since mid-2001, I have been working as the Chennai correspondent of *Outlook*—my first reporting job. Here, to my own surprise, I have had greater success in writing occasional analytical articles and news reports on brahmin hegemony[47] than in writing about the oppression against dalits. Again, my being a non-dalit, a born-brahmin has, I think, enabled me in several invisible ways. Caste functions for me 'not as an originary identity but as a social location that you cannot often exit.'[48] Perhaps this has partly enabled a tolerant reception to some views extremely critical of brahmins in a mainstream media forum. As for reporting on dalits, in this general climate of feel-good journalism, I have found it easier to bring attention to a few positive

---

[46] A 'punishment' transfer to Coimbatore came after I wrote a short piece called 'Self-respect and Nadaswaram' *(The New Indian Express,* 10 January 1999), which dealt with the marginalisation of the isai-vellalar caste in South Indian classical music and the domination by brahmins.

[47] See, for instance, 'Cauvery in a Puddle' (21 January 2002), which dealt with 'the total hijack of the South's rich classical arts into airless, Brahmins-only monopolies'; 'The Retreat of the Brahmin' (10 February 2003), which ahead of the 2003 World Cup examined why and how brahmins dominated the game of cricket; 'Shoonya Sum Game' (14 July 2003), which looked at how in a society dominated by brahmin casteism, scientific temper can be elusive; and 'Thyagraja's Cow' (8 September 2003), A report on brahmin Carnatic musicians' hypocrisy over opposing the proposed cow-slaughter ban despite being keen players of the *mridangam* made by dalit artisans which uses the hide of a slaughtered cow.

[48] As my friend Sharmila Sreekumar felicitously phrased it for me.

stories on dalits. But what we badly need today is dalit journalists; we need them as badly as we need journalists to learn to see and report caste that is all around us. Journalists can begin by looking inwards, as this letter-writer to *Outlook* suggested, following an article I did on brahmin domination in the game of cricket by giving the caste break-up of teams over the decades. He attempted a caste break-up of *Outlook*'s editorial team by scrolling down the names as they appeared in the imprint page of the magazine:

Vinod Mehta—non-brahmin—Gujarati
Sandipen Deb—brahmin—Bengali
Bishwadeep Moitra—brahmin—Bengali
Alam Srinivas—non-brahmin—Tamil
Ajaz Ashraf—Muslim
Ajith Pillai—non-brahmin—Malayali
Paromita Shastri—non-brahmin—UPite
Ranjit Bhushan—?
Koutik Biswas—non-brahmin—Bengali
Bhavdeep Kang—?
Arindam Mukherjee—brahmin—Bengali
Saba Bhowmik—Muslim—Bengali
Murali Krishnan—brahmin—Tamil
Sheela Reddy—non-brahmin—Andhraite
Soma Wadhwa—brahmin—Punjabi
Gauri Bhatia—brahmin—Sindhi
Pramil Phatarpekar—brahmin—Marathi

I could go on and on and *Outlook* has miles to go before it is truly 'national' as per S. Anand's definition. But S. Anand being a pervert, takes pleasure in such analysis.[49]

Interestingly, this letter was used only in the web edition of the magazine, and when I drew the attention of one of the senior editors to this response, he merely clarified that he and few others were not brahmin as was alleged by the letter-writer, that Vinod Mehta was not a Gujarati but a Punjabi, that there were spelling mistakes, and other factual errors. However, the

[49] Ketan Pandit, Mumbai (Bombay), India ('Daily Letters', 2 February 2003, www.outlookindia.com).

point Ketan Pandit (a brahmin?), was making was: if there are
no dalits in *Outlook*'s midst, and if it was filled with people of
'high' castes, how was it morally justified in carrying an article
that talked of the national cricket team being brahmin-dominated and hence described as not being truly national? *Outlook*,
and the rest of the media, owe Ketan Pandit an answer.

15

the relevance of the urdu-language media

m.h. lakdawala

e ven as a couple of newspapers are added every year to the already existing 2,844 Urdu newspapers in the country, the state of the Urdu press in the country is pathetic. Urdu-language papers are yet to come to terms with the modern needs of the common people.

A random survey revealed that Urdu readers believe that the standard of Urdu newspapers is deteriorating day by day, particularly in the Urdu-speaking belt. And the readership base is decreasing constantly as the number of people who read the language is also falling. The latest report by the Registrar of Newspapers for India (RNI) says that the Urdu press comprised 2,906 newspapers in 2001 as against 2,844 in 2000. [1]

Urdu is the fourth largest press in the country, after Hindi, English and Marathi. Among the dailies, with 534 newspapers, Urdu ranks second, next to Hindi. There are 21 weeklies, 377 fortnightlies, 533 monthlies and 72 quarterly journals. But these numbers cannot conceal the fact that the Urdu press is facing acute problems. The RNI also notes that the circulation of Urdu newspapers fell to 5.1 million copies in 2001 from about six million in 2000, a decline of about 900,000 copies. There are hardly 20–25 Indian newspapers with substantial circulation figures. Most of the papers are printed just to maintain records and to get advertisements.

The basic reason for the pathetic editorial quality is that Urdu newspapers hardly pay remuneration to the contributors.

---

[1] http://rni.nic.in/pii2002.html.

Second, Urdu is losing its popularity in Delhi, Uttar Pradesh and Bihar, which used to be the cultural centres of the language. The critical position of Urdu newspapers throughout the country was disclosed on 27 November 2000 in reply to a question raised in Parliament, according to which only 113 Urdu newspapers have been registered in the Directorate of Audio Visual Publicity panel for the year 2000–01. Earlier, around 500–600 Urdu newspapers used to be on the panel of this agency, which issues government advertisements.

The decline of Urdu journalism began in the 1980s, as the old Urdu-reading generation of Muslims in north India approached retirement age. Uttar Pradesh has lost its position as the stronghold of the Urdu language. The gradual phasing out of Urdu newspapers and journals serves as an index of the decline of Urdu in the state, which has 25 per cent of India's Muslim population. At least 103 Urdu dailies and newspapers have ceased publication during the last five years, while another 100 are on the verge of death. This has been quoted by National News and Features, which conducted a survey of the Urdu media recently.

The survey claimed that of the 300-odd Urdu periodicals in the state, only 100 have survived the vicissitudes of adverse circumstances after Partition. The newspapers that went out of circulation recently include Lucknow's *Qaumi Awaz, Azaim* and *As-Subah,* considered milestones in Urdu journalism, as well as Rampur's *Qaumi Jung* and *Elan,* Kanpur's *Mazdoor Vahini, Noor e Bareli* and *Dukhti Rug,* Gorakhpur's *Subhe Avadh,* Bahraich's *Ghazi,* Moradabad's *Aina e Alam* and *Moonis,* Aligarh's *Mashaal e Azadi* and *Sardar Times.* Most of them had to close down due to financial difficulties. Currently, Aligarh, Bahraich, Rampur, Azamgarh and Allahabad have no Urdu daily of their own.

The Uttar Pradesh government does not support the small newspapers, while in neighbouring Madhya Pradesh small newspapers begin receiving advertisement support after being on their own for some time. The survey estimates that the obituary list of Urdu journals will include 83 more journals within a couple of years if no method is devised to boost their economies and circulation.

The declining state of Urdu journalism can be gauged from the fact that *Shama*, a popular Urdu monthly for several decades, wound up in January 2002 after 60 years of continuous publication. Though primarily a film magazine, it catered to Urdu literary circles in north India and was successfully run by the Dehlavi family belonging to the Punjabi Muslim community in Delhi. It was at its zenith during the 1960s and 1970s.

Instead of taking up contemporary issues and conducting in-depth investigations, Urdu papers are pushing stereotypes. They just rake up old issues that are now non-issues and create a fear psychosis among the Muslim community. They are yet to open their minds and see the larger developments in the world.

Development is 'no story' in the Urdu media, obsessed with the three 'E's—Emotional stories, Encouraging stereotypes and Embellishing the traditional community leadership. Important development issues relating to the environment, population, health, empowerment of women and child rights do not feature well in the Urdu media. An analysis by this writer revealed some interesting facts about the issues covered in the Urdu press. A sample of six Urdu print publications showed that only 4.22 per cent of the total space was dedicated to development issues like environment, health, women and population.

Ironically, many Urdu journalists behave like preachers rather than as professional journalists. For many, Urdu journalism is more a mission than a profession. Most writers in the Urdu media are reinforcing stereotypes and raking in emotional stories. There is hardly any space given to innovative social experimentation, mainstream Muslim entrepreneurship, social reforms or highlighting the achievements of Muslim women.

Even non-controversial issues relating to religion or gender are rejected. This writer's feature on the issue of lack of proper space for Muslim women to offer prayers and the inadequate provision for them in mosques was rejected by almost all the top Urdu dailies; ultimately, it was carried by the English media.

Most mainstream publications regularly use the services of experts and do not hesitate to present different shades of opinion on the same subject. In Urdu journalism there is no space for experts and for those who do not first conform to the basic thoughts and stereotypes of the community.

no longer an agenda setter

In the past, the Urdu press was the agenda setter for the community. Even today, the Marathi, Bengali, Malayalam and Tamil media have a crucial role in shaping the agenda of the state or region. In contrast, the Urdu media have been reduced to expressing the opinions of a section of Muslims with little or no influence in the mainstream community.

Election time is the right time to gauge the impact of the Urdu media. There are hardly any Urdu newspapers or magazines which conduct a detailed study or research on the voting pattern of Muslims. The job is left to the non-Urdu media. Apart from supporting one group, individual or party, there is no inclination or felt need to conduct opinion polls within the community.

There are no innovative ideas or original stories even during the peak of the election season. Thus, in the beginning of 2004, even *Inquilab*, one of the largest selling Urdu dailies published from Mumbai and financially the strongest, suffered a decline in readership by 4,000, and this prompted the management to replace the editor.

It is true that earlier the Urdu press used to be the voice of the people, and important advertisements of the government as well as of private companies used to be published regularly. This provided high revenue to the Urdu press, which was eager to give first-hand news by appointing more people to work and adding valuable columns. But things have not remained the same and gradually the public has started losing interest in Urdu papers due to their stale news and poor quality.

While the editors blame the common people for the decreasing circulation in the Urdu press, the latter have an altogether different story to relate. As far as Urdu students are concerned, they opt for Urdu papers as Urdu is their mother tongue, and they are comfortable with this language. However, they feel that there is very little for them in the papers, as far as the educational and literary content is concerned.

So, given the economic compulsions of the day, people do not buy Urdu newspapers, as the news is stale. Whatever information is available in the Urdu papers is already published much earlier in the English dailies and broadcast on television. People therefore prefer to buy cheaper, yet better quality, English

papers, rather than expensive and inferior quality Urdu papers.
Today Urdu papers are read by the masses who only know Urdu.
There is no denying the fact that educated Urdu-speaking people
opt for English newspapers. Even people associated with the
language, like teachers, students, professors and poets, now
prefer other newspapers instead of Urdu for better quality of
news and views.

In terms of technology and innovation, it is the regional media that have taken the lead. Urdu media-owners have not kept
pace with technological changes and are not prepared to invest
in new technology. Owners of Urdu language papers also do not
spend much on news gathering. Very few papers have foreign
bureaux and most of the world news in Urdu papers is through
the lens of Western and other foreign agencies.

Except for a few papers, a large section of the Urdu media
does not accept emails. The reason cited is that personnel who
can download the messages are not available at all times. One of
my friends, who contributes to an Urdu daily in Mumbai, sends
his article every week to a colleague in a Marathi weekly, who
in turn downloads it and couriers it to the Urdu daily in question!

the poverty of the urdu media

Despite a general perception about the pervasiveness of the Urdu
media in ordinary Muslims' lives, the community suffers from
acute media poverty. This is part of, and yet distinct from, economic
poverty. Media poverty refers to the limited access to newspapers
and magazines due to low levels of literacy and education, as well
as low levels of access to TV owing to low purchasing power. The
culture of the community is not to purchase newspapers but to
borrow or share them. Even in Urdu-knowing, middle-class
households, the Urdu newspaper is a second choice, and hence
many a time is given a miss.

This is both a horizontal and vertical phenomenon. Rapid proliferation of the Urdu media in overall terms, notwithstanding
their comparative media poverty with respect to other communities, has led to hundreds of newspapers and magazines being
published in Urdu, despite low literacy levels. In turn, the average front page of a leading Urdu language newspaper features

as many as 15 to 20 headlines, with even more sub-headlines. Moreover, the subjects and their treatment in the Urdu media can be predicted with precision, as the same topics expressing the same emotions are written by the same writers for months together.

When reporting internal, regional and global conflicts, the Urdu papers often seem to become weapons of war rather than purveyors of peace. While being loyal to their readers and supportive of their community, they project stereotypes passionately as leaders and extremists. Only some Urdu papers and only some part of the media content, for example, editorials or analytical comments, resist the pressure to conform. When it comes to religious issues, most papers follow a rigid policy. Even analytical pieces by professional and competent persons are refused in the case of religious issues.

In comparative terms, in the print media, the Urdu press lags behind not only in its financial aspects, but also in terms of professional competence and qualified personnel. Since Urdu journalism is not a well-paying vocation, hardly any talented person joins it. While content and quality are always the crucial factors that command readership, there is a blatant and obvious asymmetry in the Urdu media vis-à-vis mainstream domination and this leads to media inequity.

Distance and disconnectedness are the very antithesis of media and information, because communication is supposed to bring people together, not keep them apart. Yet the Urdu media often reinforce isolation both between communities and within the community. One reason is that the vast majority access media content in their own respective mother tongues or regional languages. While content may be common between the media in different languages as, say, in reporting a major event, each language has its own psyche and its own area of perceptual demarcation. Even though they share many substantive elements, the reader of an Urdu newspaper in Mumbai and a reader of a Marathi newspaper in interior Maharashtra, are far away from each other, and not just geographically. Within the community as well, readerships of different languages remain entrapped in their own sub-worlds. The overwhelming preoccupation with community and religion also colours readers' perspectives on several issues. As professional journalists, Urdu journalists have still to learn to operate on a broader canvas and to be open to inquiry about the world around and outside of them.

As a visiting faculty teaching journalism, this writer has often observed that the students of Urdu journalism are so steeped in Muslim issues, that to separate those concerns from the 'secular' practice of journalism is tough. I quickly realised that besides teaching them the craft of journalism, my real challenge as a journalism educator was to broaden their world-view by introducing them to a palette of issues and concerns and to encourage them to be open-minded about things they did not know enough about. This meant helping them confront their biases and prejudices about the world outside their Muslim quarter and even to interrogate some of their own belief systems.

In stark contrast to the growing dominance and omnipresence of the media, even as media poverty persists, there is virtually no substantive attempt to promote Urdu media literacy and Urdu media education on a mass level other than in the restricted scope of university departments of journalism. Media literacy refers to the need to inform and educate children and youth, beginning at the primary and secondary levels, on the factors that shape media content, on aspects of media ownership and control and on how to analyse media content, so that citizens can refine their capacity to differentiate between subtle biases and imbalances and truly benefit from the media rather than be exploited by them.

There have been instances when the Urdu media have contributed to positive and constructive development of the community. In Maharashtra, a discernible shift in favour of education is seen in the last couple of years. The enrolment of Muslims not only at the primary and secondary levels, but also in vocational and professional courses, is increasing gradually. A slew of reasons are responsible for this development. For the last couple of years, Senior School Certificate results in Maharashtra show a number of Muslims, particularly Urdu medium students, in the merit list. The leading Urdu daily *Inquilab* has played a significant role in arousing awareness. The late Haroon Rashid, when he was Editor of *Inquilab*, brought about the cultural shift in favour of education. Unfortunately, others could not build on this initiative and lost the tempo.

The media have played a great role in bringing down communal violence in Hyderabad in the last 10 to 15 years. The basic reason for communalism among youths was lack of education and employment opportunities. The Urdu media had taken up the task of providing educational opportunities to the Muslim youth, besides ensuring them employment by publishing information about job opportunities in the Gulf.

Recently, after suffering a decline in readership, *Inquilab* started concentrating on development issues and this time the focus has been on hygiene and cleanliness in Muslim majority areas. Features on non-government organisations, groups and individuals who are working on these issues have been given importance and prominent space.

is revival possible?

With so many problems with the Urdu press, what are the remedies for its improvement? There should be a change in the whole infrastructure of the journalistic set-up, including remuneration for staff and expenditure on layout and photographs, to rescue the sagging image of the Urdu press. People would like to see once again the fearless Urdu press of the past. They feel that the Urdu press has to rise above petty interests and selfish motives and play an active role by not acting as a mouthpiece for different political parties.

The problems are many, but so are the solutions. At each level, right from the common man, it is the government that is blamed for this sorry state of affairs in the Urdu press. It is high time there is self-evaluation by the Urdu media in India, otherwise they will soon become extinct. Although, on the face of it, Urdu journalism looks like an unviable proposition, if media houses agree to a 360-degree about-turn in policy and a restructuring of content, revival is not only possible but can also be profitable.

Most Urdu papers are trying to sell their product without identifying the needs of readers or bothering to find out what they actually want. Moreover, the current readership profile is middle class and middle age oriented, and this could lead to a slow and painful death. For a revival of fortunes, the media bosses must plan for the future. What better way of securing the future of the Urdu media than to invest in selling the Urdu language to young people who are not all necessarily Muslim?

There can be several inexpensive ways of promoting the Urdu language. What is needed is highlighting the advantage of knowing Urdu for a career in the mass media, especially in Hindi cinema, theatre and advertising. Once the youth are convinced that learning to read and write Urdu will help them in their careers, they will take to the language in a big way.

Even within the framework of Urdu journalism, a lot can be done to improve content and presentation. Many Marathi, Bengali and Malayalam publications have large circulations mainly because they reflect on their respective societies and are harbingers of change. In contrast, Urdu papers resist changes and present those who innovate and try to bring in social reforms as anti-community. That is why the coverage given in the Urdu press to Muslim women is so low compared to papers in other languages. Because of the communication gap between mainstream journalists and those in the Muslim community, the projection of gender issues or social reforms leads to suspicion and misunderstanding amongst Muslims.

The Urdu media can end their isolation by becoming a bridge between the Muslim and mainstream media. The community can generate resources to promote Urdu journalism—provided the Urdu media bosses are willing to re-engineer their operations, change their thoughts and refine their outlook. Taking a leaf from the consistent promotional campaign by *The Indian Express* group, the Urdu media need to launch an aggressive campaign to attract new readers. The task is thus multidimensional. There is a tough road ahead, but one that is definitely not impossible to march on.

16

iron veils: reporting sub-conventional warfare in india

praveen swami

*a*fter visiting a house-of-horrors exhibition in the United States of America, Umberto Eco wrote:

> As a rule, there are mirrors, so on the right you see Dracula raising the lid of a tomb, and on the left your own face reflected next to Dracula's, while at times there is the glimmering image of the Ripper or of Jesus, duplicated by an astute play of corners, curves and perspective, until it is hard to realise which side is reality and which illusion.[1]

I have often used his *Faith in Fakes* to illustrate the challenges and perils of reporting conflict in India, mainly to show that the evidence of journalists' eyes is not always reliable. Most of Indian media's engagement with violence has not been largely conventional, despite the enormous journalistic outpouring generated by the Kargil war. Instead, the media each day negotiate their way through the exceptionally bloody sub-conventional conflicts that have raged through considerable parts of the country over the past several decades. These wars—fought in Punjab, Jammu and Kashmir, India's North–east, or zones hit by Maoist violence—have claimed far more lives than all of India's wars with its neighbours put together.

In this paper, I offer a sketch of some of the perils and challenges of reporting internal conflicts in India. The largest of

---

[1] Umberto Eco, *Faith in Fakes: Travels in HyperReality* (London: Pan Books, 1987), pp. 13–14.

these, of course, is that journalists die, often at the hands of regimes unenthusiastic about the truth being bared. In India's sub-conventional wars, however, this is not the main problem. I suggest here that the real challenges lie in the media's unwillingness to search for the truth and their surrender to coercion: the iron veils that obscure conflict from readers' eyes are largely of the media's own making.

the structure of information

States across the world seek to regulate the flow of information to journalists and to shape media output in ways that best serve the purposes of governments. While efforts at media control may be at their most intense during times of actual war, most low-intensity conflicts also generate information structures intended to further the objectives of the state.

Government organisations dealing with the media in conflict situations generally receive fairly lavish funding. In 1989–90, for example, the Northern Ireland Information Service, the British government department responsible for media management in the region, spent UK£ 7.238 million. Its Scottish counterpart, which served a population of five million people against a population of 1.5 million in Northern Ireland, spent just UK£ 1.4 million.[2] In essence, the job of the Northern Ireland Information Service was to legitimise the United Kingdom's war on the Irish Republican Army as a battle between the forces of order and development—the state—and the criminals opposed to civilisation.

India has no similar organisation. Perhaps the closest formal conflict-related public relations apparatus is the Directorate of Public Information within the Military Intelligence Directorate, known until recently as the Army Liaison Cell. Currently headed by an officer of the rank of Major General, the Directorate of Public Information arranges visits by journalists to forward military locations, provides off-the-record briefings, and organises

[2] David Miller, 'Northern Ireland Information Service and the Media', in John Eldridge (ed.), *Getting the Message: News Truth and Power* (New York and Abingdon, Oxford: Routledge), p. 74.

interviews with senior officials. At the time of writing, officials with public information roles are being appointed in Corps-level formations. Parallel to the public relations apparatus are the public relations officers of the Union Ministry of Defence, who issue press releases on regular military-related activities and also have powers to grant journalists access to the military establishment. There is no clear division of power between the Directorate of Public Information and the Ministry of Defence.

Several alternative sources of official information also exist. The Deputy Commissioners and Superintendents of Police for each district in India are entitled to speak to the media about events in their area of jurisdiction; however, they have no obligation to do so. In some areas, officials of the Border Security Force (BSF) and the Central Reserve Police Force (CRPF) are available for comment. Officials of the Intelligence Bureau, who deal with domestic intelligence, and those in the Research and Analysis Wing, who deal with external intelligence, have varying degrees of contact with the media. No formal parameters exist for such contacts, however, unlike the United States of America, where the Central Intelligence Agency (CIA) has structured dealings with the media. Some primary government data on the scale and intensity of violence is regularly published, notably in the annual reports of the Union Ministry of Home Affairs. A welter of independent sources of data has sprung up in recent years, including the South Asian Analysis Group and the South Asia Terrorism Portal.

Almost all organisations generating data on conflict scenarios have clearly defined interests. The job of the Directorate of Public Information, quite obviously, is to shield the Indian Army from negative publicity, and to put across its point of view. To expect bureaucracies to participate in providing disclosure on information, which may discredit or embarrass them, is wholly unrealistic. Relatively high levels of institutional transparency in the West have not led to the glare of light being focused on ongoing military campaigns in Iraq and Afghanistan. By contrast, harsh restrictions on battlefield access during the Kargil war did not stop Indian journalists from travelling in the region, and, where they were so inclined, from discovering several skeletons in the military establishment's closets. By September 1999, for example, news had also broken that months prior to the war, the disgraced commander of the 121 Brigade, Surinder Singh, had issued repeated warnings of large-scale infiltration into the sector, which his superiors chose to ignore.[3] The Army denied there had been any such warnings. Soon afterwards, the documents appeared in facsimile form, along with reports that Singh's superior, Major General V.S. Budhwar, had been busy at about the same time using his troops to hunt for wildlife to inhabit a zoo he was determined to build in Leh.[4]

While the media in general are sceptical about official data, and, perhaps, occasionally lazy about the unexciting task of dealing with it, these figures often provide interesting insights. The Union Ministry of Home Affairs own published data on violence in Jammu and Kashmir, for example, shows that only about a third of all terrorists killed there are foreigners, mainly of Pakistani origin. This debunks claims made by Indian politicians that over two-thirds of terrorists in Jammu and Kashmir are foreigners. Alternatively, the same data illustrates that Indian claims to have won a decisive military victory in the Kargil war must be read against the fact that violence in Jammu and Kashmir actually escalated after the conflict.[5] Analysts have also shown, based on Indian official data, that the massive Indian military build-up of 2001–02 failed to deter Pakistan from actually escalating cross-border terrorism–and thus, in effect, sacrificed lives for nothing.[6] In 2003, the Indian Army claimed to have scored major military gains against terrorist groups in Poonch, in the course of a 'shock-and-awe' offensive, Operation Sarp Vinash. Data obtained from the Jammu and Kashmir Police, and internal Army documents, showed that the Army had in fact killed fewer terrorists in Poonch during the Operation than in past years.[7]

[3] Nitin A. Gokhale and Ajith Pillai, 'The War that Should Never Have Been', *Outlook,* 6 September 1999. The official denial of this report was enabled by the fact that it incorrectly referred to a briefing note as a letter, a somewhat frivolous ground for objection.
[4] Praveen Swami, 'The Kargil Story', *Frontline,* 10 November 2000.
[5] Praveen Swami, 'Terrorism in Jammu and Kashmir in Theory and Practice', *The India Review,* 2(3), 2003, pp. 55–72.
[6] Aparna Pande, 'South Asia After 9/11', *Faultlines,* 15, pp. 84–86. Also see Praveen Swami, 'Terrorism in Jammu and Kashmir'.
[7] Praveen Swami, 'The Hype and the Folly', *Frontline* 20 (13), 2003, www.flonnet.com/fl2013/stories/20030704007300400.htm.

Despite the growing availability of testable primary data, the fact remains that there is no substitute for the classic skills of journalism: source cultivation, a sense of curiosity and an eye for what is actually going on. In this sense, reporting conflict is exactly like reporting anything else. It requires an understanding of the subject one is writing on, scepticism about claims made not only by the State but also its allies and opponents, and careful negotiation about claims and counter-claims made by participants. Journalists in conflict situations need to be acutely alive to the fact that all informants have potentially life-threatening stakes in what ends up in print or on television.

testing the truth: the case of chattisinghpora

While the system may be set up to deny information, a larger problem are that the media are not particularly good at understanding the material at hand. How this works in practice is illustrated by the media's handling of the massacre of 36 Sikh villagers at Chattisinghpora, a small village in southern Kashmir. Carried out on the eve of the 2001 Indian tour of the US President, Bill Clinton, the massacre offers interesting insights into just how thin on fact are media narratives of major events.

Chattisinghpora is particularly interesting because of the diametrically opposed ideological narratives it generated—narratives that were based heavily on conjecture and assumption, but devoid of actual evidence. One particularly influential media commentary came from the novelist Pankaj Mishra, whose assertion that the massacre was the outcome of an Indian covert operation gained wide currency in this country and abroad. Writing in *The Hindu,* Mishra—not known for any experience of reporting either on Jammu and Kashmir or on conflict situations in India—asserted that 'the number of atrocities in Kashmir is so high and the situation in general so murky that it is hard to get to the truth'. Mishra did not see fit to provide evidence for his assertion that the level of atrocities in Kashmir was high, or in comparison to what it was high. Nor did he explain just why the situation in the troubled state was murkier than that, say, in rural Bihar. Instead, the bald assertion was used, through a series of leaps of logic, to assert that the general situation 'lends weight to the suspicion ... that the massacre in Chittisinghpura [sic] was organised by Indian intelligence agencies in order to influence Clinton.'[8]

It is worth noting, in the first place, that Mishra's article nowhere suggests that he actually made an effort to gather any evidence in support of this claim. We remain uninformed of what official and non-official sources were consulted to arrive at the conclusion, or what effort was made to assess and weigh the evidence. Mishra's position, in fact, accurately reflected widespread rumours of that time in Jammu and Kashmir, elevated to the level of facts. Nevertheless, none of the proponents of the Indians-did-it theory actually claimed to be witness to the massacre, or to have any hard facts to support the allegation. Allegations based purely on the testimony of local residents, sometimes claiming to be eyewitnesses to an event, have constituted the leitmotif of reportage on Jammu and Kashmir. In general, careful investigation of several such incidents has given us cause to be sceptical of claims like uncontested eyewitness accounts.[9] Journalists rarely seem conscious of the multiple pressures that could be operating on informants in conflict zones, and of the multiple ways in which such pressures may shape their testimony. The 'ordinary villagers' who litter the pages of newspapers could be just that—but they could also be people with ideological convictions, half-baked information, the habit of spreading rumours or the lack of inclination to tell the truth.

At the outset of the Chattisinghpora investigation, the media seemed generally willing to accept the government position— for no better reason, it needs to be noted, than the one impelling those who accepted Mishra's position that the massacre was engineered by the Indian State. One thoughtful analysis of the

---

[8] Pankaj Mishra, 'Paradise Lost', The Hindu, 27 August 2000.
[9] Press Council of India, Crisis and Credibility: Report of the Press Council of India, January and July 1991, Lancer Paper IV (New Delhi: Lancer International, 1991). The Press Council found several contradictions of fact in eyewitness testimony offered by women who claimed to have been raped by soldiers in the village of Kunan Poshpora. My objective here is not to pass any judgment on the event itself, but to note the limited and well-proved fact that participant testimony is not always credible.

affair has noted that three newspapers reported the arrest of a suspect, Mohammad Yakub Wagay, in wholly distinct ways.[10] Wagay, the scholar Kanchan L. has noted, was described in *The Hindustan Times* as 'a local conduit' for terrorists who carried out the massacre, in *The Pioneer* as a Lashkar-e-Taiba operative, and in *The Asian Age* as 'the butcher of Anantnag'. All these descriptions, incredibly, were made as the outcome of a single press conference held by a senior bureaucrat—suggesting that while the media were generally accepting of the government position, they were less than faithful to its content and nuance. When Wagay was subsequently released, the media claimed the government case had collapsed—but made no effort to find out on what evidence the arrest had initially been based, or to even explore the possibility that the government had, in fact, failed to seriously investigate allegations made by victims' relatives.

Similar chaos was generated by the killing of five people, alleged to be terrorists possibly involved in the Chattisinghpora massacre, at Pathribal. Soon after, protests broke out in the region, with villagers claiming that the five were in fact local residents who had been killed in cold blood by the Indian Army. DNA tests were carried out, and after an evident attempt to tamper with the evidence, it was finally proved that the five were in fact south Kashmir residents. For much of the media, however, this appeared to decisively settle the case. Journalists seemed unable to comprehend the simple fact that the DNA tests only proved that the five individuals were in fact south Kashmir residents, and not the question of their innocence or guilt. Sloppy reportage—notably the claim that the police had carried out the killing, although the Army itself claimed responsibility for the encounter in official documents—further obfuscated the issue.[11] Most crucial of all, the larger political contestation between the National Conference and the Union Government, of which the DNA issue was just a small part, passed almost unnoticed. For the media, each new disclosure

---

[10] Kanchan L., 'Analysing Reportage from Theatres of Conflict', *Faultlines*, 8 (April), 2001, p. 43.
[11] Praveen Swami, 'In Search of the Truth', *Frontline*, 19 (12), 2002, www.frontlineonnet.com/fl1907/19070320.htm. Also see Praveen Swami, 'Questions over Action against Police Official in J&K' *The Hindu*, 14 August 2004.

was an irritating aside, not an organic part of the narrative itself. As such, the Pathribal affair illustrates a larger media problem with complex stories:

> The appearance of reports in a piecemeal fashion tends to create a bland and unquestioning acceptance of the narrative on the evolving scenario. The continuing nature of the incident— as also of the news cycle—necessitates an objective recapturing or reassessment of the incident in its entirety, but this rarely happens and the media continues sourcing for 'side-narratives' even as the original incident is pushed into the background by the succession of events .... [T]he Press never stops to sum up and reassess, but is forever pushing forward, grasping at the latest twists and turns, in the episodic succession.[12]

While the truth, as Eco warns us, is elusive, the media at some stage abandon the very search for it, replacing it with a Mishra-type fantasy, replacing journalistic first principles with surrender to fiction. In some senses, this is just a reiteration of the old truism that truth is a casualty of war. In this case, however, the death of truth is as much a consequence of media failure as of propaganda.

censored at gunpoint: the case of punjab

A larger problem underlying this failure, perhaps, is that the Indian media long surrendered their freedoms to the censorship of the Kalashnikov. Few within the media have examined the ways in which terrorist fiat has shaped the very terms through which discourse is conducted in the Indian media on security issues; it is as if this is a shame which may not be named. I will focus here on the impact of the Khalistan movement in Punjab on the media, and the lessons it holds out for the Indian press. The experience shows just how easy it is for non-state actors to skew the discourse on violence—and, sadly, how unwilling the Indian mainstream media have been to do battle in defence of their own freedoms.

***

[12] Kanchan L., 'Analysing Reportage from Theatres of Conflict', p. 46.

Although now almost airbrushed from our collective memory by an epic act of amnesia, the conflict in Punjab claimed 21,443 lives between 1981 and 1993. As contestation between Khalistan groups and the Indian state approached its climax in the late 1990s, the media themselves became a theatre for battle. One key episode pertained to demands by Khalistan groups that newspapers publish a letter written to India's President, R. Venkataraman, by Harjinder Singh 'Jinda' and Sukhjinder Singh 'Sukha.' Harjinder Singh and Sukhjinder Singh had been convicted for the 1986 assassination of General Arun Vaidya, a commander who had played a key role in the Indian state's initial offensive against Khalistan groups. Their 21-page letter explaining the reasons for their actions was despatched to major Punjab-based newspapers, most of which carried abridged versions on 27 July, 1990. One newspaper whose correspondent had received a direct threat to his life, the *Punjabi Tribune*, chose, however, to carry the entire text.

A subsequent investigation of the media in Punjab by the Press Council of India noted the impact the *Punjabi Tribune* decision had on other publications within *The Tribune* group, the state's largest media chain.[13] The investigation, conducted by Jamna Das Akhtar, K. Bikram Rao and B.G. Verghese on the instructions of the Press Council, concluded that:

> The differential treatment of the letter within *The Tribune* group brought an immediate threat to *The Tribune* (English) and the *Dainik Tribune* (Hindi) to comply. *The Tribune* accordingly carried the full text on 28 July, [but] not the *Dainik Tribune*. The Editor of the latter is thereupon said to have received a dire warning, and the paper carried the full Sukha–Jinda letters on 29 July with an abject apology.[14]

Much of the media had to pay the price for *The Tribune*'s editorial surrender. Soon, a gaggle of terrorist groups were issuing material for verbatim reproduction to media outlets, often accompanied by threats. Terrorist repression of the media escalated to a peak in November 1990, when terrorist groups

---

[13] Press Council of India, *Crisis and Credibility*.
[14] Ibid., p. 22.

fighting for the creation of a separate Sikh state, imposed a code
of conduct. The guidelines were issued by a Panthic Committee
led by Sohan Singh, a one-time government employee, who set
up the organisation in 1989 as an apex ideological council for
terrorist groups operating in Punjab. The Panthic Code mandated, among other things, that:

- The media cease to use words like terrorist, extremist or
  subversive.
- The prefix 'self-styled' be omitted from references to ranks
  of terrorist leaders.
- No reference be made to the fact that the Panthic Committee was Pakistan-based.
- The term Sant, or Saint, be prefixed before all references to
  the Sikh fundamentalist leader Jarnail Singh Bhindranwale.
- Journalists were to take the advice and direction of the local
  leadership of terrorist groups.
- 'Memorable punishment' would be meted out to those who
  defied the code.
- Journalists were to 'accept the creation of Khalistan'.

Several elements of this code are of course significant. Not the
least among these is the now-mainstream use of the word
'militant', a term historically used to describe left-wing political
radicals, for terrorists in the Indian media. Journalists who had
qualms about receiving orders on what words they could and
could not use were further tamed by the assassination of a director
of the state-run All India Radio, R.K. Talib, on 6 December 1990.
Only papers with a strong ideological persuasion defied the
Panthic Code. On the left of Punjab politics, the resistance came
from the Communist Party of India's *Nawan Zamana,* the
Communist Party of India (Marxist)-affiliated *Lok Lehar* and six
small newspapers supportive of various Maoist factions. On the
ideological right, the *Punjab Kesari,* run by the Hind Samachar
group, defied the Panthic Code. Editorial staff and proprietors of
Punjab Kesari faced repeated terrorist attacks, and the newspaper
eventually had to be distributed under police protection.[15] New
Delhi-based newspaper organisations with enormous financial

---

[15] K.P.S. Gill, 'Endgame in Punjab: 1988–1993', *Faultlines,* 1 (May), 1999, p. 72.

muscle and political influence, notably, displayed no such gumption.

After the collapse of independent print reportage on Khalistani violence, terrorist anger focused on the broadcast media, at the time exclusively State-owned. In May 1992, one terrorist group, the Babbar Khalsa International, killed All India Radio broadcaster R.L. Manchanda. After Manchanda's execution, the organisation issued a fresh 10-point code of conduct for the media, which demanded that women anchors cover their heads, prohibited the use of the term *atankvadi* or terrorist, and sought a phased end to all non-Punjabi-language broadcasting within the state.[16] Coercion, commentators have pointed out, was not the sole mode of terrorist relationships with the media. Although evidence of collusion with terrorism is hard to come by, one study of the period has pointed to the role of some journalists in collaborating with the drafting of the Panthic Codes.[17]

In Punjab, the state responded to terrorist pressure on the media by bringing its own legal and institutional coercive apparatus to bear. Copies of *The Tribune* carrying a Panthic Committee edict, listing officials who would be punished for failing to use Punjabi in all official communication, were seized by the Chandigarh administration on 2 February 1991. Similar action was taken in subsequent weeks against *The Indian Express, Ajit* and *Aaj di Awaz. The Tribune* responded by dropping the article in subsequent editions—and the Panthic Committee with a letter to Punjab newspaper editors threatening them with execution if they did 'nothing to resist' this censorship.[18] Some newspapers, notably *The Times of India*, also faced action under the controversial Terrorist and Disruptive Activities (Prevention) Act for carrying press releases issued by the Panthic Committee. In general, however, such legal action seems to have led to little; my research suggests no journalist was actually convicted for criminal offences under counter-terror laws. As the Editor of *Nawan Zamana* noted in his deposition to the Press Council of

---

[16] Ibid., p. 66.
[17] Ajai Sahni, 'Free Speech in an Age of Violence: The Challenge of Non-Governmental Suppression', *Faultlines*, 2 (August), 1999, p. 157.
[18] Press Council of India, *Crisis and Credibility,* p. 88.

India, the state's inability to respond to terrorist coercion of the media with counter-terror of its own set up the terms of media discourse in Punjab during its troubled decade of terror:

> The Press in the Punjab has been subjected to constraints both by the Government and the terrorists. Any objective assessment would show that the threat from the latter has been a continuous process of very serious dimensions. Those worthies, who, instead of standing up to the terrorists' threats have cowed before them, are much more vociferous against the government.[19]

None of this is, of course, surprising: bringing about such compliance is the purpose of censorship-by-Kalashnikov. As Kanchan L. has pointed out:

> ... acts of terrorism constitute a political statement and have a substantial political intent. Increased and intrusive media coverage is, at once, part of such intent, and itself becomes an element of the dynamics of its realisation, as it inevitably leads to a global focus on the theatre of conflict ....[20]

some conclusions

The Indian media are in the grip of a bizarre pathology, which leads them on the one hand to uncritically reproduce state narratives masquerading as 'objective' reportage, and on the other, to equally uncritical reportage on the state's adversaries, which is valorised as fearless criticism. Although a wealth of tools and information is available, which could lead to meaningful critical discourse on security issues in India, the media have failed their audience. We are told one week that infiltration in Jammu and Kashmir has increased, and that terror-training camps continue to operate across the border; the next that peace with Pakistan is around the corner. One set of reports informs us that the Army has crushed terrorism in Jammu and Kashmir; another

---

[19] Press Council of India, *Crisis and Credibility*, pp. 94–95.
[20] Kanchan L., 'Analysing Reportage From Theatres of Conflict', p. 54.

that it is in fact principally engaged in acts of terrorism directed at the civilian population. Most disturbing of all, theatres of violence are increasingly becoming little other than stages from which the heroic reporter may declaim—a representation which rests on ignoring the reality of the millions of people who live in these supposed battlefields, or of children who go to school there. In other words, India's conflict zones are being reduced to a spectacle.

Little surprise, then, that the Indian media no longer feel the need to sift the image of Jesus from that of the Ripper; to address themselves to the task of making distinctions, of informing and of subjecting claims to the test of reason. Real introspection is needed within the media community on these issues, but introspection must first be founded on the realisation that there is in fact a problem.

17

embedded journalists: lessons from the iraq war

shyam tekwani

*t*he Iraq War has generated as much controversy for the manner in which the media have covered the conflict (or been
manipulated into covering it) as for the flimsy premises on which
the conflict was based in the first place. The recent conflict has
introduced a new word into the lexicon of journalism and has in
all likelihood changed conflict reporting forever. 'Embedding' as
a catch-phrase may be a new addition to media jargon, but as a
concept it is one of the oldest in journalism. The first conflict
reporters ever were 'embedded' journalists.

The first news reports carried in newspapers on wars consisted
of 'reports' sent by active soldiers to editors in the form of letters
and dispatches from the front. Lieutenant Charles Nasmyth of
the East India Company's Bombay Artillery was enlisted by *The
Times* to write on the Crimean War. This recruitment of junior
officers to write from the battlefront was a practice followed by
British editors until the Crimean War. But the process was a
very erratic and often frustrating one for editors who often had to
wait until a battle was over to get their reports, if at all. In 1954,
William Russell accompanied British troops to Gallipoli. Russell's
reports from the front so enraged British officialdom that he was
severely discouraged by the military, who tried to shake him off
by making life very hard for him on the field. He was not given
any rations or assistance, often forced to pitch camp outside military lines. But Russell held on despite the hardships and filed the
dispatches that were to make him famous.[1]

---

[1] Phillip Knightley, *The First Casualty* (New York: Andre Deutsch, 1975). See
Chapter 1 for a detailed account of Russell's career and the early years of war
correspondents. The book is also a useful resource for a history of war reporting.

While subsequent analysis found many shortcomings in
Russell's reportage, it was clear that his work had changed the
way in which wars would be reported. It brought home to the
politicians and the generals the fact that wars were no longer
the exclusive concern of governments but that the public would
and should have a say in the conduct of war.[2]

The Crimean War was also the first war to be covered in
depth photographically.[3] Roger Fenton was the first embedded
photojournalist and in him, perhaps, the modern-day Pentagon
saw their ideal. Fenton was sent to the war to take pictures
showing the excellent conditions under which the British troops
lived and fought and to portray their successes. Fenton's photographs were to be used in Britain as propaganda. While Fenton
did his share of propaganda, even he could not help taking pictures that portrayed the brutality of war.

Subsequent conflict, right up to Vietnam, saw the emergence
of war reporting as a specialised form of journalism and has
since thrown up some outstanding reporters and photographers
and substantial work on the subject. With every war, correspondents and photographers have adapted and emerged with newer,
more formalised strategies, contracts and specialised equipment
for the coverage of war. Alongside, governments have also
learned their lessons and experimented with various forms of
control, from outright censorship, denial and partial to total media
control. As media organisations have become more efficient in
the collection and dissemination of news from the front with the
modernisation of communications equipment, from the staid
telegraph to the dynamic and instantaneous satellite phone,
governments have become more sophisticated in their efforts to
manipulate media coverage.

Since Russell, hundreds of correspondents have travelled with
military divisions and battalions covering the war first-hand. They
travelled with a particular unit or battalion out of choice, in an
informal arrangement made on the field by the correspondent
and the unit members, usually for an unspecified duration. The
journalist was an 'independent', not affiliated to the unit in any
way and not contractually obliged to the unit, or to the military.

[2] Ibid.
[3] Peter Howe, *Shooting Under Fire: The World of the War Photographer*
(New York: Artisan, 2002).

But with the Iraq War the US government, clearly unwilling to repeat the mistakes of past governments in allowing unrestricted access to the battlefront, formalised the policy of 'embedment', literally handpicking assignments for journalists and assigning them to units. The US military's rationale for embedding media within its military units is as follows:

> We need to tell the factual story—good or bad—before others seed the media with disinformation and distortions, as they most certainly will continue to do. *Our people in the field need to tell our story*—only commanders can ensure the media get to the story alongside the troops. We must organize for and facilitate access of national and international media to our forces, including those forces engaged in ground operations, with the goal of doing so right from the start. To accomplish this, we will embed media with our units. These embedded media will live, work and travel as part of the units with which they are embedded to facilitate maximum, in-depth coverage of U.S. forces in combat and related operations. Commanders and public affairs officers must work together to balance with the need for operational security.[4]

Clearly, the US government had done its homework on conflict reporting. The Vietnam War, one of the most defining experiences in US history and a fertile breeding ground for the careers of many war correspondents, left an indelible mark on the way wars were to be covered in the future. Hundreds of correspondents from the US alone and more from the rest of the world were allowed unprecedented access to the battlefront in Vietnam, after the merest of formal procedure required to avail of the MACV (accreditation by the Military Assistance Command, Vietnam) card. The result was an abundance of coverage, and a plethora of images at the end of which no one was the wiser about the big picture of the Vietnam War. Phillip Knightley, author of *The First Casualty,* cites a Gallup poll done in mid-1967, which revealed that half of all Americans had no idea what the war in Vietnam was about.[5]

---

[4] Extract from US Defense communication, 101900Z, February 2003.
[5] Phillip Knightley, *The First Casualty.*

Although the general impression is that the US government had a hard time containing media reporting unfavourable to it in Vietnam, the government could claim many successes in its manipulation of the media even during the Vietnam War. Despite the vast numbers of US and other international correspondents roaming about the Vietnamese countryside, the US government was still able to mislead the media and lie about its massive bombing campaign inside supposedly neutral Cambodia and parts of Vietnam and Laos in 1969–70. US media were still sceptical about the genuineness of the My Lai massacre story when it emerged and it took nearly a year from the time the first reports emerged, for full-fledged coverage of the incident.

In the case of Iraq, the US military was very clear about its intentions. 'Our people in the field need to tell our story'. The purpose of embedding from the point of view of the US government was unambiguous. Less clear is how embedment panned out in practice.

Months before the current conflict in Iraq began, Knightley was quoted on BBC as saying that Gulf War II would mean the demise of the war correspondent 'as an objective, independent person trying to find out what is going on'.[6] Knightley was discussing the proposed embedding plan. Sydney Schanberg, former correspondent for *The New York Times*, whose work in Vietnam and Cambodia was featured in 'Killing Fields', on reviewing the Pentagon's guidelines for embedding journalists, recommended that editors opt for few embeds and would be better off letting their best reporters work independently of the embedding process.[7] Of course, not many followed his advice. In all about 600 correspondents participated in the 'embedded' programme in Iraq, including nearly all the major American and British newspapers and broadcast networks. Additionally, there were nearly 1,500 independent or 'unilateral' reporters. And besides the still missing 'Weapons of Mass Destruction', embedding was the biggest event of the Iraq War.

---

[6] Chris Jones, 'Peter Arnett: Under Fire', BBC News, 4 April 2003, news.bbc.co.uk/1/hi/in_depth/uk/ 2000/newsmakers/2917635.stm.
[7] In an interview with the editor and publisher, quoted by Peter Barrett. See 'US Reporters Condemn Pentagon Press Controls', *The Guardian*, 27 February 2003.

Now that hostilities are well underway (despite George Bush's claims that the war is over) and embedded reports have made it to the nightly news and the morning headlines, the debate on embedding is raging elsewhere.

While at first glance embedding seems to offer unprecedented freedom to report facts from the front, closer scrutiny reveals the opposite. Embedded reporters have to sign a contract with the military and are governed by a Pentagon document that lists what they can and cannot report. The list of what they can report is considerably shorter than the list of what they cannot report.[8] Among the clauses in the policy that concerned many in the journalism establishment is one that states that where the military allows reporters access to sensitive information (undefined) reporters must agree to a security review of their coverage and if such a review is not agreed to, then access to that information may be denied. Similarly, somewhere else the document states that reporters exposed to sensitive information should be briefed on what they should avoid covering. Most of all, the document requires that all interviews with soldiers and military staff should be 'on record', which in effect would prevent most of them from speaking freely to the media. Such requirements led many journalists including BBC's John Simpson to opt for covering the war independently of the embedding plan.

Despite such criticisms, embedding as a military tactic in public relations and media control was an unequivocal success. As a tool for war correspondents and photographers, its impact is less clear.

What embedding did to the coverage of the Iraq War was that it brought to television viewers, in particular, a sense of immediacy, a visceral reality, a feeling that one is at the very centre of a war, on the front, where one can hear the sounds and see the sights and actually gain a sense of what war is like where it is being fought. This sense of immediacy brings an element of reality into the coverage of war that was lacking in earlier war coverage. Embedding in the Iraq War brought home to many the actual nitty-gritty of waging a war. It got viewers an up-close look at the technology of modern warfare, and its hard-

---

[8] David Miller, 'Embed with the Military', in Danny Schechter (ed.), *Embedded: Weapons of Mass Deception* (New York: Prometheus Books, 2003), pp. 84–87.

ships. Embedment also enabled focus on the soldiers on the front, their fears and fancies, the dangers they face and shifts in their morale. Earlier war correspondents from the days of Russell wrote on the hardships of the foot soldier, the lack of equipment and the daily hardships in poor weather and depressing conditions, and did so despite being severely discouraged by the top brass. Embedded journalists, and through them their audience, got a first-hand look at how modern warfare is waged by the world's most dominant military force. But this very process of getting so close to a subject is fraught with risk for journalistic objectivity.

An editorial on embedding in the *Cornell Daily Sun* argues that:

> Placing a journalist alongside his subject in a potentially deadly situation can severely limit objectivity. One of the primary goals of journalism is to effectively eliminate the importance of authorship. That is to say, the journalist's opinions should not interfere with the transmission of information regarding an event. But it would be unreasonable to expect a journalist to act so staunchly and emotionlessly in what is potentially a life or death situation.[9]

The result of such proximity of author to subject resulted in what many termed a very one-sided version of the war, an Anglo-American one. A French journalist, Philippe Rochot, covering the war for French television, went so far as to describe embedded journalists as 'soldiers of information': 'They are soldiers of information, marching with the troops and the political direction of their country. They won't say anything wrong; they feel duty-bound to defend the Anglo-American cause in this war.'[10]

Rochot's viewpoint is an extreme one, not shared by most people, at least not publicly. But generally many regarded embedment as a useful tool in covering the war. While it is patently obvious that embedment gives the military more control

---

[9] Editorial, 'Embedded Journalists Cannot be Objective', *Cornell Daily Sun*, 3 April 2003.

[10] Philippe Rochot, *France 2*, quoted during Interception, *France Inter*, 30 March 2003.

over what is reported, it also provides journalists reporting from the front a greater degree of protection. Strategically speaking, embedment is a very useful device for journalists to get up close and gain personal access to soldiers and the war front. And there is no better and safer way to do this than with the support of the military machinery. After all—correspondents and photographers died covering the Vietnam War, and the only journalists who died covering the Iraq War were the so called 'unilaterals' operating independently, outside the army ambit, some killed by coalition forces themselves.

But embedment as a device to access and provide consumers of news with a true and complete picture of the conflict can only be possible if embedding were to be carried out in conjunction with independent reporting from other news sources. Major international news organisations had, besides embedded reporters, correspondents spread out across Iraq and other crucial centres in the Middle East, besides having their correspondents in London and Washington to ensure a more contextual and complete coverage of the war. Such nuanced coverage was possible only for large news organisations with the resources to have correspondents spread out far and wide, contributing along with embedded reporters to a wider pool of information. Less resourceful organisations had to rely on embedded reporters to provide a very one-sided, subjective coverage of the conflict. The alternative was to attempt to cover the war outside the army ambit, as independent journalists or 'unilaterals', an experience many journalists found fraught with hardships, mostly created by Coalition forces.

A CBC reporter had the following to say on the experience of being 'un-embedded':

What I didn't expect … is that embedded journalists would be given exclusive access to the war, leaving the rest of us shut out of the battlefield, …. By keeping 'unilateral' journalists out of Iraq, the Americans have succeeded in reducing independent reporting of the war, and I believe that was exactly their plan from the beginning.[11]

---

[11] Paul Workman, 'Embedded Journalists versus "Unilateral" Reporters', *CBC News Online,* 7 April 2003.

The Guardian drew attention to the creation, by the Coalition Forces, of a 'caste system' of journalists, giving preference to embedded journalists and freezing out reporters from organisations who chose to operate independently. The European Broadcasting Union's secretary general charged the central command of actively restricting independent news gathering from parts of Iraq. The EUB's Head of News, Tony Naets, went on record to say that the Coalition forces were giving preferential treatment to embedded journalists from countries of the coalition, shutting out unilaterals.[12] Throughout the conflict independents and unilaterals were detained by soldiers and forcibly returned to Kuwait, allowing embedded journalists and the organisations they represented to have access that they were denied. Many independent reporters lost their lives in Iraq, a number of them victims of 'friendly fire' by US forces, leading to the belief among independent reporters that embedding was the only safe option—a view that is reinforced by the Pentagon, which holds that the battlefield is no place for unauthorised journalists (read un-embedded ones). British Defence secretary, Geoffrey Hoon, in commenting on the death of an ITN crew member (an independent), said the death occurred 'because he was not part of a military organization'.[13] The protection thus offered to embedded reporters by the military can in fact be interpreted as a threat to independent journalists rather than as a reassurance for embedded journalists. Says David Miller: 'The message is clear: stay embedded and report what you are told or face the consequences.'[14] While most of the criticism of the embed process has come from British media (within the coalition) and other international media, there have been—to their credit—some damning remarks on the Pentagon's media manipulation even among American journalists. CNN's Christiane Amanpour said in a talk show on CNBC that CNN had been 'intimidated' by the White House. She rephrased David Miller's words more brutally, describing the military's embedding manipulations as a case of either 'play by the rules or f*** off'.[15] Clearly George

---

[12] Ciar Byrne, 'Independents "Frozen Out" by Armed Forces', *The Guardian*, 3 April 2003.

[13] Quoted in David Miller, 'Embed with the Military', pp. 84–87.

[14] Ibid., p. 87.

[15] Christiane Amanpour, quoted in John Plunkett, 'CNN Star Reporter Attacks War Coverage', *The Guardian*, 16 September 2003.

Bush meant every word when he warned the world 'either you're with us or against us' in the build-up to the war.

Sifting through news reports and the experiences of unilaterals from across the world, it would appear that in Iraq, while the system of embedding seemed to have worked for British and American journalists, reporters from countries that did not support the US and British-led war on Iraq appeared to have been at a disadvantage in covering the conflict. 'There was a feeling that this was a war where if your government was not actually fighting on the side of the Americans, or not helping the coalition, then you as a journalist were not really welcome at the war,' said Stewart Purvis, the former chief executive of ITN.[16] Arnim Stauth, a correspondent for the German TV station WDR, had this to say on the subject: 'We were not welcomed. Clearly journalists were either privileged or discriminated against depending on the stance their governments took towards the war.'[17]

The Chicago Tribune, in a scathing article on the manner in which the American cable network Fox News covered the war in a unabashedly pro-American fashion, concedes that every US TV network had shown a pro-American bias by 'taking most of what the Pentagon says at face value and doing nothing to hide embedded reporters' sense of identification with their military units'.[18] Surely this is a big part of what the creators of the embedding policy had in mind. And this is where homework shows. 'Scratch a good journalist and one is likely to find a vicarious adventurer who seeks to be at the scene of the action telling the Big Story,' says media scholar Lance Bennet, criticising the manner in which media organisations leapt at the invitation to 'embedding', believing it to be a ticket to the 'real' picture. Bennet goes on to say that the 'Big Story was dictated from Washington, and the scenes from inside the tanks were little more than B-movie fillers that authenticated a story told by the government'.[19]

---

[16] Ciar Byrne, 'Media Guardian *BBC* was "Distrustful" of Embedding', 22 October 2003.

[17] Ibid.

[18] Steve Johnson, 'How Fox is Winning the War', *Chicago Tribune,* 4 April 2003.

[19] Lance Bennet, *The Perfect Storm: The American Media and Iraq Political Communication Report*, www.opendemocracy.net, 28 August 2003.

But despite the brutal criticisms of the embedment policy and the scathing indictment of the jingoism of American networks, embedment as a small part of the big picture has a role to play in war coverage. It offers a slice of life as it were, a slice of war, a peek into the soldier's world, a close-up look at the battlefront. But to work, from a news organisation's point of view, or more importantly from the point of view of balanced news coverage, an embedded journalist's work needs to be contextualised by reporting from a variety of more objective sources. In any case, it is highly likely that embedding has come to stay, and will be a part of future media coverage of military operations in conflicts around the world. And when the novelty of being part of a military operation as an 'embed' wears off, and the practice is, with the advantage of hindsight, put into proper perspective, and relegated to its proper place in the range of war reporting that comprises competent coverage, embedding may well turn out to be more of an asset for viewers and reporters than for governments and militaries.

The Iraq War has not really tested the practice of embedding. This was a relatively brief conflict, with little formal opposition to the troops that had embedded reporters on board. In a more protracted conflict, where things may not be going so well for the military, the embedment policy may be under more pressure. Soldiers may be under more pressure and reporters can have access to more than just the adrenaline-thumping excitement of the brief forays into battle as in Iraq. In, all, about 600 correspondents participated in the 'embedded' programme in Iraq, including nearly all major American and British newspapers and broadcast networks. Additionally, there were nearly 1,500 independent or 'unilateral' reporters. Such huge numbers of correspondents and photographers in a conflict zone during a tough and extended war might have brought about an entirely different perspective both on the war itself and on the practice of embedment. In such a conflict embedding might actually work in favour of more factual, more nuanced reporting, rather than towards producing a well-packaged Pentagon action documentary on conflict the coalition way, as has generally been the case in Iraq.

230 Practising Journalism

In the words of BBC's Washington Bureau Chief in a radio discussion on embedding and the coverage of the Iraq War:

> ... Was the citizenry well informed? Well, I think they certainly had a selection of impressions, a wide range of media that they could go to, but I think they had to do a lot of work on their own to get an accurate impression about what was going on.[20]

And work they did. As the American networks patriotically went to war alongside their troops, vast numbers of Americans seeking more balanced reportage flocked to UK news websites. Traffic to the BBC News site from the US increased by 47 per cent in the week following the outbreak of war, while the number of visitors to *The Guardian* website from the US jumped by 83 per cent.[21] If Americans were flocking in such large numbers to non-US sources for a less biased picture of what was happening in Iraq, it hardly bears mention that people across the world, anti the American position on Iraq or otherwise, were even less likely to rely on CNN (which had cornered the market on the first Gulf War in the absence of competition) and its ilk for real news.

Former *Wall Street Journal* White House correspondent and TV commentator Ellen Hume summed it up when she said: 'If you have embedded journalists, there's a reality quotient there. But it's not the meaning quotient, and it's not the entire reality.' She chose to describe embedded journalists as 'really just an arm of technology; they're giving us eyes and ears'.[22]

[20] Martin Turner, Washington Bureau Chief, BBC, Panel discussion on *Embedded Journalists: Is Truth the First Casualty of War?*
[21] Owen Gibson, 'US turns to British News', *The Guardian,* 12 May 2003.
[22] Keming Kuo, 'Iraq War's Embedded Journalists', *Iraq Crisis Bulletin,* 2 April 2003.

18

mainstream indian media: 1990s and after

bindu bhaskar

*a*re these the best of times or the worst of times for the Indian media? The Great Indian Middle Class is on a roll. Foreign media, flush with funds, have found outlets to grow. Across all platforms—print, television, radio and the Internet—there's a wave. Yet the colour of money, the pulse of circulation, the metaphor of the market that propel the profession into the twenty-first century also appear to lull its sense and sensibilities. The signals cannot be missed a decade after the Age of Liberalisation dawned on an unsuspecting nation. A corporate media-led numbing of the Indian mind is taking place.

The 1990s flirted with the sanctity of the edit page, created clutter around the masthead, witnessed a day when an upstart dotcom's advertisement could eclipse the front-page news, discovered that celebrity stalking or party hopping was more chic than civic issues and that the commodification of news could be lucrative business.

The delinking of radio and television from state control unleashed the genie of privatisation. Broadcast channels—regional, national and international—proliferated, driving the news as entertainment phenomenon into urban drawing rooms. India was the new hub and upwardly mobile television watchers dictated the flow of advertising revenue.

A seemingly staid print media competed by capitulating to colour, gloss and glamour. There were the conscientious objectors, but they too had to succumb, after a fashion, to the gung-ho mood in the market. According to the *Future of the Print Media*, a 2001 publication of the Press Council of India, one-third of the total advertising revenue of newspapers comes from foreign companies. Unlike two decades ago, when the government provided one-sixth of the revenue, it now accounts for barely 5 per cent. Small, medium and single edition publications are most hit, but who notices? Other, more glitzy brand names are established and the grand old media empires reinvent themselves to meet the demands of the changing times.

The combination of capital, technology and competition has certainly injected a degree of professionalism, perhaps even in unlikely places and among unlikely people. The compulsions of the market must be understood in tandem with the overriding importance of editorial freedoms. There is a constitutional sanction for individual freedom of expression, and it is not merely an occupational hazard if journalism loses it.

Far beyond the implications of economics, globalisation poses cultural challenges, manifest through the satellite television era of the 1990s or the FM bandwagon of the 2000s or the arrival of trendy software that allows form to manipulate content with a tap of a finger. Marketers redesign news agendas to suit rapid living. The public mindset is rewired almost instantly. The dangers go beyond the promotion of a culture of passive homogeneity that Western media scholars have warned against. There is a serious dilution of the media's critical-adversarial function as expounded by Chomsky–Herman[1] in an examination of the American media.

Unlike in the West, where the mainstream, alternative, specialist, tabloid, commercial broadcast, public service broadcast, instant, mobile and long-form magazine journalisms function within articulated definitions and spaces, recent media history in India suggests an identity crisis and fuzzy logic, with no offence to computers. At a critical juncture in the Information Age, when the future shocks the present into submission, and technology expands possibilities, Media India also dared to enter the brave new world.

A successful transition into the era of 24-hours news channels has been such a heady ride that there has been no attempt, certainly within the media, to pause or reflect. It was not as if

---

[1] Edward S. Herman and Noam Chomsky, *Manufacturing Consent: The Political Economy of the Mass Media* (New York: Pantheon Books, 1988).

the Indian media *in toto* traded sensitivity for sensation, but that they found a way to compartmentalise complexity into a time slot.

Breathless anchors feed anxious audiences a daily cocktail. Even development issues become a capsule to be swallowed at the end of a bulletin, an item that appears off and on to salvage the conscience. Newspapers, once clearly nationalistic in tone, comfortably stepped into well-heeled, self-promoting metropolitania. In fact, perspectives are increasingly shaped by a narrower set of urban, upper-caste and upper-crust parameters. The question is: Can the media afford to be exclusive instead of inclusive and must the elite and the intelligentsia give up their critical stake in shaping an egalitarian society?

The preference theory of allowing the readers/viewers to choose what they want has its advocates, but every reader/viewer is either an informed/uninformed, sensitised/unsensitised or wakened/unawakened citizen depending on how open, free and representative news and information channels are. Media organisations have branched into new specialisations and earmarked pages and programmes to accommodate diversity; but are they improving their depth of coverage, investigative and campaigning strengths, setting up research bureaus across multiple disciplines and encouraging out-of-the-box lateral thinking for creative change?

Mechanical coverage of events or studio-based polemics cannot substitute for context or background. Understanding the process behind the news requires incisive, analytical and time-consuming pursuits, but who will foot the bill? A production-controlled and management-driven media environment is calling the shots and forcing most players (read journalists) to fall in line. Willing individuals can still be found but the institutional support is missing and the documentary space is shrinking.

Locating development issues on a platter of subject choices, from politics to cinema, poses a dilemma. Before the idea of development becomes a lofty notion that journalism once knew, there is a need to nurture it, not merely as tokenism, but to revitalise it in form and character. It needs to break free from the prescriptions of format. The failure to construct an institutional process within the mainstream media will throttle the catalysis for change and diminish journalism's sense of purpose.

As C. P. Scott, Founder-Editor of *The Manchester Guardian*
proclaimed nearly 150 years ago:

Fundamentally, journalism implies honesty, cleanness,
courage, fairness and a sense of duty to the reader and the
community. The newspaper is of necessity something of a
monopoly and its first duty is to shun the temptations of a
monopoly. Its primary office is the gathering of news. At the
peril of its soul it must see that the supply is not tainted.
Neither in what it gives nor in what it does not give, nor in
the mode of presentation must the unclouded face of truth
suffer wrong.[2]

Public opinion, media content and the actions of government
interact in complex and uncertain ways. In a democracy, the task
of confrontation, when the executive, legislature and the judiciary fail to check each other, rests with the media. But journalism itself appears to be in a make-over mode because of shifting
priorities within the larger media complex and the self-indulgent,
possibly petulant, mood in the practising professional circuit.

Every Indian is a curious amalgam of distinct identities, each
coexisting with another without any palpable danger of extinction.
If anything, the divisions are getting sharper. Scratch the veneer
of educated sophistication that the elite possess and out will
tumble the disdain and discomfort relating to the Other India.
In the absence of a clear-cut geographical divide, the paradoxical
nations-within-nation idea continues to flourish within undefined
borders and boundaries. For a long time, many educated Indians
self-consciously admitted the existence of a Bharat within India.
Both sides have powerful proponents, but who dominates the
media space?

As journalism draws its numbers from the educated elite, all
discomforts extend to the media. The us-and-them divide, as
demonstrated in recent trends in the choice and packaging of
content, helps boost circulation and viewership but it cannot
shape the nation or society. Many segments of the media seem
content to abdicate their role in moulding the political and social

---

[2] Quoted in Rangaswamy Parthasarathy, *Journalism in India: From the
Earliest Times to the Present Day* (New Delhi: Sterling Publications, 1989).

consciousness or, more unfortunately, understand the nation in narrow patriotic terms.

Before the nation was invented in 1947, newspapers were instruments of dramatic and radical political and social change. No freedom fighter worth his or her salt underestimated the power of words. 'I want you to look upon journalism as an art and not an industry. Journalists are like poets and painters rather than factory workers. They are really creating works of art', C. Rajagopalachari, the last Governor-General of India, informed a gathering of journalists.[3]

India has an impressive record of an intrepid press in shaping ideas of nationalism and stabilising a nation-in-the-making through tumultous phases, responding to domestic challenges posed by authoritarian, corrupt or anti-social practices. But why, then, must it undermine its agenda-building function when unfinished agendas remain?

India has the largest number of poor people on the planet. India also has the greatest concentration of rural households that are totally landless—60 million households. Landlessness and rural poverty are closely linked. In fact, a recent World Bank report showed that landlessness is by far the greatest predicator of poverty in India—even more so than caste or illiteracy.

Development journalism gained international currency over the decades, but its growth and impact in specific regional contexts, particularly in India, appears uneven and limited, despite relentless efforts by a committed band of practitioners. One real problem is that the band is too small and scattered. Voices that speak for the oppressed resonate through the mainstream media too randomly in an era when their relevance should have magnified, given the sharp inequalities shaping the multinational and intra-national world.

At a time when there seems to be just that odd and occasional introspection within the profession, it is relevant that commentators outside, particularly in academia, have made poignant statements about the media's social significance. Nobel laureate Amartya Sen has discussed the remarkable fact that

---

[3] Quoted in Parthasarathy, *Journalism in India*.

no substantial famine has ever occurred in any independent and democratic country with a relatively free press. Sen, who witnessed as a child the country's last famine in 1943, four years before Independence, lists multiparty democracy, facing elections and criticisms from opposition parties and independent newspapers as critical factors that led to the elimination of famines.

Citing a comparative example, he points out:

China, although it was in many ways doing much better economically than India, still managed (unlike India) to have a famine, indeed the largest recorded famine in world history: Nearly 30 million people died in the famine of 1958–61, while faulty governmental policies remained uncorrected for three full years. The policies went uncriticized because there were no opposition parties in parliament, no free press, and no multiparty elections. Indeed, it is precisely this lack of challenge that allowed the deeply defective policies to continue even though they were killing millions each year. The same can be said about the world's two contemporary famines, occurring right now in North Korea and Sudan.[4]

A more recent example comes from Sen's collaborator Jean Drèze, who shows how lack of media involvement can deflect attention from real issues. In a recent interview to an alternative Internet journal, indiatogether.org, he says that media interest in the drought nearly died out after abundant rains in late August and September 2002, creating an impression that the drought was over. Meanwhile, however, there had been massive crop failures in many areas, especially but not only in Rajasthan. The revised economic estimates published in the *Economic Survey*[5] brought out the seriousness of the drought. He anticipated a revival of media interest a couple of months later, when the stage would be set for 'harrowing pictures of dead cows, emaciated children and famished labourers'.

Drèze points out that lack of media concern for hunger and related issues makes it that much easier for the state to get

---

[4] Amartya Sen, 'Democracy as a Univeral Value' *Journal of Democracy*, 10(3), 1999, pp. 3–17.

[5] Ministry of Finance, *Economic Survey 2003–2004* (New Delhi: GOI).

away with doing nothing. He mentions the striking case of the neglect of health matters in the media as well as in public policy:

India's infant mortality rate has virtually stagnated during the last five years or so, yet the problem is barely discussed, let alone addressed. In fact, it has gone virtually unnoticed. This is a matter of supreme importance for the nation, but somehow it escapes the policy-making elite. Media interest in this matter could certainly be fostered through skilful activism, and this would make it harder for the government to ignore the problem. As things stand, however, a deafening silence surrounds the whole issue.[6]

The critique from outside, which is yet to percolate into the mainstream, drives home the truth about the media's influence, even though most owners themselves perhaps do not need to capitalise on this constituency. During a convocation address at the Asian College of Journalism in the summer of 2002, Prabhat Patnaik, Director of the School for Social Sciences, Jawaharlal Nehru University, Delhi, captured the public perception of the media's role thus:

The very fact, however, that the media do take humane and democratic positions on a range of burning questions is a sign of hope. Indeed, with the 'political class' increasingly being viewed with a degree of suspicion and unease, the media are being assigned in popular perception the role of moral interlocutors on behalf of society. People's moral positions may have become less certain, but this does not mean that they do not appreciate the role of the media in spheres where they do uphold morality.

While post-liberalisation India seems to shine for a few in a euphemistic mood of political consolidation and economic stability, the minorities, the marginalised, the outcastes face the risk of getting further displaced from public space and scrutiny. A recent trend of some Indian newspapers' obsessive fascinations

---

[6]Jean Drèze, 'Hunger, Malnutrition and the Media', www.indiatogether.org/2003/apr/med-jean.htm.

has perhaps enhanced their bottom-line but, as Patnaik has mentioned, it has also contributed to a 'powerlessness':

> The media may not be able to arouse the people to force the resignation of the Gujarat Chief Minister, but this does not mean that the people do not appreciate the role of the media in exposing what happened in Gujarat. To use this 'moral capital' to acquire a more powerful role in society, it is important for the media to display the same humaneness and concern for democracy in looking at the impact of 'liberalisation' and 'globalisation' as they have done in exposing the doings of a Narendra Modi. Otherwise, the loss of their power witnessed in the 1990s will continue unabated.[7]

Patnaik re-examines Sen's statement that a free press acts as a bulwark against famines in the context of Gujarat, where the large-scale loss of lives, once it became known, did not set in motion immediate preventive measures:

> The proposition about a free press was a derivative one: since a free press typically brings to light the threat of a large-scale loss of lives, it helps to prevent famines. But, as Gujarat has shown, this implicit assertion is by no means valid today: the loss of lives there, according to several reports, was with the connivance of the very entity, the State government that is entrusted with the constitutional responsibility of taking preventive measures. It may be that things would pan out differently in a famine-like situation, but the fact remains that one can no longer be sure. We have entered an era in which the power of the media has diminished. The question that immediately arises is, why?[8]

Patnaik looks at 'internal', that is, media-centric, explanations for the phenomenon. Probing the question why a society loses its capacity for feeling a sense of moral outrage, he thinks the answer might be linked to the electronic media and the print media tending to homogenise 'calamities'. As media

---

[7] Prabhat Patnaik, 'Market, Morals and the Media', Convocation Address at The Asian College of Journalism, Chennai on 3 May 2002.
[8] Ibid.

increasingly portray differences only in quantitative terms and implicitly tend to obliterate the difference between 'natural calamities' and 'human-induced genocide', the audience begins to accept the latter much as it accepts the former. He says: 'Such "internal" explanations, however, no matter how valid they may be, are not enough, since it is not only the media whose power has diminished. Such a diminution has also occurred for the entire intellectual community.'[9]

A ready explanation for the reduced public influence of the media and intellectuals is that this invariably happens under fascist governments. But as Patnaik points out:

> We do not, after all, have a fascist state, a characteristic of which is a terrorist dictatorship. We still have liberal democratic institutions, though under a government in which communal fascists predominate. Even they, however, are forced into alliance with a whole array of political parties that can by no stretch of imagination be called fascistic or undemocratic. How is it then that the media and intellectuals are afflicted by growing impotence even in such a situation?[10]

Apathy and self-interest in the elite mainstream, of which the media are a critical component, have become such accepted norms that it requires more than courage and imagination to fight the system. Too many individuals remain trapped by institutions and too few step out. Those that do must develop an alternative base, and it is heartening that their efforts have been honoured. For instance, Magsaysay awardee Aruna Roy is a bureaucrat who turned activist and campaigns to show poor rural folks how information could give them power to stop corrupt officials from siphoning off precious funds needed to dig wells, for example, or to demand the pitiful wages that are their due. Winner of numerous international awards, P. Sainath began his career as a freelance development journalist through solo sojourns into India's most deprived districts. In *Everybody Loves a Good Drought,* perhaps a rare best-seller among books devoted to development issues, he says: 'Maybe the authors of 19th

[9] Ibid.
[10] Prabhat Patnaik, 'Market, Morals and the Media'.

century fiction were more effective in expressing the reality of their times than some late 20th century social scientists have been in capturing the reality of ours.'[11]

When novelist Arundhati Roy publicised her humanitarian essays in select magazines like *Frontline* and *Outlook* in India and *The Guardian* in the United Kingdom, the reading classes responded warmly, particularly the young and buoyant set. I remember the reaction of an informed reader: 'Finally some good journalism'. Of course, a journalist remarked: 'She has the freedom to write the way she wants. Would we have been allowed to do so?'

Perhaps, this should have been a first-person narrative, a technique rarely encouraged in serious journalism except for a special occasion, as a way of seeing or commenting on a profession I left, sabbatically, almost two years ago. But I exercised the journalist's prerogative to remain detached from the situations I encountered, to present an objective, dispassionate reality. If there is one.

Parts of this exploration are reflections from a splintered self. Almost inevitably, every journalist who ventures into the professional space like an idealist without a cause, discovers disillusionment in the cracks of monolithic media establishments. Every time a journalist steps out of the institutional edifice into a seamless surreality, there always lurks a mystification about the media's link with the society they purvey.

The media are constantly reinventing themselves. This amorphous gathering of institutions, large, medium and small, and of individuals, liberal, moderate, conservative and extremist, many of whom enter the space by virtue of vague sentiments and connections, together form a sub-group of society that must identify, examine and project the concerns of the rest for some larger, but never clearly defined, social purpose.

There is an uneasy balance of power between individuals and institutions within the media matrix. An individual who *chooses*

---

[11] P. Sainath, *Everybody Loves a Good Drought: Stories from India's Poorest Districts* (New Delhi: Penguin, 1996).

to be a journalist, as distinct from those who wander in with other unfulfilled agendas or discover a platform for new, perhaps more fulfilling missions, experiences a need, and sometimes a zeal, to explore the world through a prism that filters timeless realities into momentary truths.

Going beyond being an instrument, a conduit, a channel of select information that *objectively* disseminates into a wider ambit through an osmotic process, a sensitive journalist absorbs the pains and pleasures of a society in transformation. Despite a metamorphosised media environment, some idealistic youth will wander into the profession and before they get lost amid a gamut of the glamour-struck, before they start jostling for space and learning merely to co-exist, their voices too must be heard above the cacophony.

There will always be real stories of real people. The themes will vary, sometimes they will be of joy and often times of horrors, but the importance of creating a written record, a lasting testament, will remain.

> Write it. Write. In ordinary ink
> on ordinary paper: they were given no food,
> they all died of hunger. 'All. How many?
> It's a big meadow. How much grass
> for each one?' Write: I don't know.
> History counts its skeletons in round numbers.
> A thousand and one remains a thousand,
> as though the one had never existed:
> an imaginary embryo, an empty cradle,
> an ABC never read,
> air that laughs, cries, grows,
> emptiness running down steps toward the garden,
> nobody's place in the line.[12]

The dead poet's society conveyed as many relevant realities yesterday, as it does today, or will tomorrow.

---

[12] Wislawa Szymborska, *Hunger Camp at Jaslo* (1923).

19

the importance of being earnest as well as entertaining

robert brown

t amil director Shankar was never going to please everyone when he teamed up with popular music maestro, A.R. Rahman, to make a fairly lighthearted film about the sexual awakening of six young college students. *Boys* was banned in rebel-held Sri Lanka by the LTTE and huge cuts were demanded by the Chennai censors before it could be deemed suitable family viewing in the city where it was shot. Still, even the Tamil Tigers—who denounced its 'crude sexuality' and its 'imparting false values' amongst youngsters—must have seen the funny side when the testosterone-driven young hopefuls, having formed their own boy band to woo their college classmates, attain overnight celebrity status in the music world. Their triumph at the MTV awards propels them on the cover of both *India Today* and *Outlook* and is even hailed as the front-page lead story in *The Hindu*. That certainly produced a chuckle among cinema audiences in Chennai, where such a lapse in editorial standards would be totally inconceivable. *The Hindu* is cherished by its ultra respectable readership for holding out against a tide of trivia. However, its publishing rivals have proved anything but immune to the 'celebrity virus' which has engulfed print media all over the planet in recent times.[1] Some Indian editors, indeed, seem to have succumbed to the exact same strain of the disease as their counterparts in the West. A news-stand in New Delhi isn't all that different from a news-stand in New York: often you find the same movie actors,

---

[1] Pete Hamill puts the 'celebrity virus' in the American print media under the microscope in *News is a Verb: Journalism at the End of the Twentieth Century* (New York: Ballantine Books, 1998).

rock musicians and fashion models adorning magazine covers and newspaper mastheads, although Hollywood obviously has to compete for column inches in the subcontinent with Bollywood and the country's cricketers.

The triumph of entertainment over enlightenment is now widely perceived as one of the most disturbing trends in the modern news media. Some serious-minded journalists find this trend not only deeply unsavoury but damaging to democracy, a system of government dependent upon a switched-on citizenry capable of rumbling rhetoric and seeing through spin. The issue has been encapsulated by a British editor-turned-educator:

> Journalism has always entertained as well as informed. Had it not done so, it would not have reached a mass audience. But today, say journalism's critics, the instinct to amuse is driving out the will, and depleting the resource, to report and analyse in any depth. Obsessed with a world of celebrity and trivia, the news media are rotting our brains and undermining our civic life.[2]

Others fear that the growing obsession with celebrities and consumerism has diverted newspapers from their traditional role of campaigning for social justice. As a leading Australian journalism professor has observed:

> 'It was once said that the role of the journalist was to "comfort the afflicted and afflict the comfortable". Today, comfort still preoccupies news editors but the intention is to keep a carefully defined audience in its "comfort zone", thus ensuring its continued support'.[3]

The way in which a sizeable section of the India media have succumbed to this syndrome is deeply depressing for those who remember the radical origins of the press in this part of the world:

> Traditionally, the Indian news media has been wonderfully free—hard-hitting, fearless yet compassionate. It has exposed injustice, forced constructive action and strengthened democracy through its adversarial relation with the ruling powers.

---

[2] Ian Hargreaves, *Journalism: Truth or Dare?* (Oxford and New York: Oxford University Press, 2003).

[3] Lynette Sheridan Burns, 'Comfort or Curse?' in S. Tapsell and C. Varley (eds), *Journalism Theory in Practice* (Sydney: Oxford University Press, 2000).

But for over a decade now, it has been affected by the global 'dumbing down' phenomenon. One result is a 'narrowcasting' focus on the aspirational; selling dreams, always a good part of any business, has moved centre stage. The previously subsidiary role of entertainment has become the first priority, followed by news as entertainment, while drab, non-entertaining news is gradually turfed out.[4]

Such lamentations have assumed an especially caustic edge in India not just because of the perceived fragility of civic life in a time of terror and communal strife, but due to the persistence of large-scale poverty in this part of the world. If an obsession with celebrities can be regarded as objectionable in the world's most affluent states, it is surely obscene in a country where so many people still wonder where their next meal will come from. From the time of the Raj, journalism has played a crucial role in promoting social justice across the subcontinent and many believe that it shouldn't abandon this noble function to pander to aspirational audiences. Among them, perhaps surprisingly, is Atal Bihari Vajpayee, who started out as a journalist before clambering up—and sliding down—the greasy pole of governmental power. In a speech to mark the 125th anniversary of *The Hindu*, the then Prime Minister lamented the fact that not every newspaper occupied the same moral high ground:

There is an increasing tendency in a section of the media to project trivial things in life, to give more importance to certain aspects than is intrinsically due, to highlight the fads and fashions of the rich and the over-privileged and to aggressively advertise a consumerist lifestyle, which is simply beyond the reach of the majority. All this happens to the exclusion of attention paid to the problems of the masses, their sufferings and their aspirations, even their courageous—and often successful—efforts to overcome their odds. A newspaper should be the voice of the voiceless. It should be the hope of the hopeless. But this is not always the case. The common man is often invisible in the pages of our glossy newspapers and magazines.[5]

---

[4] Antara Dev Sen, 'India's Benign Earthquake', posted on openDemocracy.net (20 May 2004).
[5] Reported in *The Hindu*, 14 September 2003.

The previous day, in a special anniversary supplement, the Delhi-based historian Mukul Kesavan had also paid homage to *The Hindu* for remaining so high-minded.

"I find *The Hindu* indispensable because it takes India seriously." No other paper does, not consistently. Under the broadsheet exteriors of its rivals beat tabloid hearts and they will always be better at producing film tattle and catwalk pictures. *The Hindu* doesn't need photos of pageants and starlets to reach the young readership crucial to the contemporary broadsheet's bottom line.[6]

This was a subtle dig at *The Times of India*, which has bolstered its circulation, if not its standing among the intelligentsia, with the sort of populist approach Kesavan deplores, especially on its now infamous Page Three. A far more explicit attack on the prevailing news values on India's largest selling English-language daily was launched recently by Vivek Sharma of the organisation Development Alternatives. In a polemic posted on a website which monitors the Indian media, Sharma caustically observed how 'examples of extreme deprivation, hunger and hopelessness are evident everywhere throughout India but the ten editions of the *TOI* selling over 1.8 million copies everyday usually look right past it'.[7]

The purpose of this essay is not to pour more scorn upon *The Times of India* for placing hedonism over human rights or to heap further praise on *The Hindu* for doing the opposite, but to give serious consideration to why the content of leading Indian newspapers is changing. It aims to pose some provocative questions: Aren't the trends in press coverage which Mr Vajpayee lamented simply inevitable consequences of the economic and social forces his Bharatiya Janata Party (BJP)-led government unleashed? Isn't it possible for a newspaper to be both socially progressive and offer its readers insight into popular culture and consumer passions? Does coverage of celebrities and lifestyle issues need to be shallow and debasing? Can't serious broadsheets brighten up without dumbing down?

---

[6] Special supplement in *The Hindu*, 13 September 2003.
[7] www.thehoot.org

Vajpayee criticised the development of a 'mass media without the masses', casually overlooking the fact that large-scale illiteracy has always made the Indian print media 'class media' rather than a 'mass media' in their reach and assumptions.[8] It is also somewhat rich of the BJP leader to berate sections of the media for pandering to the selfish appetites and aspirations of a relatively privileged segment of the Indian population. The BJP owes much of its electoral success to adopting precisely such a strategy. As one leading commentator has noted:

> We start off the 21st century with a dynamic and rapidly growing middle class which is pushing the politicians to liberalise and globalize. Its primary preoccupation is with a rising standard of living, with social mobility, and it is enthusiastically embracing consumerist values and lifestyles. Many in the new middle class also embrace ethnicity and religious revival, a few even fundamentalism. It has been the main support of the Bharatiya Janata party and has helped make it the largest political party in India .... It has no clear ethos beyond money and the here and now. It has no heroes other than cricketers and Bollywood stars.[9]

That, it should be hastily added, is the view of a leading venture capitalist and consultant who enthusiastically endorses the country's recent transformations. Perhaps because he spent his formative years in the United States, Gurcharan Das recognises that the social and cultural consequences of a free market are often far from edifying, something with which Mr Vajpayee was plainly struggling to come to terms with when he addressed *The Hindu*. The media manifestations of rampant consumerism may have been unsavoury to him, but he was somewhat naïve if he imagined that individualism and desire, defining features of the New India engendered by economic liberalisation, would not find expression on the news-stands or the airwaves.

Mass media don't always accord with mass reality, however, as the political and media villages in Delhi were somewhat

---

[8] Shashi Tharoor, *India from Midnight to Millennium* (New Delhi: Penguin Books, 2000).

[9] Gurcharan Das, *India Unbound* (New Delhi: Viking, Penguin Books India, 2000).

startled to discover in May 2004 when the general election results rolled in. Perhaps the only journalist not shocked by the
outcome of that poll was P. Sainath, who has led a somewhat
lone battle in the last decade or so to highlight the plight of the
rural poor. When these people spoke up for themselves at the
ballot box, he argued that the election result had driven home a
disconnect between the Indian elite and the Indian people. Sainath
suggested it was time for editors to examine their consciences:

> Little in the media output of these past five years had pre-
> pared audiences for anything like this outcome. The polls suc-
> ceeded where journalism failed. They brought back to the
> agenda the issues of ordinary Indians .... The failure of jour-
> nalism was far more predictable than the poll results. For
> years now, the media have stopped talking to ordinary people.
> How on earth can they tell their readers and viewers what is
> going on? There are 400-plus journalists to cover Lakme In-
> dia Fashion Week. Almost none to cover the agricultural cri-
> sis in any informed way. The labour and agriculture beats in
> newspapers are almost extinct. The media have decided that
> 70 per cent of the population does not make news. The elec-
> torate has decided otherwise.[10]

The same point was made in a less polemical fashion by Antara
Dev Sen in a post-election analysis posted on the world wide web:

> This aspirational, Eurocentric, escapist culture being wrapped
> around media users—readers or television watchers—is not
> entirely invented or alien, but neither is it truly integral to
> their lives. It becomes unreliable primarily because it edges
> out other socio—cultural considerations that have more to
> do with the daily realities of rural and urban India: hunger,
> education, health care, unemployment—those tedious, unap-
> pealing segments that line the cutting-room floor of televi-
> sion news, or are buried in single column, four-centimetre
> news items on the inner pages of dailies. If we had paid more
> attention to those news items, we may have known better.[11]

---

[10] P. Sainath, 'Mass Media vs. Mass Reality', *The Hindu,* 14 May 2004.
[11] Antara Dev Sen, 'India's Benign Earthquake'.

It remains to be seen how much the plight of the poor will now feature in the columns of the nation's leading newspapers— or in the corridors of power. In the euphoric aftermath of Sonia Gandhi's election triumph, it did not slip everyone's memory that the process of economic liberalisation which has wreaked such devastation across rural India was inaugurated by the man she insisted should be prime minister: Manmohan Singh. Since 1991, when he was Finance Minister, successive Indian governments have enthusiastically embraced the forces of global capitalism. They have done so at a time when that system of economic organisation has entered a significant new phase. The transformation has been summarised thus:

> We are making a long-term shift from industrial to cultural production. Commerce in the future will involve the marketing of a vast array of cultural experiences rather than of traditional industrial-based goods and services. Global travel and tourism, theme cities and parks, destination entertainment centres, wellness, fashion and cuisine, professional sports and games, gambling, music, film, television, the virtual worlds of cyberspace and electronically mediated entertainment of every kind are fast becoming the centre of a new hyper-capitalism that trades in access to cultural experiences.[12]

No one with an elementary understanding of media history should be at all surprised that newspapers have sought to cash in on this new hyper-capitalism. In free-market democracies the development of the press has traditionally been intertwined with that of advertising, which is a pervasive, intrusive element of all commercial media content. If commerce increasingly involves the marketing of a vast array of cultural experiences, then profit-driven media organisations will inevitably provide platforms for such marketing. They might do so not only in the main section of the newspaper, but also spawn additional sections and glossy supplements whose prime aim is to amuse and arouse our consuming desires.

Rifkin also makes the point that 'the metamorphosis from industrial production to cultural capitalism is being accompanied by an equally significant shift from the work ethic to the play ethic'. Again, it is not surprising that newspapers should respond

---

[12] Jeremy Rifkin, *The Age of Access* (London: Penguin Books, 2000).

to this new *zeitgeist*. Even when the work ethic held sway, the appeal of newspapers and other forms of popular culture stemmed in some measure from their provision of a daily dose of pleasure. The 'play theory' of mass communication was first advanced by William Stephenson four decades ago but it wasn't taken seriously at the time in academic circles, where more conventional explanations of media consumption were preferred. Today it is more widely recognized that play deserves serious and sustained attention. In the words of Theodore Glasser of Stanford University: 'The day's news enlightens and entertains, of course, but it also extends to readers, viewers and listeners an extended and welcome opportunity to enjoy themselves'.[13]

Some serious journalists would be offended by the suggestion that their purpose is to provide enjoyment. For them, 'truth is violence, reality is war, news is conflict' and 'journalism's heroic figures are the combative interviewers who won't take no for an answer, the war junkie following death around the world, the adversarial investigative reporter, the crusading paper or programme'.[14] Earnest muck-rakers have traditionally despised the 'smiling professions', all those who interface with the public in the name of pleasure, entertainment, attractiveness, appeal. In the media context these practices are now associated with TV presenters, lifestyle and consumer journalism, PR, advertising and spin doctors.

Much ink has been expended in Britain on the 'dumbing down' of the news media, popular culture and public discourse. One seasoned newspaperman in London was even moved in 1997 to pen a West End play about the transformation of a conservative Sunday broadsheet into a racy tabloid. No one doubted that the object of Michael Bywater's biting satire was Britain's biggest selling broadsheet, *The Sunday Times*. His play was entitled The Shallow End, which was the mocking term applied to the section of that paper's sprawling newsroom at Wapping in east London where the ever-expanding style, travel and popular culture sections were assembled.

---

[13] Theodore L. Glasser, 'Play and the Power of News' in *Journalism: Theory, Practice and Criticism*, Vol. 1 (London, Thousand Oaks, CA and New Delhi: Sage Publications, 2000).

[14] John Hartley, 'Communicative Democracy in a Redactional Society: the Future of Journalism Studies', in *Journalism: Theory, Practice and Criticism*, Vol. 1 (London, Thousand Oaks, CA and New Delhi: Sage Publications, 2000).

The Sunday Times was not the only title to undergo such a metamorphosis, a fact recognised by a leading commentator long associated with its chief rival on the news-stands, *The Observer*. In a sombre essay aimed at fellow reflective practitioners, Anthony Sampson argued that 'since the 1980s the frontier between qualities and popular papers has virtually disappeared'.[15] He deplored the fact that 'in the last 20 years most people accept that there has been a fundamental change in broadsheet newspapers' away from 'consistent coverage of serious events towards short-term entertainment, speculation and gossip.' The author of several penetrating books on aspects of international capitalism, Sampson was astute enough to identify the chief underlying factor:

> Today the broadsheets compete fiercely for advertising, which imposes its own conditions—still more in the present crisis of newspapers which have cut their prices while newsprint has become more expensive. The advertisers determine the allocation of space—the pages devoted to consumers, travel, entertainment—which look more and more alike.[16]

Advertising is even more dominant in the Indian newspaper marketplace. As a result of Murdoch-style price wars, even a highbrow title like *The Hindu* now draws 80 per cent of its total revenues from selling space. Appalled by the way the advertising tail is wagging the editorial dog, some people believe that there is only one real radical response: that it is time to get the advertiser to be less of a determinant in the making and selling of news. Serious newspapers should raise their cover price to a serious level and persuade serious-minded citizens to pay a sizeable premium for a newspaper which is truly independent. But it is hard to envisage any Indian newspaper adopting the sort of 'Independent Pricing Policy' he advocates. Editors and proprietors here are more likely to draw lessons from the British media marketplace, which is every bit as savagely competitive as the one in which they are forced to operate.

Roy Greenslade, who made an effortless transition to a senior editorial executive post at *The Sunday Times* after editing the

---

[15] Anthony Sampson, 'The Crisis at the Heart of Our Media', *British Journalism Review*, 7(3), 1996.
[16] Ibid.

tabloid *Daily Mirror*, accepts that Britain's broadsheets are now publishing material that would never have been previously countenanced in what was regarded as the 'serious' or 'quality' press. But he defends them against the dumbing down indictment, contending that Sampson's substantive point that they have abandoned their public service remit is 'badly flawed'. According to Greenslade, who now combines media punditry on *The Guardian* with a professorship in journalism, the broadsheets have simply taken advantage of improved reproduction and increased pagination to incorporate the tabloid agenda without unduly compromising their authority and their central mission to inform and explain. The proliferation of soft features does not mean there is less space devoted to foreign stories. 'The owners and editors of broadsheets haven't been dumbing down: they have been wising up,' Greenslade argues. 'They know they have to go on trying harder if they have any hope of retaining their diminishing audiences in the face of the threat from the electronic media, such as 24-hour TV news and the internet.'[17]

Greenslade invokes a retailing analogy, suggesting that 'the old corner shop of eight poorly-printed, monochrome pages with its restricted editorial diet had been transmuted into a new supermarket offering scores of well-illustrated pages and a seemingly limitless range of content.'[18] Today's multi-sectioned newspapers can certainly be compared to supermarkets, though hypermarkets might be a more apt comparison. Readers, like shoppers, have to pick from the vast array of products on offer, choosing to fill their minds, as they fill their trolleys, with wholesome fare or otherwise. What worries some critics and custodians of standards in the media is how many people plump for junk journalism along with junk food. For them, the continued popularity of 'supermarket tabloids' in the US is a truly sad indictment of American civilisation.

But the 'dumbing down' thesis has never held much sway in some quarters. John Hartley, a British academic now based in Australia, defines journalism as 'the sense-making practice of modernity', the very foundation of democracy and the primary wiring of popular culture. He is among the optimists who view the 'tabloidization' of journalism not as a diminution of its

---

[17] Roy Greenslade, *Press Gang* (London: Macmillan, 2003).
[18] Ibid.

ambition but as an extension of its reach.[19] A leading media don, Felipe Fernandez-Armesto, took to the airwaves in Britain recently to argue that, instead of fearing the triumph of trash, we should start taking pride in pulp:

> Maybe we shouldn't get too high minded about programmes or papers that other people like. We hear a lot about the obligations of the media to education and public service but their over-riding obligation is surely to do what they do well. That includes escapist television, tabloid trivia, pulp fiction and pop art. Public service includes serving passive, stressed-out audiences and catering to raucous, rollicking public taste.[20]

Pete Hamill, who has had the rare distinction of editing both of New York's rival tabloids, believes that what distinguishes a publication isn't so much what it covers but how it covers it. 'As a newspaperman and as a reader, I'm not against celebrity journalism,' he argues. 'It just must be journalism.'[21] The sort of celebrity journalism he admires most are the big-name profiles published in leading glossy magazines such as *Vanity Fair*, *The New Yorker*, *GQ*, *Esquire* and *People*, where the journalist is given time and space to explore his subject in depth. Most of the finest writers of such profiles, Hamill notes, have worked in other forms of journalism, covering wars or sports or foreign affairs. Because they have wide experience of the real world, they have a sense of proportion about the big names. They have no interest in being publicists but are, equally, not afraid to celebrate human beings who have added something valuable to the world:

> That level of celebrity journalism certainly belongs in newspapers. The examination of individual celebrities can tell us something about celebrity itself and how it functions in the creative American imagination. It can help readers to understand what they are really looking at when they go to a play or a movie or park in front of the TV set.[22]

---

[19] John Hartley, *Popular Reality: Journalism, Modernity, Popular Culture* (London: Arnold, 1996).

[20] Filipe Fernandez-Armesto, 'Pulp Nation', BBC Radio 4,

[21] Pete Hamill, *News is a Verb*.

[22] Ibid.

What proportion of entertainment coverage in India attains such standards? Not very much, would appear to be the answer. For a whole host of reasons, India doesn't have anything on a par with the leading American glossy magazines which Hamill holds up as exemplars of the sort of celebrity journalism he applauds. Emulating them will require substantial investment, for the in-depth profiles which have become the trademark of these publications can be as resource-intensive as any form of investigative journalism. The coverage of entertainment in the Indian press is all too often fawning and superficial. It has what Hamill would call a 'nose-pressed-to-the-glass quality'. Readers are seduced by bright colour blurbs on the front page into reading about big name celebrities. Some newspapers, it seems, will seize upon any banal utterance or action by a celebrity to sprinkle a little stardust on their masthead. On a visit to India in the autumn of 2003, one of the first things that grabbed my attention in Chennai's airport terminal was a tantalising headline on the front page of *The Telegraph*: What are Liv Tyler and Kate Moss doing in Scotland?' Being a Scotsman, this naturally tickled my curiosity, but it was hard to fathom why Stella McCartney's star-studded wedding on a remote Scottish island would be remotely interesting to the paper's core readership in Calcutta. However, someone at *The Telegraph* evidently found it appealing. An alluring portrait of Liv Tyler was strategically located on the masthead to hook admirers of this particular Hollywood actress. Alas, the story inside consisted of a few skimpy paragraphs supplied by one of the international news agencies. Anyone who purchased the paper for this feature would surely have felt downright cheated.

Coverage of celebrities and consumer passions doesn't have to be crude and debasing. Delivered with subtlety and sophistication, it can broaden the scope of a broadsheet, brightening it up rather than dumbing it down. That has arguably been the experience in England of *The Guardian*, which has become significantly more entertaining without becoming any less enlightening. Indeed, this progressive daily very often deploys wit as a weapon in its radical armoury, proving that it is possible to be both humane and humorous. It treats its readers as rounded human beings who don't necessarily care any less about Third World debt just because they are curious about Manchester United's latest multi-million pound transfer signing.

Although he was once described as 'legendarily serious' by its
Delhi correspondent, the present Editor-in-Chief of *The Hindu*
is evidently a great admirer of *The Guardian*, extolling its virtues in his own editorial columns. N. Ram could do worse than
to study its pages closely as he endeavours to address his own
paper's most daunting strategic challenge—its ageing readership profile. To hook and hold a new generation of readers, *The
Hindu* will have to take popular culture more seriously than it
has done up to now. Entertainment might be escapist but it is
also an integral part of people's lives. Throughout the developed
world, entire university programmes are now devoted to popular culture and you will find gangster rap being written about
with great seriousness in the pages of *The New York Times*, a
newspaper which once published editorials denouncing brass band
music as 'a devastating vice' and 'a giant evil'.[23]

The importance of being entertaining as well as earnest seems
to have been absorbed by at least one leading Indian editor.
When the website tehelka.com was re-launched in early 2004 as
a weekly newspaper, Tarun Tejpal pledged not only to preserve
its crusading spirit but to serve up some fun and frivolity too.
'We have no intention to be joyless,' he assured subscribers to
the self-styled *People's Paper:*

> Among the endless lessons of the last three years has been a
> crucial one on the lightness of being. Burdens are light when
> borne by laughter. The paper must then reflect all aspects of
> our lives, serious and trivial, high-brow and low-brow: it must
> attempt to be what each one of us is, all things in ourselves.
> Of course it must be all ordered, for it is in the ordering of our
> values that we proclaim our true selves.[24]

[23] Lawrence Levine, *Highbrow/Lowbrow: The Emergence of Cultural Hierarchy in America* (Cambridge MA: Harvard University Press, 1988).
[24] Tarun Tejpal, 'The Soul of the Business', tehelka.com, 2004.

PART IV
Implications for the Future

20

the public sphere of print journalism*

robin jeffrey

*W*e need a Hindi version of *Citizen Kane*. The time is right
for it. The Indian newspaper industry throbs with the buc-
caneer capitalism, Himalayan egos and desperate politics of New
York in the 1890s. India is transforming itself, and the print
revolution—and especially the daily newspaper revolution—of
the past 20 years is helping to propel that transformation. 'A
million mutinies now' was the best thing about V.S. Naipaul's
book of that title. Millions of mutinies are, indeed, going on, and
the fact that people now read about them in their newspapers,
and read about *themselves* in their newspapers, helps to explain
the mutinous environment.

What is the 'newspaper revolution' and what is it doing to
India? Imagine the morning scene 27 years ago (1976) at a cos-
mic, all-India bus stand peopled by characters from an R.K.
Laxman cartoon. Around each daily newspaper available from
the hawkers, 50 people would be jostling to get a glimpse. Now,
think of the same bus stand in 2001. The population has grown
by 400 million. Where there were 10 people for every square
metre of bus stand in 1976, there are now 16. Nevertheless, the
crowds around the newspapers have thinned considerably; there's
now a newspaper for every 17 people. The Common Man and
Common Woman stand a chance at least of reading the headlines. They are also more likely to be able to read—65 out of
every 100 in 2001; only 35 out of 100 in 1976.

If you were an aggressive newspaper proprietor, you would
also be proclaiming to anyone who would listen that *your* paper

---

*This paper was earlier published as 'Breaking News' in *The Little Magazine*,
4 (2), 2003.

was known to have six readers for every single copy printed. At that rate, you could argue, India in 2001 had virtual newspaper saturation. (You wouldn't be right, but you could argue it!)

In the early years of the twenty-first century, daily newspaper circulation in India's 13 major languages stood at about 58 million copies a day and had more than doubled in 10 years. The transformation—the rapid, new availability of daily print—is stunning. In languages like Hindi, it is reaching a par with New York city in the 1890s, when Joseph Pulitzer, William Randolph Hearst and two dozen dailies fought for the eyes and the pennies of millions of people newly exposed to reading and to print. Since the early 1990s, circulation in Hindi has more than trebled from under eight million copies a day to more than 25 million. And Hindi is not the biggest grower. That distinction belongs to Assamese, where circulation appears to have grown from 45,000 to 320,000 (though the circumstances of the statistics for Assam are special). Telugu, however, where the statistics are less clouded, has gone from 360,000 dailies a day to 1,700,000.[1]

Anyone familiar with the Indian newspaper industry will begin to put faces and personalities to these references to Hindi and Telugu expansion. Mention Telugu newspapers and one thinks of *Eenadu* and Ramoji Rao. *Eenadu* is the dominant daily for more than 70 million Telugus (more people than live in France). Started in 1974 on an ancient flatbed press in Vishakhapatnam (which had a population of about 200,000 then) with a print run of 4,000 copies, *Eenadu* in 2003 published from 23 centres and has an audited circulation of more than 900,000 copies a day. As rivals have given up trying to compete commercially, *Eenadu* controls—temporarily, at least—more than 90 per cent of the daily circulation in Telugu, validated by the Audit Bureau of Circulations (ABC). Such validation is important because it brings the mass-market advertising that shapes newspaper industries in expanding capitalist systems.

The *Eenadu* story has the ingredients for an Orson Welles film, or perhaps, with the legendary pickle factory, an Arundhati Roy novel. Andhraites, after all, like to recount that one of the

---

[1] Where these numbers come from is a story in itself. The Registrar of Newspapers for India and the ABC are the two sources I consult. There is an essay considering the virtues and vices of each in the journal *Asian Survey* for September 1994.

sources of the wealth that allowed Ramoji Rao to start *Eenadu* was a pickle factory. But it is the Hindi press that the film needs to be made about, because the battles being fought there are so unpredictable, so intense and so formative of India's political future that they have a truly epic quality.

Look at the players. There was a time, only 15 years ago, when if you talked about Hindi newspapers, you were at once referred to *Navbharat Times (NBT)* the poor, 'vernacular' relation of *The Times of India*. When *Punjab Kesari*, a cheeky, downmarket paper from provincial Jalandhar (not just provincial, but Punjabi too!), began outselling the *NBT* in the mid-1980s, the event passed almost unnoticed, such was the lack of interest in the goings-on of the 'vernacular press', even among politicians who may sometimes have had better sense.

At that very time, for example, Rajiv Gandhi's government supported a venture called *India Speaks*, an attempt to digest and report on Indian-language newspapers around the country. *India Speaks* had the aroma of a British institution, the Vernacular (or Native) Newspaper Reports, begun in the late 1860s to try to keep tabs on what was going on in the bazaar. By the time the Narasimha Rao government came to power in 1991, there was a growing awareness, even in Delhi, of a fact that state politicians, especially in the south, had known for a long time: the Indian-language press had readers and influence. With his remarkable command over languages, Narasimha Rao seems to have been among the first to pay serious, regular attention to Hindi newspaper owners and editors. In 1993, the Delhi editor of *Punjab Kesari* expressed delight that the Prime Minister had begun to consult him. 'He (the PM) was trying to convince *me!*' the editor said. 'The politicians never used to do this sort of thing with Hindi editors.'

Today, it would be a foolish politician who did not keep the owners and editors of Hindi newspapers flattered and informed. Consider the state of Rajasthan in the past 10 years, and the saga of *Dainik Bhaskar*. In 2002, *Bhaskar* (founded in 1958 and based in Bhopal) was the highest circulated Hindi daily in India. It sold 1.4 million copies a day and was published from more than a dozen centres. At the Census of 2001, Rajasthan boasted the greatest increase in literates of all the Indian states. In 1991, there had been 13.6 million literates or about 39 per cent of

Rajasthanis over the age of seven. In 2001, there were 28.1 million, a doubling of the number of literates in 10 years. If you were a newspaper proprietor, this meant an addition of 14 million potential customers. In what other business did the market grow so fast? The proportion of literate Rajasthanis rose from 39 per cent in 1991 to 61 per cent in 2001.

We can, of course, always dispute the figures. Critics regularly contend that much of census data is unreliable. It is collected, they say, by lazy, harried officials who fill out forms to keep their superiors happy but without troubling to interview the intended respondents. The *Dainik Bhaskar* story, however, lends credence to the census results for Rajasthan. Unlike census officials, newspaper proprietors have a keen interest in counting the newspapers and the takings.

In 1996, *Bhaskar* announced it was starting a Jaipur edition. It was intending, said one of the owners, not so much to capture readers from other papers but to sell to *new* readers. This sounded like a big gamble. By most measures, Rajasthan was 'backward' and spread out. 'Who will read it?' said one wit, reflecting the stereotypes about Rajasthan. 'The camels in Jodhpur?'

Jaipur already had a well-run local Hindi daily in *Rajasthan Patrika* of the Kothari family, which had its own rags-to-riches story and felt confident enough to have a dispute, and a break, with the Audit Bureau in 1995. When *Rajasthan Patrika* left the ABC, it was selling 365,000 copies from its single centre in Jaipur. When *Bhaskar* brought its five editions into the ABC system in 1997, they altogether sold only 350,000 copies a day.[2] The change was remarkable. By 2002, *Bhaskar* was the leading Hindi daily, not just in Rajasthan but in India. Its 1.4 million copies a day were published in six states from 20 centres. *Rajasthan Patrika* rejoined the ABC in 1999 and was selling 605,000 copies from 10 centres.

Bhaskar's Jaipur experience was written up as a case study for business and marketing courses as an example of what thorough market research and sustained implementation could achieve. But if the example was important for its commercial lessons, its social implications were even greater. As *Patrika* and *Bhaskar* confronted each other around the state, daily newspaper penetration in Rajasthan trebled. Between 1991 and 2000,

---

[2] The five centres were Gwalior, Bhopal, Indore, Bilaspur and Raipur.

261 The Public Sphere of Print Journalism

the crowd around each daily newspaper at the imaginary
Rajasthan bus stand dropped, as did India's, from 50 people to
about 17. Did the competition between the two newspapers—
and the other Hindi dailies also in the race—make people literate? I don't think so. More likely, newspapers began to discern
that literacy was growing as a result of greater prosperity, educational programmes and spread of television.

Television? Yes. There's a persuasive argument that television exposure encourages people to learn to read and write. With
its tantalising, six-second grabs, television introduces people to
topics and stories they've never encountered before. But television rarely provides background or puts things into context.
People look to newspapers to do that the next day. At one stage
in the early 1990s, some Indian-language newspapers added readers by publishing local-language summaries of Hindi epics on
Doordarshan, the State-run television network.

Television also spreads the snob value of literacy. In the villages, to see people reading was once unusual. On TV, on the
other hand, the rich and powerful are always picking up and
putting down pieces of paper of one kind or another. 'The newspaper is seen as a status symbol,' wrote the American scholar,
Kirk Johnson, of a village in Maharashtra in the 1990s. It is
'reserved for those with a greater education; people who receive
the newspaper are thought of as intelligent and are sought for
advice in important matters'.[3]

A newspaper is a cheap status symbol. For the price of a cup of
tea, you can impress the neighbours. 'What do you do if you are
unemployed?' a Malayali friend used to say about Kerala in the
1970s. 'You buy a diary and go to Trivandrum (Thiruvananthapuram).' The diary suggested you were an important person, and
you bustled round the state capital, looking as if you were on the
way to engagements. It used to be said of the grey, conservative
Daily Telegraph in Britain that you didn't read it, but you bought
it, because it made the neighbours think you were 'deeper' than
if you bought the lower-brow *Express* or *Daily Mail*.

But what's the fuss about? Is newspaper reading important?
You can bet your boots and *chappals* that it is. It changes the

---

[3] Kirk Johnson, *Television and Social Change in Rural India: A Study of
Two Mountain Villages in Western Maharashtra* (New Delhi: Sage Publications, 2000).

way people connect to the world. The Canadian media guru
Marshall McLuhan sometimes claimed that exposure to print
was the necessary condition for mass production and the industrial revolution. The implication was that until people were ac-
customed to seeing ordered lines of type every day, in a line, in
columns, with a beginning and end, they weren't ready for factory life. Writers on 'nationalism' put the newspaper at the centre of ideas about the modern nation. How can a person in
Chennai imagine they have something in common with a person in Jalandhar if they do not read 'Indian weather maps', 'Indian sports reports' and such in a newspaper every morning?
"Newspapers," someone once said, 'give the nation the chance
to have breakfast together.' The great Malayalam daily,
Mathrubhumi runs the line in English under its masthead: 'The
national daily in Malayalam.' It's a subtle statement about the
partly unconscious role that newspapers perform.

Then there's the 'public sphere', a concept often associated
with the German social theorist Jurgen Habermas. The 'public
sphere' is that 'space' between family life and the State or
government where people in modern times carry on debate about
how their world is going and how it ought to go. The public
sphere and newspapers grow up together. One can't have
Habermas' public sphere without the presence of the newspaper.

If there is any validity in contentions such as these, what
does it mean for politics in India? Newspaper exposure in India
is now as great as it was in Britain or the US, when vigorous
two-party democracies entrenched themselves in the middle of
the nineteenth century.

In a thoughtful, critical review of *India's Newspaper Revolution*, Krishna Kumar argues that the local-content emphasis of
expanding Indian-language dailies has led to 'the fragmentation
of the public sphere'.[4] By this he means, I think, that 'some of
the largest circulation dailies' ignore great national issues—'the
grim implications of ... the nexus between politicians and criminals, communal propaganda of the Sangh institutions and the
nuclearisation of India and Pakistan'. Most Indian language dailies 'have parochialised the reader' by covering national issues
only in the most casual, unthinking way. According to this

---

[4] Krishna Kumar, 'India's Newspaper Revolution', *Economic and Political
Weekly*, 27 July 2002.

interpretation, the spread of the Hindi daily press has contributed to trivialising public life and distracting people from the serious concerns of the nation.

I would argue a bit differently: public spheres have not so much been fragmented as created. In rural India 30 years ago, a newspaper might have reached a high-caste pensioner or schoolteacher every week or so. It would have contained translated material from English-language newspapers in the great cities or from wire services. But in the same village in the 1990s, *Dainik Bhaskar* and *Rajasthan Patrika*—with colour photos, lots of advertisements, big headlines and racy language—arrive in time for breakfast *every* morning.

What do such papers say and do? It is true that they cover local news, deep and wide. Peter Friedlander, an Australian-based scholar of Hindi, examined such local coverage in *Punjab Kesari* and *Dainik Jagran* after the nuclear tests in 1998. One of his examples suggests the *creation* of a public sphere where in the past no such possibility could have existed:

'telephone pole: may fall down at any time'

'*Jalandhar, 4 June (Rajendra)*. The residents of the Laksmipura area have demanded the removal of Telephone Pole No. 2219 because it is half uprooted and might fall down any moment and cause an accident. It is noteworthy that it is tied up with rope.'[5]

This is the most basic sort of village-*ghat* journalism. What did the residents of Laksmipura do *before* there were newspapers to proclaim the danger of Telephone Pole No. 2219?

Such stories are repeated every day wherever local dailies are produced. Because of the indignation they can breed, and the fact that such reports endure—they are part of the *public record*—citizens relish them, buy the newspapers to read about them, and officials are forced to take note of them. If Telephone Pole No. 2219 falls down and injures someone in three months' time, angry citizens will point out that it was a *public* issue long before. Heads may be expected to roll. Therefore, before that,

---

[5] *Punjab Kesari*, 5 June 1998, p. 10.

the mills of the administrative gods may be expected to grind, and Telephone Pole No. 2219 may get repaired. That's how a 'public sphere' can work. To be sure, these are not nation-shaking debates; but in thousands of small ways, they are nation-building and citizen-empowering.

Public spheres—abstract arenas where citizens have an opportunity to reflect on what concerns them—do not have to be liberal, positive or scientific. Indeed, the owners of Indian-language newspapers, especially in north India, come from social groups that one might expect to be sympathetic to the sentiments of the Hindu fundamentalist Bharatiya Janata Party (BJP). The Chopras of *Punjab Kesari*, the Kotharis of *Rajasthan Patrika*, the Guptas of *Dainik Jagran*, the Agarwals and Maheswaris of *Amar Ujala* and the Agarwals of *Dainik Bhaskar* might all appear, at first glance at least, to come from the urban, merchant-caste, north Indian tradition that was once considered the soil of the Jana Sangh and then the BJP. If a number of the Hindi dailies colour the world saffron, that isn't surprising. What may be regrettable is that there are not enough Hindi newspapers capable of painting a multi-coloured world.

In his prize-winning book *Politics after Television*,[6] Arvind Rajagopal argues that India has a 'split public'—an English-using, big-city elite and, in north India, a Hindi-using majority in the small towns and countryside. The formulation recalls earlier suggestions that the country was divided between 'India' and 'Bharat'. For Rajagopal, Hindi language publications provide a much more potent site for Hindu majoritarian ideas than they do for arguments about secularism, science and rationalism. This is *not* to say that this expanding Hindi press does not create a public sphere. Rather, it is to say that the most effective songs in the public sphere so created are those sung by Hindu chauvinist choristers.

You can't have a public sphere—a place where people who don't know each other and never see each other contend about how the world should work—without media. And the print media, especially the daily newspaper, are the original, and still a fundamental, component of such a space. For much of India, particularly rural north India, regular exposure to print in

[6] Arvind Rajagopal, *Politics after Television: Religious Nationalism and the Retailing of Hinduness* (New York: Cambridge University Press, 2001).

this way is an experience of the past 15 years. It is not that the people's public sphere has been fragmented; rather, they have entered a public sphere for the first time. It is not the coffee houses of eighteenth-century London (à la Habermas), or the Indian coffee house of yesteryear's Connaught Place; but it is a public sphere nonetheless.

For those of us who would like to believe that literacy, reading and newspapers lead to rationality, reflection and debate, the problem is that this is not necessarily so. A public sphere can just as easily be shaped and colonised by metaphysical bigots who advocate the eradication of all those who oppose them. In the case of Hindi in north India, the newspapers that have entered the lives of millions of people in the past 15 years use metaphors and cadences that often have powerful Hindu overtones, in keeping with the background of the proprietors and the journalists they hire. (You are unlikely to get a steady job on a Hindi daily unless someone near the top thinks you are reliable. But that might be said to apply to senior editors on Rupert Murdoch's newspapers too.)

Arvind Rajagopal captures these ideas of language and metaphor in *Politics after Television*. Hindi media, he writes, use 'forms of expression, principally religious in character, that were excluded from the English language media'. In 'fluent and racy prose', Hindi language newspapers transmit different information in a different way from English language newspapers. In Hindi, at least, Hindu chauvinist politics have an advantage because they work with vocabulary, allusions and images that are part of the cultural landscape. Translations of English language or English ideas into Hindi do not resonate in the same way. There is nothing soul-stirring in *agni-rath-chalanan-niyantran-pattika;* probably better to stick to 'railway signal'.

Mass politics, which grow with mass markets and the newspaper revolution, will favour Hindu chauvinist exponents until those who have other ideas find an effective vocabulary in Hindi. It appears that not enough of those of the 'secular' persuasion write well enough or often enough in Hindi. I was once at a seminar where, after listening to a very distinguished scholar from one of India's finest universities, an exasperated hill Brahmin, who was a teacher of Hindi overseas, said, 'But Professor Blank, you never write in Hindi, and when they translate you, it doesn't read well.'

The newspaper revolution is part of capitalism, but it is neutral in struggles between 'liberal democracy' and 'religious majoritarianism'. If advertisers can still advertise and proprietors can still sell ads, newspapers will simply reflect the contents that their readers think are important and that their proprietors therefore think should be written about. If foreigners take advantage of the new rules allowing investment in Indian newspapers (up to 26 per cent), it will be because they judge that readers, and the advertisers who pursue them, will continue to flock to newspapers. The foreign interests will be less interested in the content of the newspapers than in the revenue.

In the midst of struggles between great proprietors, and struggles for the soul of the Indian state, millions of ordinary people will use newspapers to draw attention to themselves and their concerns. In this, they are deploying a weapon their forebears did not have. This is the newspaper revolution, and it is making India a different place.

The image in my mind is the new, sparkling-white production centre of *Eenadu* at Rajahmundry in the Godavari delta in 1993. The tallest building in the town, it dwarfed any government office, school, temple, church or mosque. And it was becoming a central institution in people's lives. It is no wonder that powerful people want to own and operate such institutions. It is time for an Indian *Citizen Kane*.

21

alternative spaces in the broadcast media

s. gautham

*W*hen the editor of this volume first sent me an email suggesting that I contribute this piece, my thoughts wandered instinctively to the early 1980s. To many people those were the tumultuous early days of the boom in Indian broadcasting, when Doordarshan initially began to emerge from the tedium of its monochrome past— Indira Gandhi had just seized the opportunity presented by the 1982 Asian Games in New Delhi to order an unprecedented expansion of the government's TV network. New words like Low Power Transmitters, colour transmission and national network were now part of the daily lexicon.

I was then in journalism school, and my home-town Bangalore, now the capital of the cyber world, like most of the country, had no television at all. Only the colonial metros of Delhi, Mumbai, Chennai and Kolkata had television—and each of them only broadcast a few hours every evening. It was a time of general excitement. In class, clever professors were cheered for using phrases like 'Doordarshan certainly packs a lot of idiocy into the idiot box'. (It is a different matter that all the channels still do. One of the problems of the broadcast expansion is the stale sameness of television, but more of that later.) Those were the days of Doordarshan's complete monopoly over the airwaves of this nation.

In the heady 1980s, Doordarshan had funds with its political bosses ordering it to expand overnight, but it needed help and was forced to turn to its oldest covert ally—the corporate sector—which was quick to invent strategies like sponsored programmes and free commercial time. Thereafter, it was a

matter of time before the corporate media entered Doordarshan
as private producers, and a matter of technology before satellite
TV helped them launch their own channels. All this helped create a bipartisan duopoly that serves both commercial and State
(read ruling party) interests, but at the same time, with one
dangerously donning the mask of being a public interest broadcaster.

I took my first job in TV because it offered twice the wage
that print did in those days. I was the youngest employee, except for the tea-boy, in a company that liked to call itself India's
first Corporate Television News Agency. We worked out of a
decaying luxury hotel in central Delhi and we had an exclusive
contract with Doordarshan. This made no economic sense—
Rs 50 a second for footage used—and all negative rights with
DD in the bargain. They never took more than 40 seconds and
they sent our crews to all the expensive, distant places. Our
bosses thought they were buying goodwill—who were we to
complain? We flew to some dream locations—Assam,
Arunachal, Ladakh. For someone just turned 20, it was more
than you could ask for.

But there was a price to be paid, a seamier side, one that we
tried to ignore—but it is a past that comes often to haunt me
now. One particular incident serves well as an example of how
manipulation worked in those days and how power was used in
the absence of transparency. This is an eyewitness account from
January 1986.

It was a cold and wintry pre-dawn at the Sarai Rohilla station
in west Delhi when a dozen ageing Ambassador taxis disgorged
a motley crowd of camera crew. This is an obscure station on
the ring railway that periodically comes into the news when it is
used as an alternative for long-distance trains, when one of the
main junctions comes up for repairs. Of the motley crowd that
gathered there, few of us had met each other before; all of us
were Doordarshan stringers and had been summoned only the
night before for a crucial assignment. There had been no briefing. We had been told to report at the station, and that we would
be escorted by a top Doordarshan boss.

At the station there was chaos; there was a DD bossman, but
he didn't know much either. But there were lots of others too—

notably, and it is not hard to uncover them—Il
Bureau) types—and several schoolteachers, who ha
haied to perform, as we were to discover, as cens
tors. Over the next few hours it transpired that we v
commandeered train to the town of Abohar in the I
from there on to the little village of Kandukhera, wl   .ere
was to be a census—a house to house survey—to find out whether
a majority of its people spoke Hindi or Punjabi!

The Kandukhera census is no longer in the public domain
and the region has fallen off the map—so has the suffering of
the Punjabi people during those days of 'terrorism'. But at that
time, it was at the centre of media attention. The solution to the
huge border dispute was seen to be in transferring the Hindi-
speaking areas of Abohar and Fazilka districts to Haryana in
lieu of the joint state capital Chandigarh, which would go to
Punjab. This was among many others, a critical component of
the famous Anandpur Sahib Resolution—prolonged negotiations
led to no solutions and there was, of course, a Commission of
Enquiry which was unable to decide whether Kandukhera, bang
on the border, was predominantly Hindi-or-Punjabi speaking and
so the census that wintry morning.

It was quite a jamboree and in Abohar we were joined by a
platoon of the Punjab Armed Police, for protection. Once we
reached the village, the cameras were to roll as the enumerators
went about their tasks, questionnaire in hand. It was a day of
high drama—many of today's top political actors were present in
full force. There was former Chief Election Commissioner M.S.
Gill, then a serving bureaucrat, and the Punjab government's
counsel at the Commission of Enquiry. There was Captain
Amarender Singh, the current Congress Chief Minister of the
state, then a Member of Parliament—but from the Akali Dal—
and of course hundreds of security men. A senior editor, then a
young reporter, was roughed up when he discovered that a local
leader was being pressured to declare in favour of one language.
But none of this made the TV news despite the presence of several
dozen cameras. At sundown, the videotapes were taken away,
and we were back on the train to Delhi.

This story is quite outrageous any which way you look at
it—an independent broadcaster, more importantly its news

division, albeit state-owned, was called in to provide a record of events, to instruments of the state, without a by-your-leave. This is akin to a private party engaging the services of a matrimonial videographer!! Two decades down the line no one knows what happened to the images we recorded, or to what use they were put. Doordarshan's archiving technologies are, of course, well known and another slice of history now lies buried and forgotten.

I tried several times after this to ascertain from the accounts department of my employers whether this was a regular assignment—if we were actually paid—but I never did get any answer. The company itself is now defunct. It is another matter that the border issue is still unresolved; it is perhaps no longer an issue and in any case, nobody cares.

This is but one example from a million others and some will argue that with the corporatisation of Doordarshan and the boom in satellite TV, it is no longer possible for DD to get away with such temerity. But the equally well-known fact is that the corporate media too manipulate the news; only they do it with more panache and a touch of class—not in the crass and clumsy manner of Doordarshan in its days of hegemony.

One case that comes to mind is the media trial that hounded the unlucky lecturer in Arabic at the University of Delhi in the aftermath of the dastardly terrorist attack on Parliament in December 2000. Geelani was arrested on the evidence provided by one of the other accused, was tortured in jail and almost lost his job even before the trial was over. The meat of the evidence seemed to be the fact that he shared a hometown with the other accused and a chat on the cell phone with his Kashmir-based brother. Over the next year, he was sentenced to death—a committee of lawyers and activists came to his defence, and led by some of the country's leading luminaries, he was finally acquitted by a two-judge bench of the Delhi High Court, though the police have decided to appeal the acquittal.

To coincide with the first anniversary of the attack on Parliament, and coincidentally quite close to the day of the first judgment which condemned him to the gallows, Zee News began to air promos of a film—a reconstruction of the conspiracy before the attack on Parliament The channel, by its own claims, conducted no investigations of its own; it did not speak to anyone remotely acquainted with the accused. The channel claimed without a modicum of embarrassment that the film was based solely on police reports. Is it ethical or is it manipulative to simply fictionalise the police case without giving the accused a right of reply? Or is it just a battle for television rating points? It is certainly not wrong for a reporter to use police files as material—but to convict a human being before the courts announce their legal verdict, especially when it is well known that the case is controversial?

In the days running up to the broadcast, Geelani's defence lawyers had sought and obtained a stay on the telecast of the film from the Delhi High Court. They had argued that though the film claimed to be based on the police chargesheet, it in fact made allegations against Geelani that went far beyond the prosecution's case. Responding to an appeal by the channel, the Supreme Court vacated the stay on the grounds that judges could not be influenced. The film was finally telecast a few days before the first judgment that sentenced Geelani to death.

A year later the final judgment by Justice Pradeep Nandrajog of the Delhi High Court that acquitted Geelani also raised many fundamental questions on the role of media trials. Justice Nandrajog held that media trials do not vitiate the trial itself because propaganda or adverse publicity does not influence professional judges. But in her writings, lawyer Nandita Haksar suggests that the larger point has been missed—for can such films not create a climate of fear and mistrust? The fact is that today, even post-acquittal, Geelani cannot get a house on rent or buy a second-hand car.

In the days of Doordarshan monopoly, privatising broadcasting was often cited as the panacea for freedom in TV news. This is one of the greatest fictions of Republican India.

The other great fiction is that we are a benign and tolerant democracy committed to the freedom of expression. We have to constantly remind ourselves about the methods of media manipulation. The job of the corporate media is to make the universe of discourse lucrative for their corporations. In other words, it is telling us what to think about the world before we have a chance to think about it for ourselves. The job of the state media is to do that for the state. The Indian media are therefore no failure—they are a massive success story.

an argument for a public broadcasting service

One possible solution—and perhaps the only possible solution on a large scale—is the creation and sustenance of a parallel, autonomous and genuine public broadcasting platform. In an early textbook on broadcast journalism, this writer had attempted to puncture the enthusiasm of young recruits by suggesting rather scandalously, even if correctly, that television was not a communications medium. It is a *sales* medium, I insisted. It sells its audience to its actual and only buyers, the advertisers, who pay for the time and end up paying all our salaries! The logical corollary therefore seems to be that television should serve the advertisers' interests.

However, this is an entirely unacceptable argument because it is the audience which pays for the advertising through increased product prices. And it is the same audience that pays, through taxes, both direct and indirect, for the entire broadcasting infrastructure. As consumers and taxpayers, the people pay for television.

In February 1995, Justice B.P. Jeevan Reddy had this to say in a Supreme Court judgment on the airwaves:

> Diversity of opinions, views, ideas and ideologies is essential to enable the citizens to arrive at informed judgment on all issues touching them. This cannot be provided by a medium controlled by a monopoly—whether the monopoly is of the state or of any other individual group or organization. As a matter of fact, private broadcasting stations may be perhaps more prejudicial to the free speech right of citizens than the government controlled media .... The broadcasting media should be under the control of the public as distinct from the government. This is the command implicit in Article 19(1)a.[1]

---

[1] Union of India versus the Cricket Association of Bengal, judgment delivered on 9 February 1995.

In a concurring judgment in the same year, Justice P.B. Sawant said:

> The airwaves or frequencies are a public property. Their use has to be controlled and regulated by a public authority in the interests of the public and to prevent the invasion of their rights .... A citizen has a fundamental right to the best means of receiving and imparting information and as such to have access to telecasting for that purpose.[2]

The mere re-invention of Doordarshan as Prasar Bharati is a chimera that successive governments have used to deflect attention from the real issue. As the recent brouhaha over the telecast of the Indo-Pak cricket series and the intermittent controversies over its retiring and new board members continually remind us, its actual working on the ground is no different from any other channel, except that its staff have to dance to the tune of the party in power.

Supporters of a truly independent public broadcasting service are often accused of seeking alternative initiatives that are 'too serious' and 'not for everyone'—a sort of elitist ghetto of the airwaves. It is an argument that is often cited against all manner of independent expression, quite often disparagingly—art cinema, pseudo-secular—these are all common labels. This is an unfortunate, parochial view. A broadcasting platform genuinely in the public interest should provide the widest possible cultural choice, and address itself to the broadest spectrum of the audience. More importantly, a parallel system must be guided by three essential values:

Autonomy from political or commercial interests.
Access that works from an expanding production base, that interfaces emerging technologies with the creative means to express them, that works against monopolistic controls.
Plurality, which is committed to the free expression of diverse and contending ideas, and which provides space for experimentation and innovation.

This is no cakewalk, but no tall order either. There are several models across the world that have tried to work, made mistakes,

---

[2] Ibid.

changed course, failed, and survived. There will be serious issues like funding and administration that have to be tackled. A vigorous public broadcaster ought not to be framed in 'opposition' to either the commercial or the official broadcaster. As an alternative competitor, if you like, it will have to provide fresh energy in the formats and styles as well as offer space for varied points of view. All this can only benefit broadcasting. Political and public pressure to make it a reality are needed and India today is sorely lacking on both fronts. Other alternatives have to be sought in the interim.

In the meanwhile, the media machine continues to make merry as it races towards its own goals. And other issues continue to be brushed under the carpet. One of these, of direct concern to the issues being discussed here, is censorship. Television often uses a finely lubricated and impossible to contest sleight-of-hand, and a darkly subtle form called scheduling. Several years ago, I made an half-hour programme on the law that governs adoption of children in India for Doordarshan. It was an ordinary, pedestrian programme, one episode in a longish current affairs series. It was accepted without cuts, and was never shown. The excuse was that they were trying to schedule it and would do it when they could. Off the record, my producer was told the commentary had too much Hindu–Muslim stuff!

This was a programme on orphan children. Now the law very clearly says that only Hindus can adopt children, who must also be Hindu. It is a serious problem and every time Parliament tried to enact a uniform law it fell through because of protests from some Muslim and Parsi protestors, who felt it would violate their personal laws. The programme had an interview with an expert in Islamic law who explained that an enabling legislation was no compulsion on any Muslim to adopt. The programme suggested that a child-centred legislation would only be in the interest of the orphan child, and not cause offence to any community's personal law. But it was never shown.

Over the years several other programmes have been consigned to dustbins but a few have taken their battle to the courts and won justice. Many of these have been briefly in the media attention, but by and large the powers that be have had the upper hand. Doordarshan has effectively used its scheduling prerogative to delay, and quite often avert, the screening of award-winning documentaries on several occasions, despite being mandated to screen them by the courts.

In the last few months, the campaign against censorship by India's diverse independent documentary filmmaking community has thrown up a glimmer of hope that indicates several pointers to the future direction of free expression and the productive and democratic use of public spaces.

This edition of the story begins in 2003 when the circulars first came out calling for entries to the Mumbai International Film Festival for Short Films, organised by the Government of India's Films Division, for many years now India's leading showcase for the independent documentary. The community of filmmakers was in for a shock when it discovered that for the first time, it was mandatory for all Indian filmmakers to obtain a censor certificate before they could enter their films before the selection committee—curiously, foreign filmmakers were exempt from this requirement.

The clause hid behind an archaic article in the Cinematograph Act, which had never been invoked in the 13 years of the festival's existence. In fact, as a matter of convention, censor certificates are never part of any film festival globally. India's documentary fraternity, normally a disparate body of individuals of every political persuasion, were quick to come together and, in a matter of days, more than 200 independent filmmakers threatened to boycott the festival. After a few weeks of sustained campaigning the clause was withdrawn, but this was no victory. When the final entries were announced—all the filmmakers in the forefront of the campaign found their films rejected. Not good enough, according to the selection committee—which of course has its prerogative to choose films for the festival?

The irony was that many of these films were made by reputed filmmakers and had won awards at other international festivals. That should have been reason enough for the organisers to ensure they reached Indian audiences! Fuelling more suspicion was the fact that many of the films were on overtly political themes—the Gujarat riots, the Narmada agitation, dalit rights, and so on. Also rejected were other films on 'awkward' themes like alternate sexuality and sex workers' lives. Clearly, a whole package that the selectors did not want the rest of us to see.

There was no transparency in the selection procedure itself, and in a departure from the past, the 2004 edition of the festival also did away with the information section that traditionally provided space for films not selected for the competition. The final proof of the mess came in the form of protest resignations from high-ranking members of both the jury and the organising committee of the festival and the voluntary withdrawal of their films by many filmmakers whose films had been selected.

This, however, was not the big victory: that was played out just across the road during the festival itself in the form of *Vikalp*: *films for freedom*—a parallel festival which screened about 50 films rejected by and withdrawn from the Mumbai International Film Festival (MIFF) 2004.

Over the course of that one week in February 2004, I believe the foundation has been laid for an important step forward for the battle against censorship in this country. Even as the films were being screened in two locations across the street from each other, not just the films themselves, or even the issues raised by the films that were being shown or not being shown, but how they were being screened become more important than the films. It represented a spontaneous release of energy from the growing and vibrant documentary filmmaking community in India. And an equally enthusiastic response from an eager and enthusiastic audience, starved of opportunity. Vikalp eventually had more registered delegates than MIFF. Members of the selection committee accepted in public forums during MIFF that decisions had been taken behind their backs.

MIFF and Vikalp have provided the catalyst for the documentary makers and the audience to find each other as well as give the former an opportunity to reclaim public space. This is a campaign that must not lose momentum and will have to be sustained. There are those who will try and find ways to suppress these voices. And that is the battle in the future—this convergence of official and unofficial censorship.

Vikalp was not a flash in the pan triggered by the backlash generated by anger at the shenanigans of the MIFF mandarins. Less than a fortnight after the lights came on after the last screening at Vikalp, they were dimmed in a large tent in Puri Beach. This was BYOFF or the Bring Your Own Film Festival, with no entry formalities, no bureaucracy, no hierarchy, no hassles, just sun and sand and cinema. Land up with your film and we will screen it. If you have no film, come to watch, lie in the sand, go for a swim, and take a walk. There was no censorship for 'entries' and no selection process.

Over 100 films were shown. Both the film makers and the audience paid their own way—there was no scramble for free passes, no grovelling before the organisers—scenes that have become the norm at sponsored jamborees like the International Film Festival of India. Screenings continued beyond midnight. It had to be extended by a day, because it had promised before it started that it would wind up only when everybody was ready to leave.

The fact that without any funds or institutional patronage, a film festival was organised and drew crowds is testimonial enough that there is a craving for information that is not being provided for either by the State media or the corporate media. In the absence of a public broadcasting infrastructure, independent film-makers (or media practitioners) and their audiences have to create their own spaces, or reclaim for themselves those that have gone waste or been hijacked. These are some of those spaces.

22

censorship ké peeché kya hai?*

k.p. jayasankar and anjali monteiro

the man who would not mistake
his wife for a hat[1]

Censorship makes four basic propositions, all related to *meanings*:

1. One structure is always attached to one meaning. No man can possibly mistake his wife for a hat; after all a wife is a wife and a hat is a hat, and that's that. Certainty should be privileged over all ambiguities. Reason is in and such madness, out.

2. Meanings (and hence, language) are *instrumental*. They are *used* by men who have no right to mistake their wives for hats. These wise men (and censors, if you could call them so) pour their ideas into transparent words, like oil or sherbet or Coca-Cola into a bottle. As the bottle takes on the colour of the liquid, so do words neutrally take on the colour of the speaker's ideas. Censors can distinguish between *kokam* sherbet and Coca-Cola.

3. Meanings are within the *conscious control* of the speaker/ sender/user and they can be accurately *transmitted* to the

---

* In the unlikely event of the allusion being lost, the title borrows from the 'infamous' film song from the Hindi film *Khalnayak:' Choli kè peechè kya hai* .... (What is behind the blouse ....). This is a revised version of a piece entitled 'Let a Thousand Meanings Bloom' that appeared in *The Economic Times* (24 November 1996).

[1] With due apologies to Oliver Sacks. The allusion here is to his *The Man who Mistook his Wife for a Hat* (New York: Touchstone Books, 1985).

listener/receiver/another user. The man who mistakes his wife for a hat could effectively transmit his ideas to a receiver.
4. If his message is effective, the receiver, in turn, might probably mistake (God forbid) his wife for a hat as well. In other words, meanings have predictable impacts on the receiver. The censor plays God in averting such eventualities; (s)he is the patriarchal filter of (erroneous and scurrilous) meanings...

Given the above, a censor could, to use an unfortunate tautology, censor. A man who mistakes his wife for a hat is potential censorship material. If his folly comes to light, he will be consigned to the censor bins of society.

hiranya-kasipu, macbeth and humpty dumpty

Hiranya-kasipu obtained a *var* or boon from God Siva: he would have control over all the worlds and would not be slain by *day* or *night*, *inside* or *outside*, by *man* or *animal*. He was slain at *twilight* (neither day, nor night), on the *threshold* (neither inside, nor outside), by Nar-simha (man–lion, neither man, nor animal). Having gained control over all the worlds, men and hats, he, like the censor, rested on *his* meanings, *his* interpretations. Death to the censor, in its many avatars, lurks in the interstices of words, in the interline spaces of sentences and in the sanddunes of syntax.

Macbeth is a non-*swadeshi* example. He is equally pig-headed about meanings and the woods of Birnam, and about his invulnerability: no man born of a woman can kill him until the woods of Birnam come to Duncinane. This comes to pass. Yet another censor bites the dust.

Lewis Carroll's Humpty Dumpty is another hero in the censor's pantheon: 'When *I* use a word, it means just what I choose it to mean, neither more, nor less'. He can 'explain all the poems that were ever invented—and a good many that haven't been invented just yet'. A manager of meanings par excellence, he remarks: 'They've (words) a temper, some of them—particularly verbs: they're the proudest—adjectives you can do

anything with, but not verbs ....' And they all come to him for
their wages and overtime, but not for long. After his fence-sit-
ting stint, after his fall, all the king's horses and all the king's
censors couldn't put Humpty Dumpty together again! Let us
refrain from the refrain about another one biting the dust.

table, *kokam* sherbet, coca-cola and other objects

Let us ask the censor to transmit the idea of the object 'table' to
a being from outer space.[2] S/he is sure to start off with the idea
that a table is a four-legged wooden structure with a flat surface. S/he will soon discover, like the men with wives and hats,
that s/he will have to invent ways to account for the varied number of legs: for instance, 'n ' (being the number of legs) could be
any whole number (3.33 legs, definitely not) between zero and
infinity. Then comes the problem of not mistaking it for a stool,
cot or a hat. Specify the uses? Write, play, eat, do nothing, collect bribes under, sleep on (why not?), cook, work, nothing un-
printable, mind you, we're censors .... After having written a
compendium running into several volumes, the censor rests
happy: the table has been tackled in watertight terms, with all
statistical variants and for all time to come. Then the alien has
a close encounter with a 'water table', a 'statistical table' and a
'timetable'. Des-table-ised, the censor starts all over again ....
These are the wages of regarding language as a set of lexical
entries that catalogue a 'world out there'![3]

---

[2] K.P. Jayasankar and A. Monteiro, 'The Plot Thickens—A Cultural Studies
Approach to Media Education', in B. Tufte, T. Lavender and D. Lemish (eds),
Global Trends in Media Education (New Jersey: Hampton Press, 2003).
[3] The first powerful critique of a commonsensical approach to language origi-
nates in the work of Ferdinand de Saussure. Structuralism and semiology
draw on his work to critically examine various systems of meaning and
knowledge. The Saussurian position on language can be summed up as
follows:

(*i*) Saussure designates language as a system (*langue*) of which the sign
is the basic element. Langue is a system of differences: the identity of
each sign is governed by its opposition to other signs, and not by its
material condition; (*ii*) The speaking subject's relation to this system is

The word 'table' is a sign in a system of meanings, to which the alien has limited access; it becomes meaningful only in the context of a shared historical and ideological space. While common sense might tell us that we use words to name our worlds, to transmit our ideas, we have perhaps to turn this relationship on its head to understand how language structures the world for us, how wives remain wives, and hats, hats.

The implications of this for the censor's rule book are nothing short of profound. The whole is more than the sum of its parts. The censor mistakes the trees for the wood; (s)he regards it as a concatenation of discrete elements, making it possible to eliminate unhealthy species from the whole, to make it follow the dictums of her/his li'l black book. The time has come to rethink the differences between *kokam* sherbet and Coca-Cola, wives and hats.

Meanings are like eels, they slip out of your grasp. How will the censors deal with someone who chooses to read the unprintables in the Oxford Dictionary of English? They have been able to do precious little with film songs that play on double entendre. Dada Kondke, the popular Marathi filmmaker/actor has been their bane. During the Emergency, all newspapers were under a tight regime of censorship. *The Indian Express* responded by leaving its editorial column blank. The censors had a taste of

---

one of compliance. The codes of this system do not obtain from the speaking subject. The subject does not 'use' language, rather language speaks through the subject; (iii) The sign is the basic unit of language, which attains its value due to the relations internal to it, viz., that between the signifier and the signified. The relation between a sign and a thing is fictional. Thus, langue is a system without terms, without a speaking subject and without things .... Structuralism denotes a break from the classical tradition in which language stays in mimetic harmony with the world, language as a representation of nature and the world. The sign with its internal relationship effects two shifts: 1. By conceiving of the sign as an interplay between signifier and signified, without any concrete historical materiality other than this relationship, it breaks off with a world outside. The world and the word do not share the responsibility of living up to each other. 2. The sign being a relational entity, within a system of oppositions implies a retrenchment of a subject. This is a shift towards 'signification', from an act of mere representation.

K.P. Jayasankar, 'The Speaking Subject—A Preamble to Vedanta' (Unpublished Ph.D. Thesis, Bombay, 1989).

the gaping abyss of meanings. Can they control *shunyata* (emptiness) like they claim to do with men and hats?

A conversation with Kalyani:[4]

K: Does everybody die?
J: Yes ....
K. This stone here?
J: No.
K: Why?
J: Only living things die, the stone is not a living thing ....
K: What about our *living* room?

Kalyani listens to the story of Red Riding Hood. Kalyani's parents are eager to expatiate on a critique based on gender. She discovers an 'ecological' slant instead: 'Why do you think the wolf is out doing naughty things? Because the wood-cutter (the hero of the story) is cutting down trees. The wolf has no place to stay ....'

How would the censor plug such oppositional readings? Do meaning filters work or should it be, to use a much maligned term, a process of 'empowering viewers/readers' to read between the lines'?[5] The answer, my friend, is blowing in the air waves ....

the 'impactors' who mistook their 'impactees' for blank slates

Any process of empowerment has to rethink the conception of the viewer as *tabula rasa,* a blank tablet on which the media write their messages. This brings us back to the issue of the man who mistook his wife for a hat and his impact on other men. The crucial question is whether one could talk about 'impact' at all, if by impact one understands a uni-directional behavioural change that can be predicted and controlled. If the media were so powerful as to corrupt anyone, why is it that, say, development messages do not 'corrupt' any one? How many of

---

[4] Kalyani Monteiro-Jayasankar is the 13-year-old daughter of the authors. She was three at the time of the first conversation and almost five at the second.

[5] K.P. Jayasankar and A. Monteiro, 'The Plot Thickens'.

us would give up smoking after seeing anti-smoking media artefacts? It is simplistic to assume that we are Pavlov's dogs, salivating at the sound of the media bell! This preoccupation with the 'harmful' impact of our above mentioned man with wife with a mistaken identity on other men with wives and hats, sets up a hierarchy between the all-knowing, immutable censor as opposed to a malleable passive audience. All censors bracket themselves out of this mythical circle of 'impactees' and perceive these effects only on the 'powerless' beings like youth, children and the illiterate rural populace with their rustic headgear. These naive beings should not mistake their wives for turbans.[6]

Where does this land us? In a relativistic, censor-free semiotic paradise where a thousand meanings bloom?[7] Our purpose is not to celebrate a *laissez-faire* economy of meanings, but to question the oft taken for granted terms of the debate on censorship. Can we function with the conceptual crudity of the censors, who can not see beyond their noses, their hats, which makes possible the excision of an aesthetically pleasing kiss from a feature

---

[6] At the heart of this is a set of 'dividing practices'. See M. Foucault, 'Afterword: The Subject and Power' in H.L. Dreyfus and P. Rainbow (eds.), *Michel Foucault: Beyond Structuralism and Hermeneutics* [Sussex: Harvester Press, 1986], which posits a normal, modern 'Us' versus a traditional, deviant 'Them'. The whole enterprise of censorship as well as development communication privileges this relation of power between hats and turbans (A. Monteiro and K.P. Jayasankar, 'The Spectator–Indian: An Exploratory Study on the Reception of News, *Cultural Studies,* 8(1): 162–82, 1994).

[7] 'The seminal work done by cultural studies theorists like Stuart Hall, David Morley and Ien Ang demonstrates that the emergence of dominant/popular cultural codes, values and ways of seeing is a complex phenomenon. The media are only one among many systems that play a role in reproducing the dominant culture. The meaning of a media text does not lie merely in the text itself, but emerges from its articulation in a social field, its interplay with other elements and its incorporation into *specific* practices. In other words, while there is an agenda of the text, there is also the agenda of the reader and the meanings constructed will depend on the discourses that are brought to bear in *specifc* reader–text encounters'. There has been an ongoing debate within cultural studies on the question of the autonomy of audiences to construct their own meanings at variance with the agenda of the text. For instance, John Fiske (cited by D. Morley, 'Populism, Revisionism and the "New" Audience Research' in J. Curran et al. (eds) *Cultural Studies and Communications* [London: Arnold, 1996]), celebrates the notion of a 'semiotic democracy', where individuals situated within varying subcultures interpret media texts in polysemic ways. We do not fully endorse Fiske's view and would not romanticise the ability of readers to resist the agenda of the text consistently.

film on the grounds that the rule book says no, and the passing of song and dance sequences bordering on surrogate fornication, because the rule book does not say no?

We have traditions in India which allow us to read aloud, in family settings, verses from *Geeta Govindam* or *Soundarya Lahari*. Pornography is different from eroticism, because it makes only one single 'preferred reading'[8] of the text, privileging it over all other readings. A text like *Geeta Govindam*, with its explicit references to the erotic, transcends the logic of pornography. It does not reduce its structures to one meaning, nor does it allow the reader to constitute him(her)self as a privileged voyeur. This is what makes a *bhakti* reading of it possible. How can the censor, with his/her basic propositions, deal with the complexity of representation and reading?

The censor, by concentrating on the most obvious and visible forms of transgression, disregards the subtle ways in which the media reproduce norms of the dominant culture, be they related to gender, class or race. These, by the very nature of the relationship between media and culture, cannot be censored out. They belong to the realm of the 'normal'.[9] They form the very fabric of the text.[10] It is perhaps the reproduction of these levels of meaning that is more insidious and lethal.[11]

We need to go beyond thumb rules, beyond the censor's simplistic propositions, beyond impactors and impactees, men and hats, to look at our media and culture as a terrain of struggle over meanings. The choices are not general and moralistic: they are specific and political. Beneath the *choli* of meanings, there exist many layers, the skin, tissues, muscles, pure pornography, or as a paediatrician in Goa put it, breast milk!

[8] S. Hall, 'Encoding/Decoding' in S. Hall, D. Hobson, A. Lowe and P. Willis (eds), *Culture, Media, Language* (London: Hutchinson, 1980).

[9] R. Barthes, *Mythologies* (New York: Hill and Wang, 1972).

[10] One of the authors has functioned on the Regional Panel of the Central Board of Film Certification and has had the frustrating experience of being confronted with a film which did not have a single 'objectionable' shot, as per the censor board's guidelines, yet was totally obnoxious in its overall construction of gender.

[11] This relates to the point being made by Rustom Bharucha, who, in a seminal analysis of *Hum Aapke Hain Kaun?*, explores how the seemingly innocuous 'appears to the idiom most deeply related to the "banality of evil" in our times' (R. Bharucha, 'Utopia in Bollywood—"Hum Aapke Hain Kaun .....?"', *Economic and Political Weekly*, 15 April 1995: 801–04).

23

news in the age of instant communication

mahalakshmi jayaram

a n average urban news consumer (UNC) today is spoilt by the array of devices that bring in the news. This allows for choice not only in the mechanism adopted to receive the news but also the time and method of delivery. For instance, on her way to work, having gotten an email alert on her mobile of an event, let's say a major train accident, our UNC may choose to tune into her car radio for an update, where she gets the latest 'official' news of the accident (assuming radio still remains the preserve of the State in India). On reaching work, the UNC may immediately log on to her favourite news site—bookmarked on her PC (Personal Computer) or turn to her news aggregator, which is programmed to search her favourite news sites and compile a news digest for her. Depending on her choice, she potentially has access to details about the accident, an official reaction to it, background data on the reasons for the accident or other statistics on similar accidents. As the day progresses, our UNC can keep herself updated on the accident and relief efforts. Her site may give her the latest news every minute, should events be so fast paced.

By the end of her working day, she might already have seen pictures of the accident along with lists of those injured, have information on emergency numbers, and even read a blog or two from witnesses at the site, apart from having seen audio/video clips from the accident site.

On reaching home, our UNC (who we assume is a real news junkie) can still tune into prime time television news for an interview with an official or a discussion by experts on rail safety.

And the next morning, her newspaper will offer an editorial and/ or analysis of the accident apart from details, which she already has read.

The point of this rather breathless description is not to start worrying about our UNC but to realise that journalists/media houses/news providers need to be aware of the changed media ecology in which both they and the UNC operate. News in this new technology-driven media environment is no longer a matter of *getting* the story but one of *getting the story to the reader at a time and place of her/his choice*, in a manner suitable to her/his needs. It would, however, be a serious mistake to assume that in this scenario anything goes as news—the fact that in some media systems anything does go as news has nothing to do with the technology. As always, technology is a tool to be used by human beings towards a certain end.

This essay discusses the implications of this new and diverse media ecology from two angles: first, the impact on news production and delivery or how certain technological tools can transform the very process of news gathering and dissemination and the impact of these changes on newsrooms, particularly on specific journalistic practices such as gate-keeping, framing and agenda-setting; second, the impact of these changes in the media on the larger social context within which the media function—on the functioning of democratic processes and creation of a larger public sphere (as conceptualised by the philosopher Jurgen Habermas) and thereby raising certain questions about the relationship between journalists and their audiences/consumers.

instant news gathering and delivery

As a teacher of journalism and former journalist, the tremendous advances in telecommunications hit home in unexpected ways. One is the speed at which practices become obsolete or marginalised. Take the teleprinter, for instance. The ubiquitous clacking with the occasional bell to warn of a 'news flash', a sound so closely associated with the newsroom, has been replaced across all newsrooms—even in the smallest small-town evening paper—with the computer monitor.

The days of the reporter/stringer/correspondent laboriously hunched over a qwerty keyboard hammering out the latest story (with the mandatory cigarette stub hanging from the corner of his pursed lips) as a sweaty typesetter hangs over his shoulder and an impatient telegraph attendant waits to transmit his report, are not even the stuff of myth and legend any more. The telecommunication revolution over the last couple of decades has certainly erased distance and denied time in the newsroom, where anywhere and anytime are 'here and now'.

The socio–economic and cultural shrinking of the world is not just visible in the widespread impact of globalisation but also in the responses of newsrooms to events across the world. As with the flapping of the butterfly's wings, the death of a minor chieftain or the collapse of a local government could set off events of banner headlines, and hence the newsroom that ignores the former is unprepared for the latter. And the readers/viewers of that newsroom are less aware of the multiple processes that culminate in the event of the banner headlines.

So if the newsroom is to track the smallest of tremors at whatever distance, it is imperative that news workers be aware not only of events across the world but also have the technological firepower to make available such information at short notice to their readers/consumers. However, mere technology will not do, because consumers of news must be helped to make sense of disparate and often remote pieces of information and it is crucially the job of a news worker to make information relevant, to establish the social, cultural and economic networks which assign significance to events outside of the reader's immediate universe of experience.

While the older print media have sought to produce this relevance through analytical reports, backgrounders and in-depth features around a particular event, these have inevitably followed in time—the time lag being a function of space available in the medium itself. Crucially, the newer online media have the advantage of incorporating these elements with the first report, thanks to technology. The impact of being able to provide 'more story per story', to borrow an ad line, works both to whet a reader's appetite and satisfy her need.

new means of formatting/ conceptualising a story

Media researchers point out that hypertext is a structure that is assumed to be more compatible with the characteristics of digital media than traditional narrative forms, such as journalism's inverted pyramid. Hypertext or hyperlinks allows a reader to find her own way through a story and by doing so, at times, find her own story. In a news context, a reader's first encounter with a news report/story on a news website would be just a couple of sentences: it could be the traditional lead in a news story or a brief summary/teaser blurb/introduction to the whole story with a link—MORE/FULL STORY/READ ON—for the whole story. The reader's choice and control begin here. If she chooses to click on the 'MORE' link, she is given access to a set of stories which make up the whole—typically, the link would take her to a three-para introduction to the story with a set of links with more details, data, interviews, background and even, hypothetically, the reporter's notes. Take, for example, an analysis evaluating the performance of a set of mutual funds. The initial introduction might summarise the reporter's overall conclusion regarding the performance of the mutual funds—their success or failure, or even a comparative picture of a certain section doing better than others—backed by a list of reasons. The hyperlinks could then lead to detailed stories on individual fund performances, interviews with market analysts, perhaps even offer readers a set of tools to evaluate fund performances over time, list detailed portfolios for each fund, etc.

An analytical article in the more traditional print media would be constrained by the need for linearity and by space, forcing the reader to follow the reporter's trajectory. Depending on the publication's constraints, the reader either sacrifices detail and depth or is taken through several pages/columns before reaching the reporter's conclusion. Sectioning of the story and providing additional details and tools to understand the story as well as the processes by which a reporter arrives at his conclusion enhances, as has been shown by research, a story's credibility.[1]

---

[1] Robert Huesca and Brenda Dervin, *Hypertext and Journalism: Audiences Respond to Competing News Narratives* (MIT Communications Forum, 2003).

Access to sources and tools allows the reader to experience the reporting process and thus evaluate the reporter's conclusions in a more practical manner, which a traditional analysis does not.

It is important to stress that not all readers may choose to go through the process of using the tools provided, but the very presence of these tools adds to the transparency of the reporting process. For a reader who chooses not to actively engage with the intricacies of the analytical process followed by the reporter, the site still provides the basic analysis and conclusions of the reporter.

Huesca and Dervin emphasise that 'hypertexts embrace notions of contradiction, fragmentation, juxtaposition, and pluralism, rather than pursuing 'truth' that is at the heart of the traditional journalistic enterprise'.[2] This approach is described not only as more responsive to the qualities of new, digital media, but as more compatible with challenges from postmodern perspectives that 'no longer believe[s] in a single reality, a single integrating view of the world, or even the reliability of a single angle of perception'.[3] And such sectioned writing need not be confined to the business pages—an analysis of growing incidence of infanticide would lend itself equally well to progressive reader enquiry, including perhaps a separate section with interviews with the social actors—mothers, village elders, social activists, doctors—and a range of data, etc.

In addition to the use of hyperlinks to section or break up a story into separate units, hyperlinks also allow access to archives, previous or related events and finally to external sources of information and opinion—for instance, the earlier example of the mutual fund analysis could provide links to the mutual fund companies themselves and also to other financial analysts/media organisations, even as the story on infanticide could provide links to NGOs or government data and policy statements.

According to some media researchers, offsite linking opens up new content, but links only within a particular site lead to a dead end, denying the very philosophy of hyperlinking and the

---

[2] J.D. Bolter, *Writing Space: The Computer, Hypertext, and the History of Writing* (Hillsdale, NJ: Lawrence Erlbaum Associates, 1991); J. Murray, *Hamlet on the Holodeck: The Future of Narrative in Cyberspace* (New York: Free Press, 1997).

[3] Ibid.

World Wide Web. However, offsite hyperlinking and the more logical step of deep linking (bypassing a site's home page to link directly to a certain page or fragment of information within that site) raise issues of exclusivity and copyright.

Thus, while the process of sectioning has often been reviled, or accused or blamed for adding to the fragmentation of the reader's world, when used with care and in a systematic fashion, it allows the construction of a much larger universe of information as well as for more perspective, context and background that may be necessary to understand an event or process.

As researchers Huesca and Dervin point out:

As audiences respond to competing news narratives, journalists will need to rethink and enlarge their professional role from arbiters of reality and truth to *facilitators of social dialogue and cartographers of information and communication resources* .... In future journalists will be better served by professional skills that emphasize the development of multiple modes of gathering, processing and presenting information. This will include self-reflexive modes such as placing reporters' notes and interview questions online which reveal the constructed nature of news narratives and bring journalists into social dialogue with users. Rethinking the role of the journalists in this way suggests the dismantling of the edifice of expertise, objectivity and truth and the constructing of systems of flexibility, responsiveness and sense (emphasis added).[4]

interactivity

One of the key factors which sets apart the new media from the 'older' print and broadcast media is the possibility of interactivity. It is crucial to understand this term in all its shades and possibilities to realise the kind of impact interactivity in a holistic sense can have on journalism practice. It is also important to understand the difference between interactivity as seen in the

[4] Huesca and Dervin, *Hypertext and Journalism*.

'letters to the editor' section of a newspaper and a phone-in broadcast and the possibilities offered in the new/online media.

True, interactivity goes far beyond the generally understood
meaning of the term, which has often been reduced to the binary of pull technology as opposed to the push technology of
more traditional media. Here 'pull' refers to the reader/viewer/
browser's effort in pulling in information/news using the technology and tools available on her computer as opposed to the
push technology of traditional media that pushes information/
programmes/news to the reader regardless of her need or re-
ceptivity. Understanding the complexity and possibilities of
interactivity offered by the Internet will allow journalists and
media organisations to choose the appropriate tools depending
on the desired result of closer dialogue with readers/audiences
and, in turn for the readers, enhance the democratic possibilities inherent in dialogue and wider communication.

To begin with, interactivity has to be seen as going beyond
reaction, which can be classified as 'feedback'. Thus the traditional 'letters to the editor' sections are reactive messages to
media reports. However, interactivity also has to take into account monitoring and filtering and finally allow for two-way communication. That is to say, messages from the media elicit
responses from the reader/audience, which in turn leads to a further response from the media. The initiator of the communicative process need not always be the media organisation/reporter.
For instance, reader's complaints regarding lack of civic amenities in an area/municipality could lead to a sustained series of
reports/investigations by a media organisation, that might also
invite readers from the area to participate in the news gathering/
investigative process even as it seeks to bring the stakeholders
and authorities concerned together for a process of dialogue or
discussion on the problems.

These processes may seem familiar and similar to those already used by more activist traditional media. However, the use
of specific technology made possible by the Internet allows much
greater degree of audience responses and participation that, most
importantly, may or may not be monitored. The 'comment on/
respond to this article' link offered by a few news sites is one
such option.

Interestingly, few mainstream Indian news websites offer this option. Sunil Saxena, Vice-President (Content and Services), *The New Indian Express* group, who is in charge of nine websites hosted by the group, views this as a very vital option for building site identity and loyalty. The website, www.newindpress.com for instance, does offer this option, though the responses on this site are monitored and moderated.[5] Despite the often large amounts of hate speech and venom generated in these sections, Saxena points out that it creates a sense of community, not only with other users of the site but with the site itself as a forum for discussion, and hence builds user loyalty.

The speed of being able to respond almost in real time is another crucial factor which encourages users—unlike the 'letters to the editor' sections of most newspapers which are viewed as severely restricted arenas of expression, leave alone dialogue and participation. Roshan Tamang, News Editor, *The Times of India*, Delhi, agrees with Saxena on the sense of participation and involvement engendered by the option. He said, 'On average, responses received on the CMS (Content Management System) feedback module goes over 5,000 a day. On days when there are big newsbreaks, this figure shoots up by over 30 per cent'. The online edition definitely encourages more readers' response as compared to traditional feedback. In fact, 'interactivity' or the involvement of the readers/users is a primary aim of all online news sites. However, the number of responses received depends on how provocative the story is.[6]

The actual process of monitoring/moderating responses from readers remains extremely subjective. However, in these online response sections, the role of the media organisation is merely that of a facilitator—despite being the authors of the reports discussed, the journalists seldom respond to the readers/browsers and an email link/address to the reporter is rarely provided. Other options for interactivity, such as chat rooms and discussion boards, also open up avenues for dialogue and participation by users of a site.

[5] Sunil Saxena, personal communication in February 2004.
[6] Roshan Tamang, e-mail interview in February 2004.

chat rooms and discussion boards

Chat rooms allow participants to 'talk' to remote persons in 'real time'—once again erasing time and distance. News sites often play host to celebrities or experts. Viewers or subscribers to their sites are given the opportunity to interact with these experts and ask questions, creating a virtual meeting ground with famous authors, business and investment gurus, sports or film stars, academicians, politicians and even government officials. Often transcripts of these chat sessions are subsequently provided through links on the site, which enables an ever-growing audience—a crucial difference from live call-in shows on radio or television that also allow for a degree of audience participation/interaction.

Discussion boards differ from the earlier response option and chat rooms in being topic-or issue-based, which may or may not correspond to a specific news report or event, though news reports may be the trigger for a discussion. This is liberating, as readers or visitors to a site may, and often do, suggest issues or set up discussion boards on topics of interest. These virtual forums for discussion and debate make it possible for site users to share ideas and responses unfettered by geographical, social or economic constraints which otherwise seriously would hamper communication.

Thus the technology of the Internet erases difference and makes possible the formation of much larger, global communities of interests. In recent times this process has seen the coming together of people sharing concerns—from anti-war and anti-globalisation protestors to victims of cancer and other medical conditions to fan clubs and astronomers.

However, it must once again be mentioned that the ability to set up such facilities does not make it imperative for the owners to participate or, in other forms, take responsibility for such forums of dialogue. Thus news sites that offer these options seldom have their own journalists joining these discussions; there are, on the other hand, several news groups, listserves and other discussion forums exclusively for journalists. The issue at hand is the ability or need for the media person to be accessible and accountable to his reader/news consumer through a process of dialogue.

In looking at the impact of increased interactivity on newsroom practices, it is useful to consider a grid proposed by Mark Deuze, Assistant Professor at the Department of Communication, University of Amsterdam.[7]

Fig. 23.1: Impact of Interactivity on Newsroom Practice

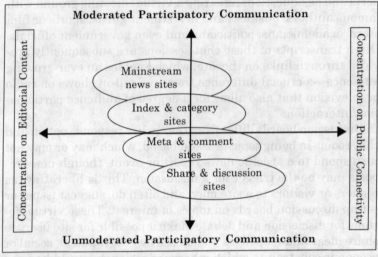

Source: Deuze, 'The Web and Its Journalisms'.

Professor Deuze's grid allows a mapping of sites based on interactivity offered as well as in terms of the monitoring of content. Locating news sites in the grid furthers an understanding of the preferred interaction between a newsroom/media organisation and its viewers/readers. More interaction and transparency would tend to indicate a newsroom willing to share its proprietary role in news gathering and dissemination.

✳ The valourising of the role of the audience as news producer, however, raises interesting questions regarding two of the basic journalistic functions: gate-keeping and framing, with the journalist as a necessary filter/arbiter of what is news. As the adage goes, the media may not tell the reader what to think, but they

---

[7] Mark Deuze, 'The Web and Its Journalisms: Considering the Consequences of Different Types of Newsmedia Online', *New Media and Society,* 5(2), June 2003.

certainly decide what the reader is to think about and also *how to think about it.* This has, of late, led to animated debates on the content of newspapers and television broadcasts and the agenda-setting function of the media.

The gate-keeping function is crucially linked to the credible-informational function of the media—as recorders of history and truth. This has meant a well-defined set of values and hierarchical processes that ensure the filtering of news before it reaches the reader/audience. However, given the ease of access and lowered costs of new telecommunication technology, one is no longer bound by the older paradigm of 'we publish, you read'. Every person connected to the Internet is potentially a publisher and nowhere is this phenomenon more evident than in the exciting, equal and participatory communicative space of blogging. A blog or weblog refers to an online journal and is a personalised response to a range of issues from politics to quilting, to life, the universe and everything. Blogs have been likened to 'signed columns' in newspapers except that in the equal online world, anyone can now have a blog and be read, unlike the offline world where recognition of expertise is as much a social process as an academic or professional one.

The celebratory view on blogging hails the new Babel, the proliferation of voices suddenly made visible (most blogs are still largely confined to text though options to add graphic elements, audio and video are increasingly available) with a variety of formatting and layout options provided free by several hosts. Indeed, increasingly accessible technology has made it possible to report/witness/listen-in to several restricted events such as board meetings, war and conflicts, anti-establishment protests, court hearings .... The list is growing exponentially as bloggers and their readers discover the joys of empowerment, of instant journalism with ready-made audiences without having to go through the often insurmountable filters and checks of traditional publishing. The most celebrated examples are the blogs by Salam Pax from Baghdad, written as letters to a fictional friend Raed during the second Gulf War in April 2003.

In a situation where traditional media access was severely restricted, these blogs provided a worldwide audience an uncensored version of the attack on Baghdad and its impact on Iraqi citizens in the city. These blogs, widely published on several

news sites, such as www.guardian.co.uk, challenged the official
media accounts and, in turn, forced media organisations to shed
their inhibitions and official shackles to report more accurately.
Is this what happens when the gate-keeper becomes redundant?

Several media commentators and journalists now have their
own blogs, which are very popular. On the flip side, Chinese
authorities have banned access to blogging sites.

Blogging also reflects disenchantment with and distrust of the
established media in the West as the impact of corporate ownership on content becomes ever more tangible. Blogging in this
situation speaks to a sense of authenticity and bearing witness.

Interestingly enough, the growing world of blogs reflects a
far older news tradition that existed before the consolidation of
newspapers as industrial products in the late nineteenth century and the birth of the modern newsroom.

The earliest newspapers or newsletters were compilations of
bits of information gathered by printers and publishers, not yet
glorified by the title of editor. Early papers in Europe relied on
postmasters to collect and send information about events in the
districts and small towns. As with some of today's blogs, sensitive information was often published abroad first. Svennik Hoyer,
Professor Emeritus with the Department of Media and Communication, University of Oslo, writes in 'Newspapers without Journalists' that 'demonstrations in Stockholm in January 1783 were
reported in French, but not Swedish newspapers, even though
the reporter was Swedish'.[8] News gathering then was a diverse
activity involving prominent citizens, priests, local schoolteachers, lawyers and paid hacks.

To quote Hoyer again:

> During the seventeenth and eighteenth centuries, compiling
> news was a common freelance activity among writers. An au-
> thor would earn a living by writing for booksellers, for the
> stage or for the public through journals or newspapers—or for
> all .... Printers for their part relied on these mobile writers to
> provide content .... The literary market contained many cat-
> egories of writers: hack writers, newsmongers and reporters

---

[8] Svennik Hoyer, 'Newspapers without Journalists', *Journalism Studies,*
4(3), November 2003.

acting as leg men, who collected news in parks, in downstairs servant quarters, in ale houses and gin shops, from prisons, police headquarters, executions, hospitals, the morgue ....[9]

The similarity to modern beats is no coincidence. Hoyer goes on to quote an eighteenth-century journal, the *Weekly Medley* which says, 'Newswriting consists in gleaning up as many paragraphs as possible, consistent or inconsistent, from the fruitful harvest of scattered reports'.[10]

Early US papers counted Congressional representatives and professors among their 'correspondents', a term first used in the mid-nineteenth century. Nerone and Barnhurst, award-winning authors of *The Form of News*, point out that:

'Correspondents wrote long informed letters from distant places; they included an authorial voice and were expected to opine. Routinely correspondents were anonymous, but often they were well known and only partially disguised personages.... The correspondent was a 'manly commentator' on important affairs'.[11]

The technologies of the Internet via blogging have, it would seem, once more reverted to information/news gathering outside established structures. The implications of this for the 'material and imagined network of relationships' that constitute the world of news and newspapers I will be discussing this further in the final section of this essay.

However, there have also been the less enthusiastic voices questioning the credibility of these 'voices from below'. In the third world context, these questions become even more problematic, given the socio-economic constraints on access to computers and then the online world. Despite the large number of enthusiastic bloggers in India, there is still only silence from the heartland and the ghettoes of minorities and dalits—the consequence of speaking the wrong language, being of the wrong

---

[9] Ibid.
[10] Ibid.
[11] John Nerone and Kevin G. Barnhurst, 'US Newspaper Types, the Newsroom and the Division of Labour, 1750–2000', *Journalism Studies*, 4(4), 2003.

caste, of being forced to live on the wrong side of the fence. Journalistic questions have also been raised. These questions relate not just to credibility but also to the ethics of a reporter publishing his weblog, which might compromise his reporting for his media employers or might go against the editorial line of the organisation.

news as sense making

So what does all this mean for newsroom practice and journalism education? Looked at through the framework of changing media ecology, a journalist will perforce have to understand the active nature of the audience/news seeker. Under ideal conditions, as Professor Dueze and others suggest, one can no longer talk just of a news consumer but must use the Alvin Toffler term of prosumer—a producer–consumer of media products. This prosumer not only has a choice of delivery mechanisms but also an array of formats to choose from for diverse information needs. These needs may be a function of time, space and information relevance, apart from the better-defined news values such as proximity, impact and currency. This prosumer not only constructs his own version of an event as he navigates the narrative via hyperlinks, he also joins in the process of news production by using interactive options wherein his experience adds vital context and detail for the next user/reader.

Interestingly enough, some of the well-defined paradigms of news work have already changed and will change further, given the ease of technology. The 24-hour news cycle of the newspaper world has already been rendered obsolete by continuous 24/7 television news channels and even these are being challenged by the constantly updated websites. Thus, deadlines become continuous and geographical proximity/distance in a globalised world of call centres and outsourcing is a slippery slope.

Some researchers such as Bardoel[12] have suggested that future information products will clearly be demarcated into instrumental and orientating categories—the former will deal with

---

[12] J.L.H. Bardoel, 'Beyond Journalism: a Profession between Information Society and Civil Society', *European Journal of Communication*, 11(3), 1996.

functional, specialised information for specific niche audiences, as in subscription sites, whereas orientating journalism will provide more general information including background, commentary and explanation, typically sites attached to media or news organisations. While this may be an extreme manifestation in highly wired societies, journalists must be aware of the need to address the diverse information needs of their viewers.

So stories online will necessarily have to complement and supplement reports available on other media. But each medium will also necessarily have to leverage its special strengths, that for the new media/online media rests on technological mediation and emphasis on formatting as well as increased interactivity to ensure not only a measure of transparency but also an essential sense of participation in the reader.

Sectioned, internally hyperlinked stories with access to sources, official data, in addition to possible discussion with reporters and sources—all of which are technically feasible—will become vital value additions to retain audiences even as these participatory mechanisms ensure a site loyalty. No longer can online newsrooms merely 'shovel' content from the print edition onto the site and be done with it. Geographical beats are already making way for the thematic as the local connects closely with the global—not just in terms of the technological access but also in terms of global impact.

Journalists also cannot any longer remain mere arbiters of truth/news but must move to become more credible interpreters and guides through the gargantuan supermarket of information that the web has become. It is precisely because of this information overload that online news seekers are returning to the notion of gate-keepers or sense makers[13] to help them make judgments which are too crucial to be left to software like 'knowbots' (personalisable pieces of software that will search the exponentially expanding online universe to find content that matches the users' identified interests). Witness the debates over the credibility of google news' entirely non-human operation.

---

[13] B. Dervin, 'From the Mind's Eye of the User: The Sense-making Qualitative–Quantitative Methodology', in J.D. Glazier and R.R. Powell (eds), *Qualitative Research in Information Management* (Englewood, CO: Libraries Unlimited, 1992).

One of the more immediate consequences of the increasingly diverse media ecology has been the fragmentation of media audiences. Two parallel processes have hastened this fragmentation: the Murdochisation of television news across the globe with its attendant corporate control over content and the ever easier access to an explosion of information and sources on the Internet and its subsidiary, the World Wide Web. The former has driven serious information seekers, who refuse to succumb to homogenization, to the latter, where choice of source and content is ubiquitous and everybody is, potentially, a reporter. What is the likely impact of this process on the idea of the nation–state? The bursting of the dotcom bubble and the attacks on New York's world trade centre have put paid to the sanguine premise of the death of the nation and the emergence of a global citizenry using technology to participate in a world sans borders.

Closer home, the mixed impact of globalisation on third world economies and societies has served to widen the existing inequities. The fragmentation of audiences in the world of media is paralleled by an increasingly divided society with unequal access to basic services such as education and health care and also information. In third world societies like India, it is again the elite with historical advantages of caste, class, education and wealth who have access to the online world for special interests and global communities. This access allows a further disengagement from the offline/hard reality of the majority of the nation.

How can the media in this fragmented universe of special interests and niche media, return to the notion of a larger, more inclusive community—a notion vital to tackle the vast inequities in society? I do not believe that the media have a choice on the need to bridge the divide—of which the digital divide is but a part. To not do so is to retreat further into the virtual that will inevitably implode. As Jane Singer in her perceptive questioning into the role of online journalists points out:

> But online, when one is talking about a community, the community is one defined and selected by an individual. Individuals choose communities of interest that they want to be part of online. In doing so, they also choose which communities they do not want to be part of, what they choose not to be interested in. That choice can lead to powerful bonds, the

formation of personally relevant connection with no geographic or other logistical limitations, the building of bridges in a up-dated incarnation of McLuhan's 'global village' (though one that still excludes those who cannot pay the hefty toll) .... But there is a danger if these are the only communities that people choose to identify with. And it's a danger that journalism has always been a buffer against.[14]

Ironically, research has also revealed that the more mature an online user, the less number of new sites she visits. In other words, as familiarity with the medium grows, the user identifies a set of trusted sites to which she returns, only rarely seeking information outside this set.

Quoting Daniel Hallin, Nerone and Barnhurst describe the professionalised news culture of the late twentieth century 'as its high modern period. In this moment, a rationale of objectivity and expertise predicted that authoritative news media could provide a reliable map of the world for readers across a political spectrum'.[15] This high modernism of news culture was supported by media monopolies and a strict division of labour in the news-room—between reporters and editors and between the 'sacral news-editorial personnel' and the 'profane business side' of a news organisation. However changes in technology and chang-ing economic considerations have signalled an end to this pe-riod. Multimedia technology has converged the reporter, editor and photographer into one even as it has collapsed the distinc-tions between print, broadcast and online journalists. Converged newsrooms are becoming a reality as media organisations le-verage the advantages of simultaneous news gathering with multiple delivery mechanisms to segmented audiences. The chal-lenges to the established newsroom and media practices can no longer be wished away nor can techno-scepticism hide the need for change.

But the euphoria over technology should not obscure the long and difficult processes by which journalistic credibility is built up. When everyone becomes a reporter, all truth runs the risk of becoming relative and all news just a series of personal

---

[14] Jane Singer, 'Who are these Guys? The Online Challenge to the Notion of Journalistic Professionalism', *Journalism*, 4(2), pp. 139–63, 2003.
[15] John Nerone and Kevin G. Barnhurst, 'US Newpaper Types'.

accounts of personal events, which other individuals make sense of as they wish. Objectivity is no longer a hallowed principle but a negotiated position, hard won. As actors in the public domain, journalists and news workers must continue to play the vital role of mediators and interpreters.

To return to our UNC, the task is not merely to inform her but to broaden her world to include others historically excluded, to give her access to contexts which determine the contours of her present experience, to offer her a mode of engagement with processes and events that constitute her world of news.

24

teaching computer-assisted reporting in south india

steven s. ross

j ournalists inside and outside the United States have an almost mythical view of the power of the American press. This is due partly to the First Amendment to the United States Constitution, which states that Congress has no power to regulate the press. It is also due partly to American journalists' almost total shield against charges of libel. When American journalists cover stories outside the USA in the company of journalists from the developing world, the latter cannot help but notice that the Americans are superbly equipped and superbly paid, by local standards anyway.

But the view is indeed mythical. As reporting scandals in 2003 make clear, American journalists often are rewarded more for good writing than for good reporting or clear thinking.[1] As the year came to a close, it seemed as though every journalism school in the United States was holding a seminar on sloppiness and jingoism of US reportage on the Iraq War. This author first taught outside the United States in 1971, and has done so regularly after joining the Columbia University faculty full time in 1985. Although journalism and the teaching of it are idiosyncratic and although there are large variations in press freedom (due to economic as well as political pressure) from country to country, the basic principles of curriculum design and teaching demeanour remain the same. This essay describes these principles as applied to classes at the Asian College of Journalism in Chennai, in October 2002, the measured outcomes and plans for future classes.

---

[1] Steven S. Ross, 'Beyond Blair: Shortcuts to Disaster', 17 June 2003, at http://www.poynter.org/dg.1ts/id.38111/content.content_view.htm.

why teach analytic journalism?

The goal is not necessarily to teach the writing of huge multi-part investigative extravaganzas, but rather to help the journalist determine that he or she is reporting on the right story, and not simply reporting well on the wrong one. The analytic process also exposes flaws in journalists' initial reasoning about the story. It is not enough to teach the mechanics of computer use, or even the techniques of good online searching. Analytic journalism raises the bar for everything a journalist does. Think of it this way: The duties of today's journalist can be divided roughly into three basic functions: Hunter–gatherer of information; Filter; and Explainer.

As the wealthiest, most educated readers go online, many believe they can bypass journalists almost entirely, to hunt for and gather information on their own. The truth is, they can't. And no technology currently on the horizon will reliably gather information from those who do not want it to be gathered.

The simple fact is that many sources of information, in corporations and in government, are not about to make information available to just anyone. And much raw data that is or will be available needs careful checking and comparison with other data to rise to the status of 'information'. The public is certainly not going to pay us a high premium for undigested or half-baked data. The half-digested and the unbaked they can get themselves!

Journalists' role as filter, deciding what is going to go into the paper or the news broadcast, will soon be obsolete. The news hole is about to become infinite, thanks to the web. This is already true in the Western world, and is arguably also true among the elites of the less developed world.

New jobs are already emerging for journalists to serve these new markets. If we don't package the news for specialised markets, members of the markets themselves will continue to rise to the occasion. Often, they have produced products that appear to be news but are actually captives of news sources.

Only in our role as 'explainer', as storyteller, do journalists appear to have a reasonably secure position. To 'explain', they have to do more than 'report'. Think about the tangled origins of many of the territorial arguments that rattle us today—Kashmir, Palestine, the Korean Peninsula. They endure because both sides of the argument have some validity. Helping readers to understand both sides requires more than simply listening to what a Prime Minister or a general has to say.

In India in the past 30 years, why have the incomes of coalminers risen much faster than for those who work making bicycles? And what might the government do, if anything, to change the situation? Why does the Government of India at all levels lack financial resources for infrastructure improvements, while China seems capable of making the investments it needs in this area? Is it due to inefficient tax policy or inefficient collection? What role does relative (to China) lack of private foreign investment play?

Journalists could also help dispel the notion that government never works in India, by highlighting examples of where it does work, at least in specific instances. The highway programme of one state might be held up as a model, or the medical programme or education spending in others.

Is it enough to describe the plight of workers who dive near-naked into fetid sewers in Chennai to clear blockages, or can we also investigate machinery to do the job, changes in sewer design, and perhaps retraining programme for sewer workers? And what about the money these changes will cost? Is there a better use for the money spent?

The web, in particular, can help journalists expand their audiences. Imagine stories in 20 or more dialects and scripts, both printed and 'spoken' using an automated computer-generated voice. Imagine text and animated graphics working together to explain complex topics. Imagine new forms of storytelling such as games and simulations to explain complex topics. Perhaps readers would enjoy becoming 'mayor' for a day in their city or town!

But such imagination is impossible unless journalists themselves can be educated to understand the complexities and nuances of the principles that guide their lives, and the lives of their audience. It is not enough to teach the mechanics of animation, in other words. One has to teach the underlying economics, history, philosophy, political science.

The vision I have described is not limited to print journalism. True, printed words are better than video for delivering vast amounts of background information and for jumping from place to place within the data heap. Most people can read two or three times more information than they can listen to in a given amount of time. But this does not mean television will go away. Already, every broadcast network in the developed world has websites with database links. But quite aside from all that, some stories are just told better in a 'television-style' news story than in any 'print style' story we can imagine.

What is the effect of prevailing interest rates on mortgage payments or company investments in job-producing factories? Or the real worth of an athlete's multiyear contract? How many times was 'good' mentioned in the news last week? Evil? Indeed it is the routine story, done better, that serves readers and listeners better than the occasional blockbuster—and makes all of journalism more fun for its practitioners. The routine story, done better, also serves as a more secure base for finding the blockbuster.

My teaching is designed to help journalists overcome gaps in conceptual knowledge and to give young journalists the ambition to fill those gaps. It is also designed to overcome their unfamiliarity with the software, the hardware, the math. Those who have had some exposure to the techniques of computer-assisted reporting may be surprised that the majority of my exercises revolve around using spreadsheet software rather than database software. This is even more so in India.

There are several reasons for starting with spreadsheets: Spreadsheet software is cheap and runs on smaller computers than can database software. Many of the stories that we can do with a spreadsheet are natural extensions of stories most media do now; thus, it is easier for reporters to get permission for these stories than for major new series. A spreadsheet also serves as the ideal vehicle for importing text data into a computer. It is far easier to identify and repair translation errors when moving from text to spreadsheet than when moving from text directly to specialised database software. Once the data are in the spreadsheet, they can be translated automatically into a format that can be used by database software. In fact, some database packages can read spreadsheet files directly, with no translation needed.

A spreadsheet thus can be used as crude database software. And, after more than 15 years of teaching computer-assisted reporting to more than 10,000 students and professional report-ers, I am convinced that students will better understand the function of specialised database software if they first use a spread-sheet to sort through data. That's because in a spreadsheet, each row is a database record and each column is a data field—just as would be the case in a printed data table.

All spreadsheet software can produce graphics of reasonable quality—graphs to help journalists visualize a story line, or graphs that can help illustrate the story itself. Spreadsheet graph-ics files can be read directly by drawing software, so that design-ers for print or broadcast can easily produce final images. Few database packages can produce graphics directly; those that can are far from intuitive in their operation.

Spreadsheets are weak, but not unusable, in statistical pro-cessing power. But SAS, SPSS, and other statistical software can read spreadsheet files. And there are add-on templates that bring statistics into the spreadsheet itself. Statistical processing is particularly important to those who are investigating rela-tionships such as the reasons behind low incomes of working mothers or patterns of credit abuse.

teaching principles

Throughout my career teaching abroad—starting in 1971—I have adhered to some basic principles. Americans and Europeans are often guilty of confusing 'poor' with 'dumb'. These principles help get past the confusion and also leave a solid foundation that can be expanded upon long after I leave a place.

Never teach a watered-down class. On average, journalists outside the United States have more rigorous undergraduate education than do Americans, especially with regard to math, science, political science, history and economics. There certainly are exceptions, but often they are temporary. Young journalists in Bosnia, for example, had their education disrupted by a half-dozen years of war.

Always strive to train on world-class equipment. In this age of easy worldwide communication, journalists compete every-where and compete across borders. It is actually more impor-tant for journalists in less developed countries to have access to the latest technology than it is for Americans; in least developed countries (LDCs), the overall support of the journalists' media organisation is likely to be less than in the United States or Western Europe.

Never describe your teaching methods as 'the American way'. Everyone abroad, it seems, has many first-hand examples of bad reporting by Americans.

Prepare carefully and test materials; avoid phrases that can be mis-translated.

It is usually best to cover what can be covered well in the time allotted, rather than to skim over many subjects lightly. The idea is to leave a real knowledge base, and real skills, behind. I make up for that by distributing CD-R discs with extra lessons and by being available by email long after classes are held and I have returned to my regular teaching job in the United States. My CDs include AVI video (with my voice-overs) to explain tough topics; I usually allow local media organisations to use, modify and copy my teaching materials royalty-free as long as they tell me what they are doing. One common modification: providing voice-overs in a local language, such as Mandarin Chinese or Croatian. Where there is a choice of material to teach in a restricted time frame, give local organisers an opportunity to choose what they want.

Allow enough time for translation where necessary, and for students to ask questions as you are lecturing. Do not let questions pile up for the end of a session. Stay on track by using PowerPoint or other lecture aids.

No matter how large the class size, keep the teaching interactive by constantly asking the students questions. Otherwise, it is easy to 'lose' students, especially if they are weak in the language you are using. At the Asian College of Journalism in 2002, I taught to a class of 80, partially in lectures and partly in 20-person computer labs. I tended to toss out questions to students for every PowerPoint slide presented and for every operation demonstrating Excel or other software. Call directly on students who are not in the habit of speaking up in class—especially women. Engage them in examples and role-playing to explain tough concepts. Use local examples where possible. It is useful to get students thinking about stories based on local, available data but analysed in new ways with the help of software tools.

Work on the gathering and evaluation of information as well as the analysis. Most journalists today can do basic web searches online. But as in the United States, they search inefficiently and search mainly web sources. They ignore parts of the web that cannot be searched through Google or other external search engines. They ignore non-web sources such as LISTSERVs, Internet Relay Chat and USENET. They are unaware of indexing tools such as askSam Systems SurfSaver[2] that can cut search costs by reducing the need for connect time to do repeat searches.

Teach method, but provide lists of currently useful links. Do not be afraid to look into the future and describe near-term advances expected in the next year or two.

Do not reinforce the bad habit of talking only to official sources. Stress that the computer is not a substitute for talking to people most affected by an action or who might be closest to a story.

chennai, 2002

I will now describe how these principles were applied to teaching at the Asian College of Journalism in the fall of 2002. The course has been described as the first of its kind in South Asia.[3] It was taught in nine morning sessions, each scheduled for three hours, with one formal monitored lab class lasting another three hours and numerous assignments requiring additional, unmonitored lab time. Lectures were handled with the aid of a projector attached to the video output of a laptop computer. This allowed live demonstrations as well as Powerpoint. Because it was not possible to go online live reliably, all websites visited were saved ahead of time on the laptop's hard drive for access at the podium. The language of instruction was English, with occasional clarifications by students for other students' benefit (see Appendix I for the teaching module).

Not all of the lab assignments listed in the syllabus accompanying this article were actually mandatory, due to lack of lab

---

[2] At http://www.asksam.com; a free version of SurfSaver is no longer available.
[3] N. Ram, speaking at Columbia University, April 2003, upon acceptance of the Alumni Award of the Graduate School of Journalism.

time. The idea was to cram the equivalent of a course that would normally require more than half of a 15 credit-hour semester and carry a weight of two credit hours, into a space of two weeks. Many students completed exercises that were not mandatory, using their own time.

Judging by outcomes, the course was extremely successful. The Mercy Hospital exercise was successfully completed by all but three of 80 students at ACJ (for a success rate of 96 per cent). The successful completion rate among students at Columbia University's Graduate School of Journalism, when this exercise was taught under comparable conditions at the start of the school year, was typically 80 per cent. ACJ students' searches for and evaluation of subject-specific websites was at par with their peers at Columbia.

Note that in comparison with similar courses taught in the United States and Western Europe, this course is heavy on use of spreadsheets (Excel, OpenOffice) but does not cover use of database software at all. As I have already noted, I stress spreadsheeting over database work in most circumstances. But outside of North America, the availability of large databases is uncommon. Where such databases do exist, they are usually not large (several hundred records at most). Analysis can be carried out with the data filtering and sorting features of spreadsheet software.

On the other hand, courses taught in North America and Western Europe rarely mention the use of geographical information system (GIS) software to track and visualise patterns of (for instance) poverty, disease and environmental degradation. This course mentions use of GIS and future courses will spend more time with this advanced class of software. GIS use is just becoming widespread among journalists in the United States and a few nations of Europe (particularly the Netherlands).

Courses taught to journalists in North America also tend to ignore the teaching of statistical methods and the evaluation of sources of information. This course devoted lectures to each of these topics (see Figs 24.1A to 24.5A in Appendix II).

appendix I

The planned Chennai syllabus, October 2003. Underlined material was linked to specific lectures, exercises and explanatory material on the course CD, which was made available in the labs.

analytic journalism, asian college of

journalism, october 2002

steven s. ross

Day 1: Lecture. Introduction. I'm not there to teach 'the American way'. American journalists have serious shortcomings in their education, even though they have nice toys. Numbers and spreadsheet basics. Exercise is Mercy Hospital.

Day 2: Lecture. Internet searching. Booleans. More than World Wide Web. Whois database. How the Internet works and how it is expected to evolve (for example, soon videos will be searchable, like text). Multiple versions of Yahoo, etc. When web portals won't work. Listserv, chat, Usenet. Exercise (in labs): Finding India-related bills in US Congress at *http://thomas.loc.gov*.

Day 3: Lecture. Evaluating what you find on line. Ways people can fool you. Tracing email headers (two hours). Data cleaning. Quick exercise: Send each other emails and see where they come from by looking at headers. Start to establish an online web-only account, to see how information for directory can be faked. Find 5 websites on any one topic and evaluate them.

Day 4: Lecture. Using spreadsheets to 'fill in' missing data—a key skill when data is hard to get! Lecture example: 'Sarajevo Trolley'. In-lab exercise, using data file from India.

Day 5: Lecture. Infographics. Doing 'pretty' graphics with spreadsheets. Lab exercise: Finding some data and graphing it from links below.

Day 6: Lecture. Business information, startups. Municipal budgets. Balance sheets, income statements, security, international and national finance. In-lab exercise: <u>BUSINESS</u>. Start with <u>spreadsheet</u> that includes revenues, profit, share price and number of shares outstanding. Calculate market value, ROI, EPS, PE ratio, margin. Sorting data. Spreadsheet data table as database.

Day 7: Lecture. <u>Data structures</u>. CSV, TXT, HTML, emerging XML standards, PDF. Getting information out of websites that have data in them, and placing the data into spreadsheets. In-lab exercise, going to specific websites and getting data, using links below, and putting an HTML table into spreadsheet. Also, getting data from <u>text file</u> and converting to spreadsheet.

Day 8: Lecture. <u>Basic statistics</u>. Confidence limits. Odds. <u>Polling</u>. Lab exercise: Find studies by government and activist groups on a topic of individual student's choice. Evaluate with respect to underlying science (if any) or statistics. <u>Reading</u>.

Day 9: Lecture: Wrap-up. The future. Demonstration of <u>Geographical Information Systems</u>. Ethics.

Key sources for exercise materials:
India Labour Statistics *http://labourbureau.nic.in/*
vslabourbureau/schemes.html
India Yahoo *http://in.yahoo.com/*
Statistics page in India Yahoo *http://in.dir.yahoo.com/*
government/Statistics/
Bureau of Statistics *http://mospi.nic.in/*
Census *http://www.censusindia.net/*

appendix II

Fig. 24.1A: Course Syllabus On-screen as HTML File

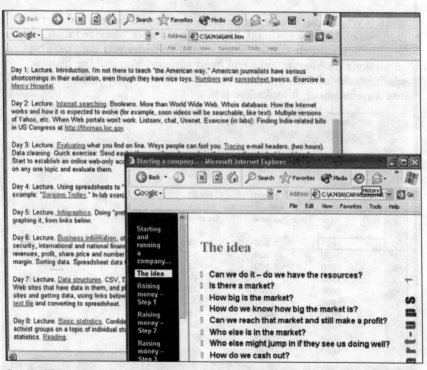

Source: The author.

Fig. 24.2A: Initial Data for Mercy Hospital Exercise

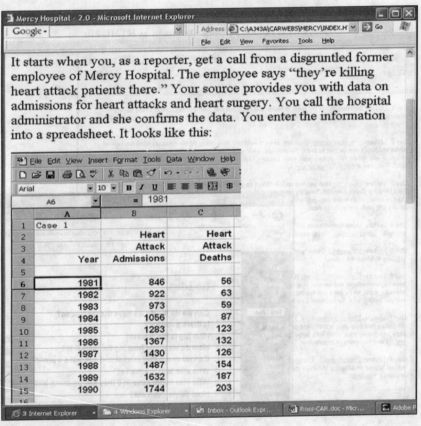

Source: The author.

Fig. 24.3A: Analysis and Comparison of Data

Year	Heart Attack Admissions	Heart Attack Deaths	Ratio, Deaths/ Admissions
1981	846	56	6.62%
1982	922	63	6.83%
1983	973	59	6.06%
1984	1056	87	8.24%
1985	1283	123	9.59%
1986	1367	132	9.66%
1987	1430	126	8.81%
1988	1487	154	10.36%
1989	1632	187	11.46%
1990	1744	203	11.64%

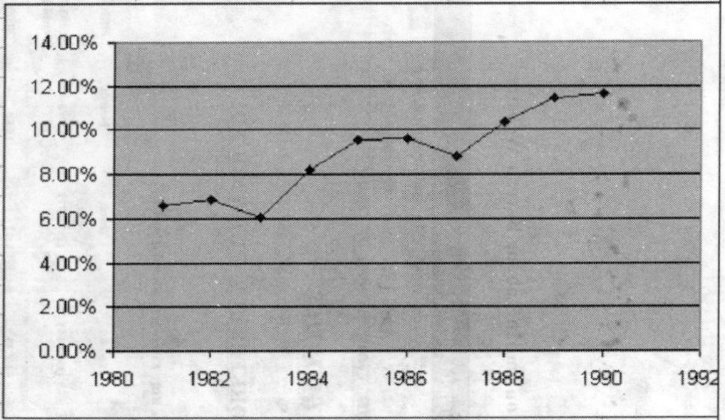

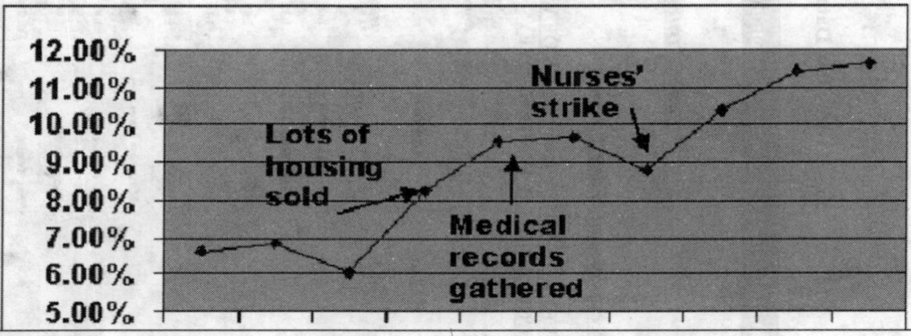

Source: The author.

Fig. 24.4A: Raw Data on Indian Labour Bureau Website

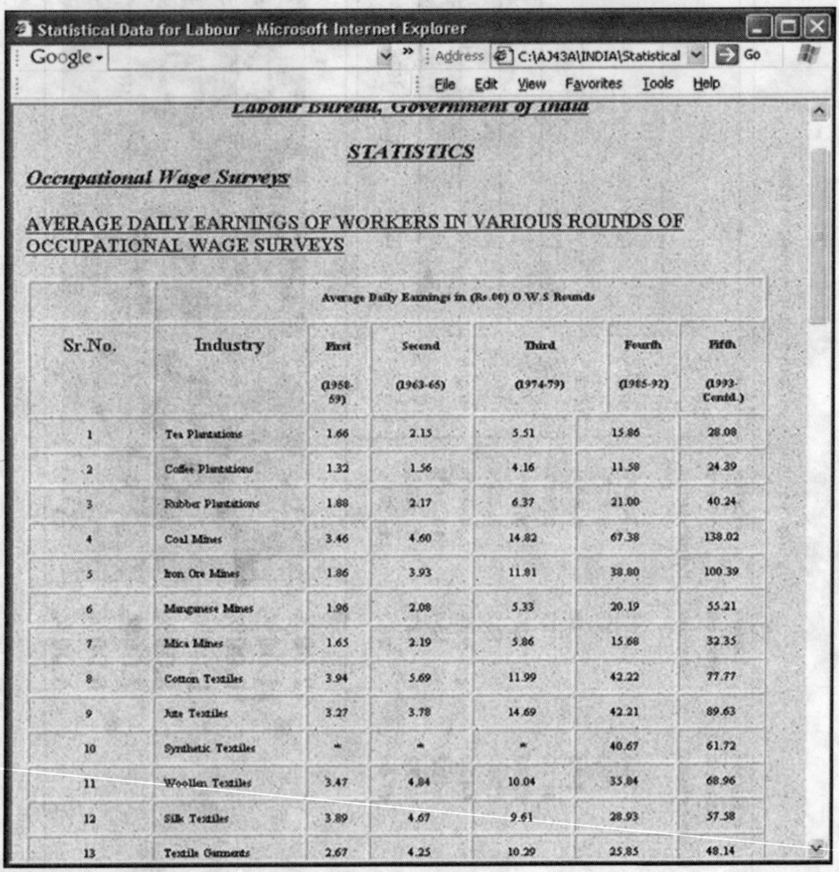

Statistical Data for Labour - Microsoft Internet Explorer

Labour Bureau, Government of India

STATISTICS

Occupational Wage Surveys

AVERAGE DAILY EARNINGS OF WORKERS IN VARIOUS ROUNDS OF OCCUPATIONAL WAGE SURVEYS

	Average Daily Earnings in (Rs.00) O.W.S Rounds					
Sr.No.	Industry	First (1958-59)	Second (1963-65)	Third (1974-79)	Fourth (1985-92)	Fifth (1993-Contd.)
1	Tea Plantations	1.66	2.15	5.51	15.86	28.08
2	Coffee Plantations	1.32	1.56	4.16	11.58	24.39
3	Rubber Plantations	1.88	2.17	6.37	21.00	40.24
4	Coal Mines	3.46	4.60	14.82	67.38	138.02
5	Iron Ore Mines	1.86	3.93	11.81	38.80	100.39
6	Manganese Mines	1.96	2.08	5.33	20.19	55.21
7	Mica Mines	1.65	2.19	5.86	15.68	32.35
8	Cotton Textiles	3.94	5.69	11.99	42.22	77.77
9	Jute Textiles	3.27	3.78	14.69	42.21	89.63
10	Synthetic Textiles	-	-	-	40.67	61.72
11	Woollen Textiles	3.47	4.84	10.04	35.84	68.96
12	Silk Textiles	3.89	4.67	9.61	28.93	57.58
13	Textile Garments	2.67	4.25	10.29	25.85	48.14

Source: The author.

Fig. 24.5A: Data After On-screen Analysis

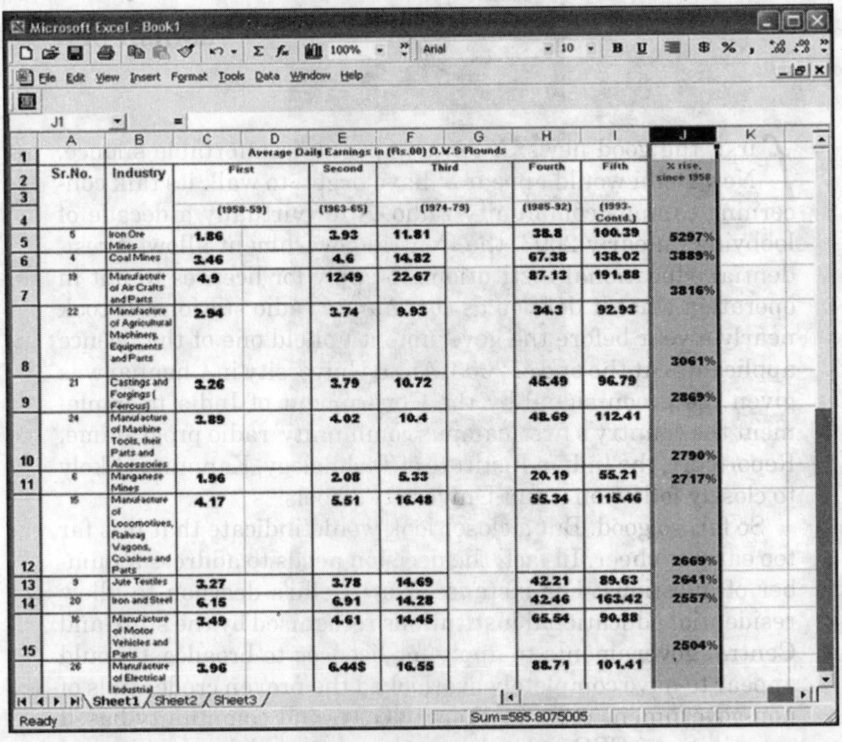

Sr.No.	Industry	Average Daily Earnings in (Rs.00) O.V.S Rounds: First (1958-59)	Second (1963-65)	Third (1974-79)	Fourth (1985-92)	Fifth (1993-Contd.)	% rise, since 1958
5	Iron Ore Mines	1.86	3.93	11.81	38.8	100.39	5297%
4	Coal Mines	3.46	4.6	14.82	67.38	138.02	3889%
19	Manufacture of Air Crafts and Parts	4.9	12.49	22.67	87.13	191.88	3816%
22	Manufacture of Agricultural Machinery, Equipments and Parts	2.94	3.74	9.93	34.3	92.93	3061%
21	Castings and Forgings (Ferrous)	3.26	3.79	10.72	45.49	96.79	2869%
24	Manufacture of Machine Tools, their Parts and Accessories	3.89	4.02	10.4	48.69	112.41	2790%
6	Manganese Mines	1.96	2.08	5.33	20.19	55.21	2717%
15	Manufacture of Locomotives, Railway Vagons, Coaches and Parts	4.17	5.51	16.48	55.34	115.46	2669%
9	Jute Textiles	3.27	3.78	14.69	42.21	89.63	2641%
20	Iron and Steel	6.15	6.91	14.28	42.46	163.42	2557%
16	Manufacture of Motor Vehicles and Parts	3.49	4.61	14.45	65.54	90.88	2504%
26	Manufacture of Electrical Industrial	3.96	6.44S	16.55	88.71	101.41	

Note: The new column shows percentage increase. The data have been sorted so that the largest percentage increase is at the top.
Source: The author.

community radio: luxury or necessity?

ashish sen

f irst, the good news: After a year of uncomfortable silence, New Delhi would appear to have begun to walk its talk concerning campus community radio. After virtually a decade of lobbying, in early 2003, the Central government allowed residential educational institutions to apply for licences to put in operation what it defined as community radio stations. It took nearly a year before the government upheld one of the licence applicants. At the end of 2003, Anna University in Chennai was given the green signal by the Government of India to implement the country's first 'campus community' radio programme. Reportedly, the Indian Institute of Technology, Kanpur, is likely to closely follow on Anna University's heels.

So far, so good. But a closer look would indicate that it is far too early to cheer. In fact, the decision needs to address a number of questions. For instance, New Delhi's decision to allow residential educational institutions recognised by the state and Central governments to apply for licenses to broadcast would appear to have completely overlooked the proven credentials of non-government organisations (NGOs) and community-based organisations (CBOs), which have demonstrated the viability and impact of community participation in radio. It needs stressing that in terms of grassroots experience, these NGO and community-based initiatives are demonstrably ahead of the educational institutions, which have no tradition or practical experience of community broadcasting. Furthermore, many of these initiatives applied for licenses in as early as 2000, long before the campus community initiative was conceptualised.

One of the reasons cited by official quarters for the absence of community radio legislation is the lack of demand. While it is true that community radio advocacy needs to go beyond preaching to the converted, it is not realistic to restrict it to a clutch of initiatives any longer. In the aftermath of New Delhi's campus radio initiative which was mooted in early 2003, there have been several universities across the country which have not only evinced interest, but also introduced community radio as a part of their media pedagogy. These include Anna University in Tamil Nadu, Indira Gandhi National Open University, and Jamia Millia and the Indian Institute of Mass Communications in New Delhi. At the same time, several development-oriented NGOs at the grassroots level have initiated or facilitated endeavours which demonstrate community participation in radio. Some of their experiences are articulated in the following voices:

We can't use government radio. It is used as a tool for propaganda. They will go to a village and say that they have given so many buffaloes to this village, we have given so much land to this village .... that kind of radio will not allow poor women to discuss their own problems and issues ..... (*Metalukunta Susilamma—from Pastapur village in Andhra Pradesh*).

You people often come to shoot work on the Gene Bank in our village. But there are seasons when it is impossible to shoot and you are not able to come. Maybe we can do our own recording and give it to you. (*Laxmamma*).

We want people outside to know about issues that concern us. (*Ipappally Malamm from Pastapur*)

My experience in Namma Dhwani community audio production is huge. Because of this we are reaching 22 villages and thousands of villagers ... (*Balu, from Boodikote village, Karnataka*).

These are a few of the many underprivileged voices from rural India, where more than 60 per cent of the country's population resides. They also represent communities which, notwithstanding their exclusion from the media mainstream, are actively engaged in building and developing community media of their own. Initiatives like the Pastapur media centre in Andhra Pradesh and the Namma Dhwani project in Karnataka demonstrate not only the relevance, but also the viability, of community media centres and their impact on development and governance in the country. But in the face of exclusion by law, it is worth reflecting how long they will continue to wait in the wings.

While community radio as it is understood across the world has yet to find expression in India, given the absence of legitimacy, a range of community-based audio initiatives have come up in the country. These, in the main, conform to two categories:

model 1. community participation in radio programming

Examples: KMVS initiative in Bhuj, Gujarat, reaching out to 150 villages in Kutch district, Gujarat; and the AID initiative in Jharkhand, Bihar, reaching out to 45 villages in Lesliegunj and Punki divisions.

features

In this model, the initiative buys time from AIR and broadcasts, usually on a weekly basis, during a particular time slot. The Dhrishti Media Collective supported the KMVS's programme on the Story of the Saras Crane, which received the Chamelidevi Jain award in 2001. Similarly, the AID initiative in Daltongunj receives technical support from a media collective in Jharkhand. There is substantial community participation in these programmes through a team of community reporters and community members taking on the roles of the protagonists. The communities also take an active role in facilitating feedback mechanisms.

model 2. community management and ownership

Namma Dhwani, facilitated by MYRADA and VOICES, reaches 35 villages in the Kamasamudram region of Kolar district, Karnataka; and the Pastapur Media Centre, facilitated by the

Deccan Development Society, reaches 75 villages in Medak district, Andhra Pradesh.

features

Both initiatives are rooted in community participation and have community ownership as their goal. They have their own production centre and regularly narrowcast programmes produced by the communities. These are disseminated through tape recorders at sangha meetings or at community centres. Through capacity-building efforts, the community volunteers are substantially conversant with audio production and today the centres are substantially managed by the volunteers/reporters.

In Namma Dhwani, the accent is currently on inclusion through cable. Three years of community engagement and participation in radio/audio resulted in the community managing the production and dissemination of programmes through narrowcasting at self-help groups and community meetings. Other innovative measures followed—such as the loud speaker narrowcast when the village *santhe/mandi* would meet every Tuesday, and more recently, the School Audio effort through cable paved the way for a cable audio initiative in Boodikote whereby household cable audio connections are provided, enabling two hours of daily community cablecasting in four languages: The programmes are cablecast in Telugu, Kannada, Urdu and Hindi.

However, notwithstanding differences in their approach, all the four initiatives appear to have a common vision: to ultimately ensure that community broadcasting becomes a reality. Summarised here are a few of the best practices that these initiatives have yielded:

gender
All the four initiatives, in different ways have promoted the voices of women. The Namma Dhwani initiative's management committee, which meets twice a month to take stock of the programming and management, has representatives from 11 self-help groups in the area. Almost all of them are women. The studio manager is also a woman—Mangalagowri.

A team of seven dalit non-literate women, headed by General Narsammah, manages the Pastapur Media Centre.

In the case of the KMVS, the women leaders of the *sanghathan*s, who have been a part of the initiative, have asserted that they have acquired legitimacy among their counterparts working on other development issues—such as watershed sanitation.

In all these initiatives, these women have asserted that they would be ready to run a community radio station on their own. Many of the programmes have focused on women's participation in the political process, women's right to education, dowry deaths, violence against women and female foeticide.

The fact that women play a strong role in these initiatives, however, does not take away from the flip side. A study conducted by Vinod Pavarala and Kanchan Kumar of the Sarojini Naidu School revealed that 'socio-cultural barriers at the community and household levels affect women's listenership negatively'.[1]

identity

'If we have our own radio, the issues that we talk about will reach a larger community of women. Radio will enhance the credibility of our messages by lending them the weight of the medium' (*Bidakanne Sammamma*).

'We want people outside to know about issues that concern us' (*Ippapally Mallama*).

In many ways, these observations from two dalit women of the Pastapur community provide a bridge that emphasises the importance of gender as well as identity in community radio.

The KMVS initiative was not only successful in using radio as a vehicle by which to reinforce ethnic identity, but also to promote community cohesion and harmony at the height of the Gujarat riots. During the Gujarat riots, the KMVS called upon

---

[1] Vinod Pavarala and Kanchan Kumar, 'Legislating for Community Radio: Policy Framework from Other Countries', *Voices for Change: A Journal on Communication for Development*, 5(1), 2001.

the people of Kutch to practise the values of tolerance and plurality which are a part of their way of life-faith.

Namma Dhwani in Boodikote village is situated on the border of Karnataka and Andhra Pradesh. The people may be conversant with Kannada and Telugu, but they prefer to speak a mix of both. The nearest radio station is AIR, Bangalore, which broadcasts in chaste Kannada. The Namma Dhwani audio production centre and cable initiative enables them to straddle language alienation.

education

'I have made programmes on healthy foods. If through this people can gain some knowledge, then I will be very happy ...' (*Usha Rani, Class 9*)

'I have learnt to make plays and music programmes. It is very useful to me ...' (*Srimurthy, Class 7*)

'We want to hear the news. We want to know what is happening in the country and the world today' (*Sundar Reddy, Class 8*).

These are voices of children from the Government High School in Boodikote. What is unusual is that they are a part of the Namma Dhwani extended family and a part of the school audio programme that started in mid-2002. They make educational programmes. Many of these are cablecast by a cable that connects the audio production centre to the school. The subjects covered are extensive: news programmes, plays, skits, etc. Apart from expressing their own creativity and making their own programmes, there is also increased exposure to general knowledge and current affairs through these programmes. Teachers have also begun to participate in these programmes and make model lesson programmes that are then cablecast to the children.

The school audio programme was born out of a concern regarding the Samudaya Dattashalaya (a government) initiative. The initiative aimed at providing a platform for parents to meet teachers and children to discuss the progress in education. Despite its laudable intentions, the Dattashalaya had poor attendance. Only four to five parents would attend, despite the presence of about a hundred teachers and children. School Audio has changed the scene completely. Not only have parents begun to take a more active interest, but they want to know exactly what programmes are being made.

School Audio has in fact triggered off the demand for cable audio across the village. Today, the Namma Dhwani cable audio is cablecast for two hours and reaches about 250 homes in the village that have TV sets. Needless to say, the channel is popular.

other aspects of governance and culture

The KMVS-revamped magazine format programme has MUSAFARI—which resurrects Kutch history, art and culture and also attempts to reinterpret them in a contemporary context. Spaces have also been created to feature dying art forms such as *Vai* singing. The KMVS believes that through these programmes a bridge is built between tradition and modernity—questions are constantly asked even of traditional legends.

At Deccan Development Society, through regular narrowcasting, a range of subjects from education and literacy, public health and environment to food security, gender justice and local/indigenous knowledge systems have been produced, narrowcast and documented.

This is, in the words of Pastapur's Pushpalata, very distinct from mainstream radio. 'We talk about *samma* and *sajja* (some minor grains). We always talk about marginalised grains, marginalised people, marginalised language and marginalised issues. This does not interest the mainstream radio.'

Thanks to cable audio, a range of community 'clubs' have started at Namma Dhwani—Children's Club, Disabilities Club and Women's Groups. They meet about once a week, discuss relevant issues and how some of these can be developed into audio programmes. There have also been interesting insights as a result of these programmes: For instance, a programme on disability helped the community to realise that bus passes were available free of cost for people with disabilities. Till then, middlemen were charging Rs 50 to fill up forms which should have been made available free of cost.

sustainability

The models of community radio that we have talked about have been supported substantially by agencies like UNESCO, UNDP and the National Foundation of India. But underlying this support have been initiatives from the communities themselves, as well as other partnership efforts that are easily replicable and worthy of discussion. The Namma Dhwani management committee has, for instance, a community base fund where the community contributes a small amount towards the programming costs. This is not a new concept, but a part of the self-help group development paradigm. It is also, in some ways, similar to the efforts of community radio stations like Lumbini and Madan Pokhara in Nepal that have community contributions and friends of the community radio support.

Namma Dhwani has also explored linkages from many institutions to address sustainability. The studio is built in a building that has been leased from the local panchayat, while techno-managerial support has come from other sources. In many ways this has enhanced the learning–sharing process.

the way forward

So where do we go from here? How long must these voices continue to wait in the wings? Their denial of legitimacy stands in sharp contrast to the private radio scenario. While restrictions continue to handicap the pace and viability of commercial broadcasting in the country, its growth in the recent past has been impressive. The recent recommendations of the Radio Broadcast Policy Committee in October 2003—if endorsed by New Delhi—could dramatically improve its fortunes. They could reportedly permit big broadcasters to own one-third of the radio stations in the city or 25 per cent of all frequencies in the country.

This apart, the recommendations have advocated the lifting of restrictions on news and current affairs with the provision that the AIR code of conduct is followed. There are provisions that also call for non-commercial channels and the strengthening of niche channels through fiscal incentives. But what these imply for community media—if anything—remains unclear.

Notwithstanding the need for the recommendations to receive the official stamp of approval, their provisions palpably demonstrate the contrast between private and community broadcasting. In many ways, the two contrasting radio scenarios effectively mirror the overall media climate in the country.

In a country of daunting diversities in terms of languages, dialects and culture, it does not take much more than common

326 Practising Journalism

sense to underscore the relevance of community radio. Its *raison d'etre* becomes even sharper on engaging with the country's poverty map. The fact is that, in times of need, the role of the media in bridging the development gap is more keenly felt today than ever before. Globalisation's impact on the poverty map leaves much to be desired. Even the World Bank statistics point to a rise in the number of the poor, with 40 million people in India having joined their ranks during the 1990s.

Noted journalist P. Sainath vividly elucidates this point:

There was no decline at all in the all India incidence of poverty between 1990 and 1997. The absolute number of poor went up by almost 70 million. Importantly, the incidence of poverty rose in the 1990s in a phase where the Gross Domestic Product growth had picked up. The poor have not gained from the reforms. [2]

Sainath goes on to articulate that, 'India also enters the "millennium" with hundreds of millions of illiterates. Again, spending on education in India is less than 4 per cent of GDP. Far less than the 6 per cent that the government itself says is the minimum required.' In terms of quality of life, too, the picture is far from rosy. 'New nutritional data at the all India level show that average calorie intake declined steadily in both rural and urban areas between 1973 and 1994.' [3]

Against this backdrop, the central issue which underscores the relevance of community radio in the country rests on its inclusiveness. Access without inclusion handicaps participation and ownership. This may have been reflected in the spirit of AIR's local radio initiatives initially. As the first director of the first localised radio effort at Nagercoil, K. Anjaneyulu, pointed out, a local radio station must be

.... flexible and spontaneous to enable itself to function as the mouthpiece of the community. In short, local radio should identify itself so completely with the interests of the local

---

[2] P. Sainath, 'The Age of Inequality' in Romila Thapar (ed.), *India, Another Millennium?* (New Delhi: Viking, 2000).
[3] Ibid.

population that the heart of the people beats in every pulse of the programme it broadcasts.[4]

Given their origins, goals and range, local radio stations (LRS) could have become the focal point of what is currently and popularly known as community radio. While LRS like those in Coimbatore and Hospet have served their communities very well and included a high degree of community participation, this has been largely because of the enthusiasm and commitment of the station directors and not because of systemic developments. In fact, financial pressures and bureaucracy have also often handicapped the LRS. Although the idea was that locally originating programming would lead the stations' broadcast service, there has been a gradual increase in relayed programmes from the regional, national and commercial services of AIR.

There have been other limitations as well. While the LRS initiative may have reflected AIR's interest in decentralisation, community ownership and management in terms of programming was never a systemic feature of the paradigm. Further, despite the LRS's substantial network, it does not reach the length and breadth of the countryside. For instance, in Pastapur, where the Deccan Development Society works, or in Boodikote where VOICES and MYRADA partner the farmer community, there is no local radio station.

Against this backdrop, the relevance of a three-tier media structure is evident. The two tiers of public (government) and private media are already a legitimate part of media processes in the country. However, a third tier—that of community media—needs to be legitimised. Priority needs to be given to issuing of community broadcasting licenses especially to rural areas and to other regions and communities that are least developed in terms of various socio–economic indicators. This is based on the fact that the least developed regions and communities of the country are also the least served by the media.

The demand for community radio in India has often been dismissed as being restricted to a charmed circle or a microscopic minority. This needs to be questioned and remedied through

---

[4] Quoted in Ashish Sen, 'Whose Voice is it Anyway?' *Voices*, June 2002, www.ourmedia.net.org.

effective documentation, networking, capacity building and strategic alliance building. Specifically, this could involve:

(i) Collaborations between universities and community media advocates/practitioners to ensure that community radio is part of the curriculum and pedagogy.
(ii) Capacity-building awareness programmes to widen the relevance of community media in the country in general and the social sector in particular.
(iii) Developing support communication mechanisms like a community media website and handbook to document and disseminate the best practices.

Unless civil society gets its act together, public advocacy will fall short of enabling community radio to be a legitimate tier of the country's media and live up to its promise of including the voices of the excluded.

26

'youth' and the indian media

anjali kamat

On the last day of the World Social Forum (WSF) held in
Mumbai in January 2004, I was approached by an NDTV
reporter who wanted to interview me for a story on the relevance
of the ideals of the WSF to India's 'MTV-generation' youth. 'As
someone brought up on Coke and Pepsi, how do you relate to
the anti-globalisation stance of the WSF?' Indeed, I entered my
teens in the 1990s—a true child of liberalisation—and could hardly
deny the charge. But I was struck by the plethora of assumptions
behind her easy categorisation of everyone under 25 into a single,
undifferentiated generation, a homogenous identity-group defined
in terms of its insatiable appetite for consumption.

Clearly, this woman and her features editor are not alone in
condemning more than half of India's population to being
permanently yoked to all the real and symbolic evils associated
with Coca-Cola, Pepsico, Viacom and others among the world's
largest and most powerful corporations. A few months ago,
Outlook magazine had a special issue on the generation of under-
25s, a generation it called the 'Zippies':

zip*pie.n. informal (pl. zippies) (zippie*dom n.) A young city
or suburban resident, between 15 and 25 years of age, with a
zip in the stride. Belongs to Generation Z. Can be male or
female, studying or working. Oozes attitude, ambition and
aspiration. Cool, confident and creative. Seeks challenges,
loves risks and shuns fear. Succeeds Generation X and Generation Y, but carries the social, political, economic, cultural

or ideological baggage of neither. Personal and professional life marked by vim, vigour and vitality (origin: Indian).[1]

Lest this definition fools the reader into assuming that the 'zippies' deserve to be commended for their élan and ambition, most of the articles in the magazine point to the inexorably high price that youth, and ultimately the country, are paying for this amnesia-inducing 'zippiness'. Some of the phrases used by the contributors to describe the attitude of 'the scrambling minds of India's future', include: 'smugness, a desire to be co-opted'; 'total absence of an imaginary of idealism'; 'culturally emasculated'; 'apathetic and naive'; 'inhabiting a virtual space of sullen self-justification and asocial narcissism'; 'disconnected from historical or conceptual movements'; 'disconnected from what everybody calls India'; 'passport Indians, just passing through a dirty birthplace'.

It hardly bears repeating that the lifestyle choices and leisure activities of young people have almost always been a source of concern to adult society. Historically, 'moral panics' around youth culture have emerged over the assumed deviance of youth and the putative threat they pose to society.[2] Whether it is their drug use, sexuality, or simply the music they make and listen to, young people and their presumed moral depravity quickly become predictable targets of the media's periodic wrath. All too often, as in the case with hip-hop music and urban Black popular culture in the United States, this unwarranted negative media spotlight has contributed to the criminalisation of particular kinds of youth. In this essay, however, I examine how the only comparable youth-induced 'panic' in the Indian media—particularly among the more progressive and left-identified practitioners–relates instead to the absolute smugness and apathy of the youth, their disturbing comfort with the status quo, and their inexplicable disregard for rebellion.

If we are to believe most of the writers in the youth special edition of *Outlook*, for example, today's youth display an overwhelming and inexcusable failure to be enthused by anything

---

[1] *Outlook*, 12 January 2004.
[2] Stanley Cohen, *Folk Devils and Moral Panics: The Creation of the Mods and Rockers* (London: McGibbon and Kee, 1972).

serious, political or life-changing for the majority of India and the world. They are largely an unthinking, uncaring, and unquestioning lot: their complaints about India are restricted to tired clichés borrowed from overused news headlines and their critique of politics rarely goes beyond the unsophisticated fallback—'all politicians are corrupt, *yaar!*'

But where does the sudden resurgence of interest in the fate of India's youth come from? Indeed, as Sadanand Menon points out in the same issue of *Outlook,*[3] a nation and its numbers are uniquely linked. Most recently, 'youth culture' as a topic worthy of careful analysis by the media can be linked to the release of the latest (2001) census figures in October 2003, which put the number of people under 25 in India at a staggering 555 million, or about 54 per cent of its total population. Almost overnight, public discourse in urban, English-speaking India was rife with platitudes about India being 'the world's youngest nation'. The products of over a decade of liberalised markets, satellite television, American-style fast food, beauty contests and ever-more-aggressive Hindutva, are now seen to form the majority of the population and therefore have to be contended with as more than just a bunch of kids.

a nation and its youth

If nationalism bears an anxious relationship to women, who are constructed as symbols of the nation and repositories of its cultural traditions, youth too form an important group that must carry the representative burden of a nation's expectations and prove the rightness of its emotional–material investments. In the early years of globalisation and the satellite television explosion, pressing the youth into the service of the nation might have borne a more direct link to a particular kind of nationalist rhetoric about protecting impressionable young Indians—and by extension the (constructed) purity of Indian culture and tradition—from the onslaught of Western consumer culture. This narrative of preserving a type of culturally unsullied Indian-ness

---

[3] Sadanand Menon, 'Mad Cow Disease of Self-Consumption', *Outlook*, 12 January 2004.

against an aggressive brand of Westernisation certainly has not disappeared—as evinced, to cite just one example, by the Shiv Sena's often-violent denouncements of Valentine's Day, that most consumerist and symbolically non-indigenous of 'holidays'. But, for the most part, the Hindu nationalists seem to be winning the Gramscian 'war of positions' by steadily strengthening their hold over Indian middle-class youth through their successful use of the new technologies of communication in the age of liberalisation.

I am not referring to the overt Hindutva agenda of the pseudo-religious propaganda channels, or even to the mushrooming of websites and e-zines (electronic magazines) directly and indirectly related to a blatant Hindu nationalist agenda. Instead, I wish to turn to the incredibly popular Hindi television soaps (of the Ekta Kapoor variety, for example) that have succeeded in reinforcing the image of the modern Indian citizen as a patriotic, urban, religious, upper-caste Hindu with patriarchal 'family values', who is simultaneously (and without any contradictions) trendy, successful in the ruthless corporate world, comfortable in English and an avid consumer of American products. This is the desired national norm broadcast to the some 40 million families with satellite television[4]—and an integral tool in consolidating a middle-class consensus for the hegemony of Hindutva ideals.

Jingoism and consumerism are familiar bedfellows and even the much-maligned portal of mindless Americanisation, MTV, regularly dons the mantle of benign nationalism; blending patriotism, Hinglish-accented Indi-pop, and its trademark American pop-art inspired advertising into a cool, digestibly Indian and guilt-free product. It is no coincidence that among the seven nominees for MTV-India's 2003 Youth Icon of the Year Award were Prime Minister A.B. Vajpayee, star of an Ekta Kapoor soap, Smriti Malhotra, President A.P.J. Abdul Kalam and industrialist Anil Ambani. Chosen by over 100,000 youth from eight cities, who were polled by the Indian Marketing and Research Bureau (IMRB), the choices reflect the successful identification of these youth with a particular nationalist imaginary—one of a strong, modern, capitalistic and family-value-oriented India. Ambani,

---

[4] Satellite television penetration figures are from the National Readership Survey of India, 2002.

the ultimate winner, urged the youth to further 'harness our core values, our religion, our spiritualism', (as 'this is what the whole world wants to learn from us') but remained confident about their capability to 'propel India into the future'; 'Indian youth are very, very ambitious' and 'very competitive'.[5]

In official discourse, then, the youth of India are a beacon of hope, lighting the way to the realisation of an outsourcing-driven economic miracle. Their entrepreneurship, information technology-savvy, command over English, skills in mathematics and science— in conjunction with their 'Indian values'—all bode well for India's economic future. Thus, the previous Indian Prime Minister Vajpayee can insist that 'Indian youth are in great demand all over the world'.[6] In a similar vein, *Business Week*'s special issue on India's youth in October 1999 described the youth as 'capitalist-minded', 'best suited to exploit the new forces of the internet and cable television transforming the social landscape of India'; in short, 'a generation [that] with its materialist values and global opinions that will reclaim India's future'.

Absent from these self-congratulatory paeans to the ambitious and modern, yet disciplined and resolutely patriotic leaders-in-the-making, is an elaboration of exactly who comprises the youth under discussion. Also missing is an understanding of how the benevolent forces of the Internet and cable television might transform the casteist and communal realities of India when almost 60 per cent of rural India still has no access to electricity. Surely, the all-embracing term 'youth' was not meant to include the two dalit boys who were beaten to death in February 2004 in Uttar Pradesh because they won a series of cricket matches against the Rajput boys from the neighbouring village. But the stark reality of the digital divide, the worsening poverty of the countryside, the continued expropriation of adivasi lands, and the increase in communal, gender-and caste-based discrimination and violence are not considered issues relevant to the youth of today. Instead, most of what comprises the 'news' that's fit for youth is an uninspiring amalgam of fashion, movies, celebrities, cricket and clichéd romantic advice.

---

[5] Anil Ambani, in an interview with MTV VJ Cyrus Broacha, printed in *Outlook*, 12 January 2004.
[6] *Business Line*, 11 January 2004.

dumb and dumber: consuming youth in the age of corporate media

As several scholars and media analysts have argued, framing the post-1991 satellite television explosion in terms of widening the range of choices available to the Indian consumer is alarmingly misleading.[7] The proliferation of the number of channels seems to be nothing but an ironic façade for the concentration of transnational corporate power. In the United States, for example, six of the world's largest media conglomerates (Disney, AOL Time Warner, Viacom, News Corporation, Vivendi and Bertelsmann) own and operate more than 90 per cent of the mass media, controlling almost all of America's newspapers, books, videos, magazines, television and radio stations, movies, wire services and Internet providers. With Rupert Murdoch's Star (News Corporation), Viacom's MTV, and Time-Warner's CNN beaming down on India since 1991, and India's own Bennett, Coleman and Co. Ltd owning some of the country's most popular English-language newspapers, magazines and radio channels, India is no stranger to the challenges of cartelised media. Indian satellite television viewers in particular live under the same delusion of choice offered by the range of channels with 'imaginary content' that 'keeps us fully entertained and half-informed'.[8]

Undoubtedly, corporate ownership and advertising—and ratings-driven content—have had a corrosive influence on Indian journalism, most noticeable in the growing 'tabloidisation' of Indian newspapers. For the most part, the media appear to be content to play handmaiden to corporate interests. Advertisers can speak of 'freedom of choice' in reverent tones, and the liberal media hail the economic democracy of free markets. Coverage of non-sensational, urgently relevant news, particularly on developments affecting large parts of rural and under-privileged India—as P. Sainath repeatedly points out—has been sacrificed at the altar of market-driven journalism.[9] Narrowcasting to the

---

[7] For example, see N. Ram's 'The Great Indian Media Bazaar: Emerging Trends and Issues for the Future', in Romila Thapar (ed.), *India: Another Millennium?* (New Delhi: Viking, 2000).

[8] Mark Crispin Miller, 'What's Wrong with this Picture?' *The Nation*, 20 December 2001.

[9] See P. Sainath's *Everybody Loves a Good Drought: Stories from India's Poorest Districts* (New Delhi: Penguin, 1996).

urban elite involves the dramatic increase in the proportion of television time and newspaper space devoted to entertainment and sensational stories, and an exclusive emphasis on dramatic packaging and sound-bytes in the format of television news. Together, these changes in both the form and content of news constitute what is often described as the 'dumbing down' of the media.

Youth play a special role in this narrative as they are specifically targeted by the burgeoning leisure industry as a niche market. As media theorists have long argued, the modern constitution of youth in terms of a social group with an identifiable *lifestyle* parallels the growth of lifestyle-related research and marketing by the media and leisure industries, and the construction of youth as a distinct group of *consumers*.[10] This is best exemplified in the development of MTV as both an advertising/marketing medium and a youth medium. Crucially, for advertisers and media conglomerates, the 555 million under-25s in India form one of the world's largest captive markets.

The advertising and media industries, then, have constructed Indian youth as an imagined community of national consumers of international goods. Recent scholarship discussing consumption, citizenship and democracy in post-colonial Africa and post-war Europe and the United States, highlight the relationship between the market, the commodity and the individual as an important plane for the construction and reconstruction of national identity.[11] In these cases, the emergence of the consumer-as-citizen in political and economic discourse tied the 'freedom

---

[10] See Stanley Cohen, *Folk Devils and Moral Panics: The Creation of the Mods and Rockers* (London: McGibbon and Kee, 1972); Kirsten Drotner, 'Modernity and Media Panics', in Michael Skovmand and Kim Schroder (eds), *Media Culture: Reapperaising Transnational Media* (London and New York: Routledge, 1992); Simon Frith, *Sound Effects: Youth, Leisure, and the Politics of Rock'n'Roll* (New York: Pantheon Books, 1981).

[11] For example, see Timothy Burke, *Lifebuoy Men, Lux Women: Commodification, Consumption and Cleanliness in Modern Zimbabwe* (Raleigh, NC: Duke University Press, 1996); Charles McGovern, Judt Matthias and Susan Strasser (eds), *Getting and Spending: European and American Consumer Societies in the Twentieth Century* (Cambridge: Cambridge University Press, 1998); Kristin Ross, *Fast Cars, Clean Bodies: Decolonization and the Reordering of French Culture* (Cambridge, MA: MIT Press, 1995).

of choice' offered by the market to notions of a sovereign political democracy. Consumption offered the utopian promise of an economic democracy where individuals could be good citizens who could simultaneously 'freely' define themselves by acquiring goods and lifestyles. In the context of the political, social and cultural changes wrought by India's economic liberalisation programme since 1991, it is the 'youth' who have been primarily targeted and constructed as consumers.

Much like the situation in other Third World states where discourses and practices of consumption and advertising are complicit in enabling new forms of neo-colonial rule, consumption in India functions as a cultural and economic vehicle that sustains the interests of global capital. Yet, the alliance between the forces of chauvinistic nationalism and capitalist globalisation creates a slippage where, ironically, consumption can sometimes offer a route to capitalist prosperity that is not at odds with the ideals of a sovereign, post-colonial Hindu nationalism. Thus, the new 'shining' India has not only shaken off the outmoded shackles of the earlier Nehruvian era of socialism, secularism and non-alignment, it has finally emerged from the darkness of centuries of colonial rule and foreign invasions. Now, India can be on a world stage, on par with the global superpower that is the United States. Not only can Indian scientists show the world that India can make and test nuclear bombs, but the results of international beauty pageants prove that Indian women are the most beautiful in the world. India is finally a country that its young consuming citizens can be legitimately proud of. Eager consumers of global commodities, music television, jingoistic Bollywood cinema and tabloid news, indeed, the contradictions inherent in the easy co-existence of 'Americanisation', economic liberalisation, and creeping Hindutva-isation appears to be totally lost on them.

It would appear to be quite rational, then, for those on the left concerned with the stupor of today's youth to view their alleged 'dumbness' as both the proximate cause and effect of the 'dumbed down' media. But bemoaning the stupidity and empty consumerism of youth who grew up on satellite television and Coke reveals a dangerous circularity between the media's obsessive catering to the youth market, their uninspiring reporting on 'youth issues', and the anxiety in public discourse over the entirely vacuous pursuits of young people. Like the context discussed in Susan Faludi's *Backlash*,[12] a process of mutual reinforcement seems to be at play within the media; where repeatedly referring to the stupidity, self-absorption and political conservativeness of youth—while continuing to generously cover celebrity scandals and cater to youth-focused advertising interests—is enough to make it true.

By exclusively emphasising the liberalisation- and media-induced intellectual torpor of Indian youth, critics of the corporate media and right-wing nationalism incongruously end up subscribing to the same advertising-centred lens with which to understand and define youth—simply a category of consumers. As Melani McAlister notes, the production of a discourse that 'comes to be understood as authoritative, as common sense .... occurs not through conspiracy or conscious collaboration of individuals but through the internal logics of cultural practices, intersecting with the entirely interested activity of social agents'. Thus, 'certain meanings can become naturalized by repetition', and 'different sets of texts, with their own interests and affiliations, come to overlap, to reinforce and revise one another towards an end that is neither entirely planned nor entirely coincidental'.[13]

Framing youth as nothing more than a group of consumers not only reproduces the corporate understanding of youth as a niche consumer market, consuming in the service of the national economy, but also reinforces the myth of an uncritical, unconscious and ultimately lost generation.

who are the 'youth' in 'youth culture'?

A fundamental question that underlies this entire discussion concerns the uncritical use of the signifier 'youth', without bothering to examine just who among India's vast numbers of under-25s are included in this all-embracing moniker. By

[12] Susan Faludi, *Backlash: The Undeclared War against American Women* (New York: Anchor Books, 1992).
[13] Melani McAlister, *Epic Encounters: Culture, Media and U.S Interests in the Middle East, 1945–2000* (Berkeley: UC Press, 2001), p. 8.

associating the term 'youth' with a very particular kind of experience and aesthetic, it risks becoming a frozen category—where mere mention of the word is sufficient to guarantee the shallow, hedonistic, and apolitical character of the subject under discussion. 'Youth' is stripped of its historical and cultural specificity, and remains fixed outside of history and political intervention. Yet it is still assumed to speak for all people of a certain age bracket.

Notwithstanding some degree of shared experiences among young people growing up in the 1990s and 2000s, such a focus on the assumed homogeneity of youth experiences privileges age over every other category, including class, gender, caste, spatial location, religious identity and sexuality. To ignore the diversity of youth experiences is to treat youth as an undifferentiated 'category of essence'.[14] More unsettling, however—given that the effects of economic liberalisation, the Mandal Commission report, and the rise of the Hindu Right have been so drastically different for people of different political, economic and social locations—is that this understanding of youth privileges the young, urban, upper-middle class and predominantly Hindu upper-caste experience as the definitive condition of 'Indian youth'.

The media's determination of 'youth' issues seems to be based more on market surveys than on the actual interest the vast majority of youth display in these issues. To assume that questions of politics and economics, for example, are irrelevant to youth is to assume that no young people in India live in dire poverty, that no child has to walk miles to attend a primary school or find a health centre, that not a single youth has faced the brunt of the economic liberalisation policies, that no young person suffers the humiliation of caste-based discrimination and that no one under 25 has been adversely affected by state, police, communal or caste violence. To return briefly to the special youth issue of *Outlook* and its discussion of the relevance of the 2001 Census figures, it was most disconcerting to note the stark absence of any mention of what percentage of the 555 million under-25s the so-called 'zippies' represent. Where are the figures and corresponding analyses of 'youth culture' for the

---

[14] Stuart Hall, 'What is the "Black" in Black Popular Culture?' in Gina Dent (ed.), *Black Popular Culture* (Seattle: Bay Press), p. 30.

numbers of youth under the poverty line? Or the youth fed on a diet of Bollywood-style patriotism and glorification of violence, who actually join the army and the police? Or the young people who have lost their homes and lands to the development projects of the state? Unfortunately, the limited categories of the census can only be blamed for a portion of this blindness.

But, media barons and editors can argue that these are not necessarily the youth reading the *The Times of India*, or *The Hindu*, or who watch NDTV, Star or Zee and listen to Radio Mirchi. Based on most of the news directed towards youth, undoubtedly, their imagined young subject is English-speaking, urban, middle or upper-middle class, Hindu, probably upper-caste, and depending on whether the news is about sports or fashion, male or female. And these youth, presumably by virtue of their privileged location, are deemed to be completely uninterested in the messy details of politics and social change.

It is this last point that appears to be raising the hackles of the more progressive voices in the media. This anxiety, not unlike that of the more conservative voices who bemoan the degenerate effects of rampant Westernisation on Indian youth, brings to mind Paul Gilroy's discussion of refusing the binary Black *or* British and struggling instead for the possibility of replacing the 'or' with an 'and'. If the anxiety of the conservatives is that today's narrowly-defined youth, understood as an identity-based category, could threaten to choose between being young *or* Indian, for those on the left, the threat is the choice between being young (and chauvinistically Indian) *or* radical. In their efforts to interrogate the dangerously self-congratulatory paeans of the state to young people, perhaps the critical, progressive— and, yes, older—voices of the English-language media have been too hasty in countering this narrative with an equally monolithic picture of the twisted, amnesiac results of this past decade. What we find here is a terrifying vision of hopelessness that, despite its radically different ideological concerns and political positioning, ultimately reproduces the same anxieties of nationalism—through a discourse of legitimate memories and illegitimate forgetting.

Sadanand Menon, indicts this generation for living in blissful amnesia, incubated from the violence of recent historical memories—where the Emergency and the Bhopal gas tragedy, for

example, have been rendered meaningless.[15] Unarguably valid
in many senses, particularly with respect to the truly frighten-
ing increase in the number of young people actively allying with
the forces of the right, his argument also betrays a curious
conflation of 'Indian youth' with the same imagined subject of
media corporations and advertising CEOs: urban, upper-middle
class and shielded from the violence of today's socio-political conflicts. Amnesia is certainly not a luxury available to the Muslim
youth of Gujarat or the dalit children in countless villages and
cities across India or the adivasi teenagers displaced by the dams,
mining projects or forestry regulations modernising the country through forced migration. To them, and so many more,
foundational moments are not restricted to events of 'national'
importance like the Emergency, but seem to recur with mind-
numbing frequency during their own lifetimes. This brings into
question the 'imagined community' of the Indian nation and what
their shared historical concerns are supposed to be. Who de-
cides if a particular event or series of events have 'nationalist'
currency, whether in a reactionary or a progressive sense?

————————

As a counter-point to the dominant constructions and perceptions of youth in the English-language media, the National Readership Survey 2002 shows that the largest selling magazine is
Saras Salil, a Hindi youth magazine on politics that enjoys a
circulation of 9.35 million. Ajith Pillai, writing in *Outlook*'s youth
special, acknowledges that the popularity of a magazine that
does not shy away from politics and economic and social issues
shows that 'many have got it wrong when it comes to identifying
the interests of young people'.[16] Indeed, there is no dearth of
energy and commitment from today's young people. To believe
otherwise is not only indicative of a certain level of hopelessness, but also speaks of a more dangerous lack of imagination.
Restricting our understanding of 'youth' to a market-defined
category of consumers, a generation distinguished by nothing
besides its affiliation with Coca-Cola and MTV, imputes a still-
unrealised victory to the forces of corporate globalisation. As

———————————

[15] Sadanand Menon, 'Mad Cow Disease'.
[16] Ajith Pillai, 'Dumbed Down? Who?' *Outlook*, 12 January 2004.

Stuart Hall reminds us, the struggle over cultural hegemony is 'never about pure victory or pure domination ... it's never a zero-sum cultural game, it's always about shifting the balance of power in the relations of culture ... not getting out of it'.[17]

What does this mean for those of us in the media concerned with stemming the tide of corporatisation and confronting the growing strength of the neo-fascist Hindu Right? This is not a call for a simplistic celebration of 'alternative' youth cultures and difference, but instead, for a strategic destabilising of 'youth' as a de facto urban, middle-class and upper-caste category. We can no longer speak of youth and claim to be representative of all young people until issues facing rural and non-elite youth are considered mainstream youth issues. It is incumbent upon us to push the limits of our definition of 'youth' beyond its narrow consumer-oriented boundaries and bring to the centre categories of young people usually positioned outside this definition; including street children, youth affected by communal riots, and those from villages and marginalised communities in rural India. Unless we do this, 'youth' is a category as empty and irrelevant as the vilified pursuits of the young people it claims to represent.

A large part of the problem is the assumption that news that is not catchy, flashy and short enough to be attention grabbing is entirely lost on young people. While news that is attractively packaged is certainly more likely to have an audience, unfortunately, as our dumbed-down media amply prove, the attention to form has led to a complete disavowal of content. The same logic has led to the misconception that serious news requires no attention to form, as if sheer commitment alone will ultimately lead people to seek out unattractively produced but well-written articles. Very few media outlets seem to function on the principle that news on vital and difficult issues can be effectively packaged in arresting and creative ways without sacrificing depth or detail. Attracting a young audience requires a familiarity not only with the issues relevant to young people's lives, but also a critical engagement with the forms of cultural expression currently popular among different groups of young people—*not* those made popular through the corporate media alone—and an ability to creatively subvert and manipulate the over-used and tired forms peddled by the advertising and media conglomerates.

Whether we turn to independent media or campaigns by groups of progressive activists across the world, we can find a wealth of examples that creatively use popular and iconic artistic forms to reflect on, discuss and promote strategies for social change. Indymedia, formed out of the mainstream media blackout on the anti-WTO protests in Seattle in 1999, is a collective of hundreds of independent media organisations across the world—most of them set up and run by young people—that produce timely and detailed grassroots coverage of both local and global issues over the Internet. QUIT's (Queers Undermining Israeli Terrorism) 'Estee Slaughter' campaign in the United States, uses cleverly ironic slogans like 'Eau de Occupation' and 'Apartheid Cologne: A familiar stench in a new package', to draw attention to Estee Lauder International's direct funding connections to the violent practices of the Israeli state towards Palestinians. MoveOn.org ('Democracy in Action'), launched by two young entrepreneurs from Silicon Valley in 1998 and now a powerful organisation mobilising close to two million Americans through its Internet advocacy network, regularly raises money to fund catchy print and television advertisements on progressive political issues. Efforts like these provide a much-needed counter to the now-ubiquitous (particularly in the West) corporate appropriation of historic figures of resistance (from Gandhi to Che Guevara) to sell a particular product.

To return the focus to India, and to provide a very recent example of hope, recently, over 10,000 youth gathered in Mumbai for the Intercontinental Youth Camp, a parallel event to the World Social Forum, to discuss, debate and strategise around issues like privatisation of education, dalit rights, organising street children, fighting communalism, and holding global corporations like Coca-Cola and Dow Chemicals accountable for their actions in India. Being serious, thinking critically about social and political problems, and displaying enthusiasm and creative energy to change the world are by no means lacking in young people. But the media cannot afford to simply stop at criticising 'youth' for their self-absorption and sense of disconnect from the society and world they live in. It is up to independent and critical voices in the media to involve young people from myriad backgrounds, re-appropriate the category of youth from its narrow corporate definition, rethink the meanings of left politics, and come up with creative cultural strategies that can tell new stories, make a difference, and, in however small way possible, 'shift the dispositions of power'.[18]

---

[18] Stuart Hall, 'What is the "Black"', p. 24.

About the Editor and Contributors

about the editor

Nalini Rajan is presently Associate Professor at the Asian College of Journalism in Chennai. She obtained her Ph.D. in Social Communications, specialising in Political Philosophy, at the Catholic University of Louvain, Belgium. Her thesis, 'Within the Fragments—A Non-holistic Approach to Indian Culture' was published the same year. She has been a Homi Bhabha fellow (1991–93), a Fellow of the Indian Council for Social Science Research (1993–95), and has held visiting fellowships at the Hastings Centre, New York (1996) and at the universities of Oxford and Edinburgh (1997), among others. She has also worked for *The Economic Times,* Mumbai.

Dr Rajan has previously published two books with Sage, entitled *Secularism, Democracy, Justice: Implications of Rawlsian Principles in India* (1998), and *Democracy and the Limits of Minority Rights* (2002).

about the contributors

S. Anand works for the *Outlook* newsmagazine in Chennai. In 2003, he co-founded Navayana, an alternative publishing house which focuses on caste. He has written extensively on caste in academic journals and in the popular media. Mr Anand is the author of *Brahmans and Cricket: Lagaan's Millennial Purana and Other Myths* (Navayana: 2003).

B. R. P. Bhaskar, during his long career in journalism, has worked with several major English newspapers and the United News of India, and is now a media consultant and critic.

Bindu Bhaskar, Associate Professor at the Asian College of Journalism, Chennai, spent the early years of her career as a journalist with *The Economic Times* and *The Times of India*, followed by a tenure in *Frontline*, as Chief Sub-Editor and Special Correspondent.

Robert Brown is Senior Lecturer in journalism at Napier University in Edinburgh. He has taught at the University of Westminster in London and has been a visiting professor at the Asian College of Journalism in Chennai. Before being associated with the academia, he was Media Editor of *The Independent* newspaper in London and Deputy Editor of a Sunday newspaper in Scotland.

Darryl D'Monte is President, International Federation of Environmental Journalists, and Chairperson, Forum of Environmental Journalists of India. Some of the best journalists in India today began their careers under him, first at the *Sunday Review*, *The Times of India*, and then at *The Indian Express*.

Dilip D'Souza, a computer scientist by training, is a columnist and author of two books, *Branded by Law: Looking at India's Denotified Tribes* (2001), and *The Narmada Dammed: An Inquiry into the Politics of Development* (2002). He has won several awards for his writing, including the Statesman Rural Reporting prize, in the *Outlook/Picador* Nonfiction competition, and in *The Times of India*/Red Cross essay competition.

S. Gautham, an independent media practitioner with a special interest in documentary films, is currently based in New Delhi. He has been an editorial consultant for several productions of international television channels and has worked as a news and current affairs producer for domestic television.

V. Geetha works for Tara Publishing. She has authored and edited several books, including *Gender* (2002), *Towards a Non-Brahmin Millennium* (co-authored with S.V. Rajadurai, 1998) and *Soul Force: Gandhi's Writings on Peace* (edited, 2004).

Harivansh has been the Editor of *Prabhat Khabar* since 1990. He started his career in journalism with *The Times of India*, Mumbai, in 1977. Till 1990, he worked with *Dharmyug* in Mumbai, and *Ravivar* in Kolkata.

346 Practising Journalism

Mahalakshmi Jayaram has several years of journalistic experience with *The Indian Express*, *The Telegraph*, and *Deccan Herald*. As an Associate Professor at the Asian College of Journalism, she coordinates the new media and online journalism specialisation.

K.P. Jayasankar is Reader and **Anjali Monteiro**, Professor and Head, Unit for Media and Communications, Tata Institute of Social Sciences, Mumbai, India. They are involved in media production, teaching and research and have jointly won 10 international and national awards for their documentary films. They have also written several papers in the area of media and cultural studies as well as function as visiting faculty to various media and design institutions in India and abroad.

Robin Jeffrey is Professor of Politics at La Trobe University in Melbourne, and President, Asian Studies Association of Australia. His book, *India's Newspaper Revolution: Capitalism, Politics and the Indian-Language Press* (2000) is a bestseller.

Anjali Kamat works for the Coalition for the International Criminal Court in New York and is a freelance print and radio journalist with work experience in New York, Cairo and Chennai. She has obtained her master's degree in Near Eastern Studies from New York University and studied Arabic in Cairo. She is an organiser with the World Tribunal on Iraq and is active in Palestine solidarity work, as well as organising education programmes for South Asian immigrant youth.

Valerie Kaye has spent over two decades working as a journalist, TV researcher and producer. She also has a master's degree in Chinese Studies.

M.H. Lakdawala, Research and Creative Director of Clear Vision, has produced and directed programmes for TV channels like ETC, Eenadu-Urdu, Doordarshan and Sahyadri. He has written and directed a documentary, *Rise of Communalism in India*, and is a regular contributor to the English- and Urdu-language press.

Lawrence Liang is a lawyer and researcher at the Alternative Law Forum, and is currently working on a research project on the politics of intellectual property and the public domain.

Mukund Padmanabhan is *The Hindu*'s Associate Editor, based in Chennai. He writes editorials and analytical articles on political and legal affairs and coordinates the newspaper's city supplements published from different centres.

Pamela Philipose is Associate Editor, *The Indian Express*, and writes on issues relating to politics, development and gender. She has previously worked for *The Times of India* and the *Sunday Observer*, as well as for magazines like *Eve's Weekly* and *Down to Earth*. She won the Chamelidevi Jain Award for Outstanding Woman Journalist in 1999.

N. Ram is Editor-in-chief, *The Hindu*, and Trustee, Media Development Foundation, the organisation behind the Asian College of Journalism. He has won prestigious awards in his field, including the Asian Investigative Journalist of the Year award in 1990 for his investigation into the now famous Bofors case.

Steven S. Ross is Associate Professor of Professional Practice at Columbia University's Graduate School of Journalism. He has authored or edited 18 books on wide-ranging topics like environmental planning, product safety and liability, construction and statistics. He was appointed Fellow of the American Institute of Chemists in 1973 for his work in air pollution monitoring.

Ashish Sen is currently Director, Madhyam Communications and VOICES, and has over two decades of professional experience in print, broadcast and development communications. He was earlier Manager, Communications for ActionAid India. He began his career as a journalist with the *Business Standard*, and the Ananda Bazar Group of Publications, Kolkata, where he subsequently became Assistant Editor.

Devinder Sharma is an agricultural scientist and journalist. He has been the Development Correspondent of *The Indian Express* and now chairs the independent New Delhi-based Forum for Biotechnology & Food Security, which examines and analyses the implications of relevant Indian and international policy decisions. His books include *GATT and India: The Politics of Agriculture*, *GATT to WTO: Seeds of Despair*, and *In the Famine Trap*.

Kalpana Sharma is Deputy Editor and Chief of the Mumbai Bureau of *The Hindu*. She is author of *Rediscovering Dharavi: Stories from Asia's Largest Slum* (2000) and joint editor of *Whose News? The Media and Women's Issues* (1994) and *Terror Counter Terror: Women Speak Out* (2003). She writes on environmental and developmental issues and was awarded the Chamelidevi Jain Award for Outstanding Woman Journalist in 1987.

Nirmal Shekar is the Sports Editor of *The Hindu* in Chennai. He has spent 25 years as a sportswriter and has written on almost all the major sports in India. Widely travelled, he has often covered sports events outside the country. He was the first Indian journalist to win the prestigious Alfred Friendly Press Fellowship and worked in New York in 1984.

Praveen Swami is Chief of the Delhi Bureau, *Frontline*. He won the Prem Bhatia Award for Political Journalism in 2003 and has written extensively on Kashmir.

Shyam Tekwani is Assistant Professor at the School of Communication & Information, Nanyang Technological University, Singapore. He has spent over a decade covering the conflict in Sri Lanka and has been published in *The New York Times Magazine*, *Newsweek* and *India Today*. His most recent publication includes a paper entitled 'The Tamil Diaspora, Tamil Militancy and the Internet', in *Asia.com: Asia Encounters the Internet* (edited by K.C. Ho, Randy Kluver and C.C. Yang, 2003).

Index

30, 199; small and medium, 24, 28, 32; social conscious, 41; socially conscious, 41; spread of, literacy, 14; state-level, 33; supportive of various Maoist factions, 216; topics of discussion in Hindi, 53
newsprint, allocation, 27
newsweeklies, 119
newswriting, 297

Operation Westend, 73, 74, 77, 78, 80
Outlook, Boys on the cover of, 242; caste break-up of its editorial team, 196; humanitarian essays by Arundhati Roy, 240; issue on 'Zippies', 330; news reports on brahmin hegemony, 195; special youth issue of, 338; 'vigilante journalism' in, 190

'Page 3', 245; journalism, 8, 151; journalism favouring the, lifestyle, 59
Panorama, 81; crew, 85; editor of, 85
paparazzi, 4, 72
Pastapur Media Centre, 319, 320, 322
People, 252
petrol-pump misallocation episode, 3
piracy, phenomenon of, 165; role played by, 162
pornography, 284
Prabhakar, Manoj, 73, 79
Prabhat Khabar, success in Jharkhand, 2; ideals and values, 46–49; circulation, 48–49, 54; role as activist newspaper, 53–55, 57–58; aim of, 52; at your door, 47, 55; different editions of, 57; identity of, 53; initial stages of, 52; new published in, 56; office, 48; Patna edition of, 57; severely crippled, 47; team, 51; work at, 58

Prasad, Chandra Bhan, 180
Prayas, 67
Premananda case, 121
Press (Objectionable Matters) Act 1951, 22
Press Council, 23, 29, 53, 180, 215, 231
Press Financial Corporation, 29
Press Information Bureau (PIB), 178
press, analysis of the Hindi-language, 14; big business, 35; dalit-free, in India, 190; development of the, 248; district, 33; English language, 19, 32, 119; in the Punjab, 218; Indian, 19; libertarian, 41; mainstream, 119; mainstream nationalist, 176; monopoly, 28; nationalist, 173; native, 19; passes, 82; power of the American, 303; state of the, 23; talking to the foreign, 84; Uttar Pradesh, 176, 177; vernacular, 259, *see also* media
privacy, controversies relating to, invasion, 77; damage of the injury caused by the, violation, 78; injury caused by invasions of, 79; intrusion and, 75; invading methods, 77; invasion by journalists, 73; law, 80; right to, 75, 76; right to, against media intrusion, 72; rights enjoyed by individuals, 72; rights in investigative reporting, 4; torts, 80; unwritten, rules, 72; violation of, 79
publication, academic, 4; ordinance to prevent, of objectionable matters, 28
Pudiya Kattru, 123
Pudiya Todam, 123
Punjab Kesari, 187, 188, 216, 259, 263, 264; editorial staff and proprietors of, 216
Punjabi Tribune, 215